CONTINGENT WORK, DISRUPTED LIVES: LABOUR AND COMMUNITY IN THE NEW RURAL ECONOMY

Contingent Work, Disrupted Lives examines the effects of economic globalization on several manufacturing-dependent rural communities in Canada. In looking at such contemporary corporate strategies as plant closures and downsizing, authors Anthony Winson and Belinda Leach consider the impact of capitalist restructuring on the residents of various communities. The authors argue that the new rural economy has caused considerable instability and hardship in the lives of rural residents as they struggle to adapt in the face of economic upheaval.

Beginning with a review of theoretical and empirical literature on global changes in the economy and the effects of these changes on labour, the text then focuses on manufacturing in Ontario with an analysis of five community case studies. Winson and Leach give considerable attention to the testimony of numerous residents; they report on in-depth interviews with key respondents, including blue-collar workers in the five communities, ranging from diverse manufacturing towns to single-industry settlements. The result is an intimate contextual portrait of the workers' lives and their attempts to adapt to the rocky economic terrain of rural Canada in the 1990s.

ANTHONY WINSON and BELINDA LEACH are professors in the Department of Sociology and Anthropology, University of Guelph.

Studies in Comparative Political Economy and Public Policy

Editors: Michael Howlett, David Laycock, Stephen McBride, Simon Fraser University.

Studies in Comparative Political Economy and Public Policy is designed to showcase innovative approaches to political economy and public policy from a comparative perspective. While originating in Canada, the series will provide attractive offerings to a wide international audience, featuring studies with local, subnational, cross-national, and international empirical bases and theoretical frameworks.

Editorial Advisory Board

For a list of books published in the series, see p. 225.

ANTHONY WINSON and BELINDA LEACH

Contingent Work, Disrupted Lives: Labour and Community in the New Rural Economy

UNIVERSITY OF TORONTO PRESS

Toronto Buffalo London

© University of Toronto Incorporated 2002
Toronto Buffalo London
Printed in Canada

ISBN 0-8020-3554-X (cloth)
ISBN 0-8020-8426-5 (paper)

Printed on acid-free paper

National Library of Canada Cataloguing in Publication

Winson, Anthony, 1952–
     Contingent work, disrupted lives : labour and community in
     the new rural economy / Anthony Winson and Belinda Leach.

     (Studies in comparative political economy and public policy)
     Includes bibliographical references and index.
     ISBN 0-8020-3554-X)bound).   ISBN 0-8020-8426-5 (pbk.)

     1. Rural unemployment – Ontario.   2. Displaced workers – Ontario.
     3. Rural industries – Ontario.   4. Working class – Ontario.
     5. Deindustrialization – Ontario.   6. Globalization – Social aspects –
     Ontario.   I. Leach, Belinda, 1954–   .   II.Title.   III. Series.

This book has been published with the help of a grant from the Humanities
and Social Sciences Federation of Canada, using funds provided by the
Social Sciences and Humanities Research Council of Canada.

University of Toronto Press acknowledges the financial assistance to its
publishing program of the Canada Council for the Arts and the Ontario
Arts Council.

University of Toronto Press acknowledges the financial support for its
publishing activities of the Government of Canada through the Book
Publishing Industry Development Program (BPIDP).

Contents

Acknowledgments

This study has engaged us for a number of years, and consequently there are many people to thank for their contributions as it took shape and progressed. Our greatest debt is to the people in the five communities who generously gave us their time and shared with us their experiences, both painful and hopeful. We hope they will find that we have used their contributions respectfully and usefully. People with special local knowledge were also generous in sharing, and we thank in particular Barbara Brownell and Wendy Milne. We are especially grateful for the assistance of Ted Arnott, Denis Bertrand, Bonnie Bews, Rob Black, Gilles Bisson, Charlotte Broughton, Yves Carriere, Derek Cook, Campbell Cork, Gary Cousins, Nadine Cuccaro, Doug Elder, Marian Fraser, Rod Gemel, Ken Graham, Sherry Guillet, Ruth Hunt, Madelyne Irwin, Jack Johnson, Rick Lamarsh, Bob Lamb, Guy Lapointe, Ben Lefebvre, Kevin MacDonald, Jim MacGregor, Georgie Mantil, Claude Miljours, Ruth Penwarden, Diane Pepin, Wendy Plante, Murray Powers, Ian Rice, Tim Rimlie, Norm Rivard, George Stanclick, Les Szenasi, Steve Thorning, and Eric Turk.

Sandra Watson's talent for developing empathetic rapport, often at extremely difficult times in the lives of the people she interviewed, comes through clearly in interview transcriptions, and her contribution to the project is considerable. We have had the good fortune to work with several excellent student research assistants – Kim Knowles, Becky Stranberg, Tanya Flanagan, Chris Valiquet, and Deborah Woodman – who brought freshness and enthusiasm to the project. Anita Mahadeo's assistance with the manuscript at different stages has been most appreciated.

Colleagues have also contributed ideas, leads, and suggestions which often proved invaluable. For these we thank Stan Barrett, Hans Bakker, Tony Fuller, Ron Hinch, Kris Inwood, David Douglas, David Waltner-Toews, Derek Wilkinson, Charlotte Yates, and Ellen Wall. A special thanks is owed to Barry Smit for his encouragement with the early stages of this long project.

The study was funded by two research grants from the Social Sciences and Humanities Research Council of Canada, including one through the Eco-Research Program of the Canadian Tri Council via the Agro-EcoSystem Health project at the University of Guelph. The University of Guelph also supported both of us through research leaves to work on the project. We appreciate the assistance of the Social Sciences and Humanities Federation of Canada Aid to Scholarly Publications Programme.

Our thanks go to the anonymous reviewers for the ASPP and for the University of Toronto Press, for their thoughtful and challenging insights which have undoubtedly made this book stronger. Thanks also to Virgil Duff and Chris Bucci at the University of Toronto Press.

Lastly, we want to acknowledge the contributions and patience of our families: Anita Mahadeo, Ross Butler, Devin Winson, Rachel Butler, and Charlotte Butler.

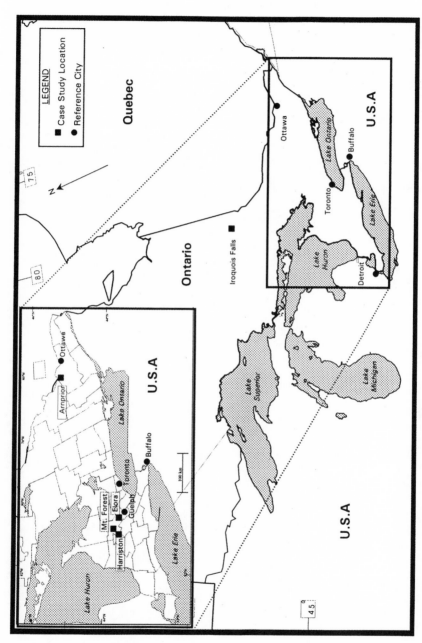

Map 1. Location of communities discussed in the study.

CONTINGENT WORK, DISRUPTED LIVES

CHAPTER ONE

Introduction

They treated us as if we were nothing. We threw a big company barbeque as a farewell thing and we invited management. Management was assigned to bring the food and this and that. Well, you know what a slap in the face is? They rented a limo, a white stretch limo, to bring these people to a country barbeque. Do you know what people thought when they pulled into that farm? They show up in a limo and all of us are unemployed. You don't drive up to a country barbeque in a white limo drinking champagne.

Bonnie Smith, laid-off Canada Packers' worker, 1991

In late 1999, while the media quoted many a politician and prominent businessperson as stating that the national economy was growing and unemployment numbers were going down, some other people saw things differently. Indeed, the majority of Canadians, according to the head of a leading Canadian polling company assessing surveys taken over the previous three years, expressed a growing sense of insecurity, aimlessness, and disengagement from society, together with the belief that the rich were not paying society their dues.[1] The poll, he suggested, is registering the fallout of unprecedented economic and technological forces that have come to bear on the Canadian population in recent times.

The subject of this book is the interaction of the new economy and the new technology in the everyday lives of everyday people who are obliged to make a living with what economists would define as less than optimal education and skills. The discussion is about people who live in small, rural communities that are fully embedded in the late industrial age, having been founded as sites for the production of manufactured goods. We look at how these people are directly affected by the transformations – sometimes slow and other times rapid and wrenching – and how these communities are being transformed. It is mostly unskilled and semi-skilled blue-collar industrial workers who have borne the brunt of globalization. In the following chapters we explore their experiences and the broader structural factors determining them.

In the 1980s and 1990s there was a proliferation of publications, scholarly and popular, on processes of globalization. Yet many of these writings have failed to shed light on the relationship between global economic processes and everyday life. Against this literature we have found ourselves worrying about what happens to people, like the woman quoted above, caught up in these processes. Our contribution addresses the grass-roots level – what happens to people in small towns and villages as companies go global and introduce just-in-time production, and as states redefine their role.[2] In this book we try to cut through the abstraction and breadth of much of the globalization literature, to look at trends affecting work in real communities and people as workers struggling to survive the globalization they confront every day.

This book emerges, as we believe the best of scholarly and creative work always does, from deeply held convictions about social justice and the potential for scholarly research to contribute to bringing it about. As in the previous writing of each of us, we make social class a central theme of the book. For us the most critical aspect of the present round of capitalist restructuring, and that which continues to require sustained attention and critique, is the way capital uses and increasingly abuses labour, and ultimately disposes of it when it is no longer as profitable as it once was. We can see this clearly in scholarly work on the use of male workers in extraction industries such as mining and large-scale manufacturing such as steelmaking (Corman et al. 1993), of women's labour in third world factories (Elson and Pearson 1981; Lim 1985), and in industrial homework throughout the world (Boris and Prugl 1996). For monopolistic resource and heavy manufacturing industries as well as the highly competitive light industrial sector, labour continues to be critical to profit-making, but in many cases it is also interchangeable, or, to put it another way, disposable. As service industries become more important to the economy, they too require certain kinds of labour in order to be profitable. Our perspective focuses on people's paid work, or the absence of it.[3]

Class is always conditioned by factors other than paid work, among which are gender, race, region, and age. These important factors are considered in our research context. Most importantly, however, we submit our study as a contribution to the literature that argues for the continued salience of class analysis. We agree with Skeggs that 'to abandon class as a theoretical tool does not mean that it does not exist anymore; only that some theorists do not value it. It does not mean the women [for example] would experience inequality any differently, rather it would make it more difficult for them to identify and challenge the basis of the inequality which they experience' (1997: 6).

The quote which opens this chapter captures one of the many ways in which class is experienced on a day-to-day basis. The quote makes very clear that class *is* practised and *is* recognized in conscious ways. How then, can class be irrelevant to analysis? Despite technological advances, capitalism continues to rely on certain kinds of labour to sustain profits, and people continue to expect capital to buy their labour so they can survive. With improved technologies, capital has become more mobile than ever, as has its ability to use relatively unskilled labour. This is in contrast to the relative immobility of labour, which puts labour at a considerable disadvantage. This extraordinarily unequal relationship, played out on the backs of millions of people leading their ordinary lives, is what sustains the central place of class in social science analysis and in politics.

Readers may feel that workers in small Ontario communities are among the most ordinary and unremarkable people we could choose as our focus. In many ways there is little romantic about their lives and their work. These are people who live in communities that have been, and continue to be, relatively resilient to the vicissitudes of capitalism. For example, the recession of the early 1990s, although much deeper in Canada than had been anticipated, and indeed than has often been recognized, was followed by a period of relative prosperity in southern and eastern Ontario. While official unemployment rates for some parts of Canada are still high, by the late 1990s southern Ontario had recovered its place as the driver of the national economy. Nevertheless, the particular workers that we concentrate on here have experienced recent economic change in significantly negative ways, sufficient in some cases to call into question their ability to survive economically. The workers we study are not the most marginal, which would suggest that workers beginning from an even more insecure position are even more disadvantaged by the negative consequences of globalization and new technology.[4]

One of our intentions is to provide, through this research and our positions as professional social scientists, legitimation for the experiences of restructuring of those who, as Skeggs (1997: 37) puts it, 'do not have access to circuits of knowledge distribution.' It was clear to us from the outset that working-class experiences and critiques of restructuring are rarely, if ever, heard by those in positions to affect policy (see Hathaway 1993). This became even clearer following the publication of a newspaper article about our research in the *Kitchener-Waterloo Record* (9 and 16 April 1996), which was greeted with derision by local municipal politicians and the community press. An editorial in the Mount Forest *Olds* (April/May 1996) clearly spelled out how marginal the workers in our study are popularly considered to be in relation to 'legitimate' debates about restructuring; it questioned the validity of the information received from anonymous informants, and asked whether unemployed workers were the appropriate people to ask about what happened following a factory closure.

In the chapters that follow we describe economic change and its effects in several manufacturing-dependent rural communities in Ontario. Global processes of economic restructuring are looked at in relation to the social fabric of rural communities. We present a detailed analysis of power, interests, economics, and historical change, and their impact on families and communities. Our scholarly training is in sociology (Anthony Winson) and social anthropology (Belinda Leach). We are especially interested in the layering of processes at local, national, and global levels, and the interface between these dimensions and across historical periods, as we attempt to understand what happens to ordinary people caught up in complex political and economic processes.

In Chapter 2 we set out our research agenda in the context of the literature. We also present our rationale for examining rural manufacturing communities as emblematic of small communities confronted by globalization. Because it is our desire to interest as wide a readership as possible, we have tried to keep this book jargon-free, and we have therefore limited mostly to Chapter 2 our sustained engagement with the extensive theoretical literature relevant to our subject. While we feel that this literature has much to contribute to the contextualization of our subject, those with a strong aversion to theory may wish to skip to Chapter 3 initially and get right into the discussion of our case study material. We hope that once engaged with the case studies, the reader may then choose to return to the conceptual discussion in Chapter 2, so as to better understand the analytical issues.

We began our research in 1992. Our work in the first phase focused on three communities in Wellington County, Ontario, and has been reported in a number of publications (Winson 1993; Leach and Winson 1995; Winson 1997; Leach and Winson 1999; Leach 1999). In 1997 we expanded the study to include two additional manufacturing communities. One of these is a northern community, Iroquois Falls, heavily dependent on a paper mill – whose location is itself dependent on the proximity of suitable forests. The other, Arnprior, is a more diversified and slightly larger community than any of the others and is located within striking distance of Ottawa – in what is sometimes referred to as Silicon Valley North, the acknowledged centre in Canada for industries related to information technology.

Chapter 3 discusses the research methods we used, and then sketches the historical and contemporary details of the five communities we studied. Manufacturing in rural areas of Ontario emerged around three major imperatives: (1) to manufacture locally the inputs necessary for agriculture; (2) to process agricultural produce into commodities and market them efficiently to local communities; and (3) to utilize the rural labour force which was unaccustomed to industrial work and for which agricultural work would provide a fall-back. In our discussion of the histories of the communities we focus specifically on the history of manufacturing. Local ownership and management was a key factor in the development of many, if not all, of these community economies. As local facilities were taken over by national and ultimately multinational corporate entities, they became more vulnerable to the global restructuring of the economy.

Our reading of much of the literature on globalization, deindustrialization, and economic change has been frequently frustrated by the absence of information about how such changes play themselves out at the grass-roots level. This frustration has been exacerbated by the reliance of policy-makers and other analysts on general statistics. For example, over the past fifteen years the public has been bombarded by the media with figures telling us how many manufacturing jobs have been lost or gained during a specific period. Much more difficult to determine, however, is how changes in job opportunities affect different kinds of communities, and for our purposes, rural ones in particular. Consequently, we report in Chapter 4 on an intensive study of changes in the manufacturing job picture for thirty-nine rural communities in Ontario whose population is between 3,000 and 7,000. Our conclusion is that, overall, rural communities in Ontario have not seen the kind of economic recovery, evidenced through employment figures (which are themselves subject to limitations), that has been reported for the province as a whole. This conclusion provides the background for our subsequent findings concerning manufacturing job changes in specific communities.

Also in Chapter 4 we look at corporate restructuring as a profit-maximizing strategy in the new political economic environment. We situate our case studies within a meso-level analysis of changes in the already-mentioned thirty-nine small manufacturing communities in Ontario over a twenty-year period. We then consider the specifics of restructuring in our case studies and examine the implications of such changes for rural community viability. Corporate strategies are extremely interesting to examine. On the one hand, they are driven by global economic processes that force corporate change in an increasingly competitive climate. This may lead to decisions to close entire manufacturing facilities, as we document for Westinghouse in Mount Forest, Canada Packers in Elora and Harriston, and Weavexx in Arnprior. On the other hand, corporate strategies are also to some extent shaped by, and themselves shape, local labour market conditions, such as the educational attainment of workers, the prevalence of part-time work, and the solidarity of local labour organizations. Chapter 4 focuses on what we might see as top-down strategies of restructuring.

Chapters 5 and 6 then turn to the people caught up in these processes and look at what happens to them. We use the concept of 'displaced workers' to describe those whose work trajectories have been disrupted by the recent phase of capitalist restructuring. Unlike some analysts, we do not utilize a tight definition of displacement, to mean, for example, those workers unemployed for a certain minimum length of time. Rather, our use of the term is intended to be more generally descriptive and to apply, therefore, to a broader range of workers for whom economic restructuring has led to displacement from what could reasonably have been expected to be the normal course of their work lives.

Our initial focus, through in-depth interviews with workers laid off from manufacturing jobs in Wellington County, led us to conclude that these workers 'skidded' (Bluestone and Harrison 1988) into quite precarious livelihood strategies. We were cautious not to generalize too broadly from these quite specific examples to other kinds of rural communities, however, and decided to extend our study to displaced workers in two quite different communities. If new jobs are being created as fast, or almost as fast, as they are being destroyed, as some analysts contend, then it is reasonable to hypothesize that in a community with a more diverse economy, driven more directly by newer technologies, workers laid off from traditional manufacturing jobs will be quickly picked up by expanding 'new' industries. Thus, we decided to find out what happened, through interviews with workers laid off from Weavexx in Arnprior.

For Iroquois Falls, industrial restructuring was not easily associated with corporate downsizing through the kinds of mass lay-offs seen in the other communities. Rather, while still substantial, labour through its union was able to ensure that downsizing was carried out more selectively through early retirements. In this community it is young people who are displaced, as the opportunities for entry into the well-paid jobs in the paper mill have shrunk to almost nothing in the past decade. Thus, the data we use for this community derive in part from a random telephone survey of young men and women who had left high school in 1992. These people told us about their work and education histories and, in some cases, about their prospects for work in Iroquois Falls.

In Chapter 5 we look at what might be considered objective data, such as the incidence of part-time and casual work in the Canadian economy and income levels among workers. Following Burke and Shields (1999), we argue against reliance on official ways of measuring employment and unemployment, and argue that there are good reasons for the distinction between what the Economic Council of Canada (ECC, 1990) described as 'good' jobs and 'bad' jobs a decade ago. While we applaud the ECC's choice of language because it refused to dress up the stark reality of the job situation in euphemistic terms, we chose to describe what we have seen in rural communities as a shift from a 'stable work world' to a 'contingent work world.'

The notion of contingent work has been used quite extensively in the literature over the past decade or so. Usually it is one of a number of terms, along with, for example, non-standard work or casualized labour, used fairly loosely to describe the nature of work arrangements emerging with restructuring. All of these terms usually incorporate forms of work like part-time, temporary, home-based, and casual, all of which are associated with lower pay, the absence or inadequacy of benefits, and frequent difficulties in qualifying for social assistance programs (Orr 1996). Christensen (1987) identifies conceptual problems with the use of the term 'contingent work' because it covers a wide range of work arrangements, lumping together such different dimensions of work as the amount of time on the job, the contractual agreements between employers and workers, and the location of work in the case of homeworkers (Christensen 1987: 15). She argues for a more rigorous definition that encompasses three types of employment arrangements: part-time, temporary, and independent contracting. To us, contingent work provides more than a useful shorthand term to cover a range of types of work, however carefully defined. We chose to use contingent because its more familiar meaning, used long before it was associated with restructuring, is especially appropriate. The *Concise English Dictionary* defines contingent as 'adj 1 (usually followed by on, upon) *conditional, dependent* (on an uncertain event or circumstance). 2 *associated*. 3 (usually followed by to) *incidental*. 4 a *that may or may not occur*. b *fortuitous; occurring by chance*. 5 *true only under existing or specific conditions*' (1991: 248). Unlike the alternative terms that are commonly used, contingent is the only one which actually connotes the importance of the relationship of this form of work to something more powerful and in control, in other words, the actions of capital. As the dictionary defines it, part-time, temporary, and contracted work is *conditional, dependent* upon the moves made by employers. As we see it, this lends the term considerably more explanatory power than any of the alternatives. Contingent work has lost the moorings, in labour regulation and union contracts, that earlier forms of work had. Whereas work in the old economy assumed that a level of employee involvement, often through unions, was desirable (even if this occurred only at the level of ideology in many cases), in the new economy there is no such participation. Work arrangements are determined entirely by the employer, or as a *New York Times* article put it, 'employers call all the shots' (Kilborn 1995: A1).

In one of the earliest analyses of contingent work, Belous (1989) contrasts the contingent model of human resource management to the 'new deal' model. As he sees it, in the new deal model unions had a central role in the way human resource systems operated, whereas in the contingent model unions play only a small, peripheral role. Moreover, Belous identified the increasingly important role of international economic forces in shaping pay levels and work arrangements and conditions, as government involvement in these issues is reduced (1989: 95).

Our use of the term 'contingent work world' tries to emphasize both the dependent nature of jobs in the new economy *and* the way in which the nature of people's jobs affects, and in some ways determines, most if not all aspects of their family life. Our major argument is that the new economy involves a fundamental shift in the stability and security of people's lives, which goes far beyond simply new work arrangements, ultimately changing lives in ways that neither we nor they see as particularly positive.

In Chapter 6 we concentrate on the narratives of the people we talked to, looking at what happens in people's day-to-day lives as a result of restructuring, and how daily routines are affected as people struggle to create and recreate family life. With contingent work we see people's lives become ever-more contingent upon the whims and strategies of their employers.

Our conclusions are far from encouraging. It becomes increasingly evident from our case studies that even in the most diverse rural community, economic change leaves many people facing an extremely precarious future. As Belous concludes, without substantial changes in social welfare systems, millions of workers will 'fall through the cracks created by the contingent economy' (1989: 116). Chapter 6 also discusses the issues for the most vulnerable workers – women, older and younger workers, the infirm, and those with few credentialed skills – and how attachment to rural localities, while potentially sustaining them, has the simultaneous effect of ensuring the contingent labour force that the new economy requires.

In Chapter 7 we ask whether economic diversity actually matters when communities face the crisis of losing a major employer. Our findings are not consistent with the predictions in the literature. We consider the limitations to an economistic approach to looking at community diversity and argue for a more social approach. We look specifically at the ways in which the presence of a strong union can make a difference to people's experience of restructuring. We caution, however, that in communities underpinned by a conservative political culture this union in itself will not ensure an ideal work world.

Looking at unemployed steelworkers' attempts (and ultimate failure) to intervene into policy debates in Pittsburgh, Hathaway (1993: 218) argues that the local business and policy-making elites were guided by principles of short-term and medium-term profitability: 'These are abstract, mathematical principles applied by accountants, economists, and managers with no sentimental or moral attachment to the people of a given community. In a world characterized by rapid change, these principles are unlikely to produce stability. Community, on the other hand, requires nurturing over time. It requires commitment. It requires stability. Obviously there is a conflict between the needs of corporations and the needs of communities.'

The tension between what people need, and what employers require, in the globalized capitalism of today is what pervades the present volume.

CHAPTER TWO

The Global and the Local: Understanding Globalization through Community Research

A central theoretical problem in the social sciences has been to distinguish the specific features of capitalism as an economic and social system. This was true, to varying degrees, of such disparate thinkers as Adam Smith, Max Weber, Werner Sombart, and Karl Marx, and, in more recent times, Karl Polanyi and Joseph Schumpeter. Even today, when social scientists have moved away from classical concerns in response to the so-called postmodern turn, others have trenchantly stayed the course, deciding that the manifest changes of the past two decades do not justify 'throwing the baby out with the bathwater.' While not averse to examining new problems in new ways, they argue that capitalism as a totalizing socioeconomic system is with us today more than it has ever been, and its impact on the lives of everyday people in rich and poor countries alike is ever-more profound. They continue to see a central role for social science in critically probing and dissecting the system that inevitably affects all of us in one way or another, regardless of whether it is fashionable to do so in certain academic circles. Some see such work progressing toward the emancipation of society from structures that oppress many while enriching the lives of few. It is in this somewhat diminished but still eminently viable social science tradition that we as authors place ourselves.

Today, the task of critically analysing capitalism confronts a rapidly changing landscape in economic, social, and political domains. An impressively rich literature has emerged that attempts to fathom this phenomenon at regional, national, and global levels. We see this book as contributing to this literature in a somewhat different way, by considering a much understudied locale in which wider processes continue to work themselves out – namely, small communities dependent on manufacturing in the Canadian context. Before we consider in greater depth the case for studying such communities, we shall situate our study within the broader theoretical literature.

At the most general level, there has been a theoretical concern to understand the processes through which the capitalist system has been able to weather periods of crisis and reinvent itself. As an analytic problem the longevity of capitalism as a system, and in particular the manifold changes in recent years that are often encapsulated with such terms as 'globalization,' has a number of dimensions, all of which are essential to understand societal change. It has implications, at the very least, for the organization of work and the deployment of workers, for the viability of communities and the persistence of uneven forms of development, for the emergence and demise of social movements, for the pace of technological innovation and, not insignificantly, for the quality of life that will be defined in any given society.

For earlier periods, and with the benefit of hindsight, there has been a degree of consensus among analysts in periodizing the predominant ways in which capitalism has been organized. The early competitive capitalist period, written about by Marx, Adam Smith, Ricardo, and J.S. Mill, was characterized by small firms. When this phase reached a crisis of falling profits, instead of being replaced by socialism, as Marx had predicted, it was replaced by a new form of 'expansionist capitalism' (Ross and Trachte 1990: 21), monopoly capitalism. During this phase, as Baran and Sweezy (1966) have theorized, monopoly firms achieved market supremacy by exploiting previously under-utilized regions. Despite its dominance during most of the twentieth century – indeed monopoly capitalism in many ways defined the century – it faced its own crisis of profitability beginning in the 1970s (see Kolko 1988; Warnock 1988). This forced a further reorganization of production in the late twentieth century.

The theoretical debate this book contributes to concerns the variety of forms that capitalism assumes to overcome periods of instability, and specifically, how to characterize its most recent transformation. It helps to address the question: What kind of capitalism do we live with now? One group of analysts herald a fundamental break with older forms of capitalism, a 'second industrial divide' after which work can be organized in different and, in some cases, non-exploitative ways (Piore and Sabel 1984). They anticipate a postindustrial period in which work as we have known it would disappear (Gorz 1982 ; Rifkin 1995). Another group of analysts propose that we have been witnessing a transition to 'global capitalism,' in which capital mobility is a dominant characteristic, targeting areas where vulnerable workers will accept low wages (Bluestone and Harrison 1982; Ross and Trachte 1990; Fink 1998; Gaventa, Smith, and Willingham 1990; Grey 1998; Harvey 1989; Peck 1996), and undermining institutional labour supports, such as progressive legislation, state entitlements, and unemployment insurance benefits. By the end of the 1990s evidence tended to favour the latter group, at least in the American context, as unemployment rates declined to levels not seen since the 1970s. The big question is not so much the lack of jobs (although this will likely return as an issue in the next recession) but rather the *quality* of jobs, as contractual, contingent labour becomes the dominant way of doing business in many sectors.

The central focus of this book is how the contemporary transformation of capitalism is reshaping manufacturing in small rural communities and affecting the lives of the Canadian individuals and families living there. Labour markets and changing labour processes arguably lie at the core of the macrorestructuring that is taking place in our society today. Understanding these phenomenon are key to discovering 'what's new about the new rural economy?' as well.

The secondary focus of this book explores the impact of capitalist macrorestructuring on the people living in rural communities. Are these communities passive recipients of external forces, or have they resisted these forces, or sought to shape them to local needs? We also wanted to learn more about the implications of restructuring for the long term sustainability of these communities.

The Global and the Local

To address our question above – 'what's new about the new rural economy?' – we use an approach that looks at global and societal processes (the macro perspective), while also carefully considering how these are played out at the local (micro) level. This chapter examines the restructuring of the work place together with the 'political apparatuses of production' (Buraway 1985), which include the governing regulatory structure of the work place, labour's right to organize, as well as a variety of welfare entitlements that condition the relationships between working people and their employers. In subsequent chapters we examine specific local communities and work places within them – places where the larger institutional changes actually work themselves out. Our research considers the various phases and crises of the capitalist model which then intersect with local traditions and resources, and together contribute to locally specific outcomes.

There is a rich tradition of work informed by this perspective. Literature about the Canadian political economy has a long history, dating back to Harold Innis who wrote in the first half of the twentieth century. Innis was centrally concerned with 'the costly and uncontrollable effect of international markets on people and communities' (Drache 1995: xiv). His staple theory argues that Canada's economic and cultural development was highly dependent on the export of staple goods (cod, lumber, and furs). As T. Dunk points out, Innis showed considerable foresight in anticipating the effect of globalization on Canada (Dunk 2002: 41). Subsequent work in Canadian political economy built on this framework, focusing much of its attention on the distortions produced by the historically high degree of foreign ownership of the Canadian economy, and also the problem of regional underdevelopment and disparity. With respect to this latter issue, a large body of literature, particularly examining Atlantic Canada, but also looking at the Prairies and the North, has emerged in an attempt to better understand the crisis in underdeveloped areas, and to address policy and economic options (see Drache and Clement 1985).

Regional disparities and the structural dependence of certain regions on the vagaries of the global economy have also been a focus for some U.S. sociologists. Among the best known is John Gaventa's work on Appalachia (Gaventa 1980; Gaventa and Smith 1990), in which he carefully documents the relative powerlessness of workers and their communities in the face of the actions of multinational corporations on whom their jobs depend.

It has often been anthropologists who have taken up local–global concerns for U.S. communities, as well as elsewhere. Eric Wolf's *Europe and the People without History* (1982) was the first systematic study of an interlinked world economy, and its effects on local communities. Wolf's work had the double effect of liberating anthropology from its preoccupation with bounded cultures and societies, while at the same time drawing attention outside the discipline to the importance of a comparative study of situated localities. Wolf advocated the integration of different disciplinary knowledges (Schneider 1995: 6–7), to carefully explore the relationship between global and the local (see as examples the essays in Schneider and Rapp 1995).

During the 1980s research within British social geography explored the interrelationships between international, national, and local capitals, and the particular spatial outcomes of these (see Bagguley et al. 1990). This literature emphasized the local and regional variation that accompanies processes of restructuring, and stressed the unexpected outcomes, especially in terms of class conflicts and commonalities. Doreen Massey, who led a major British locality study, writes that this research was intended to address the complexity of the geography of restructuring in the 1980s. As she put it 'something that might be called "restructuring" was clearly going on, but its implications both for everyday life and for the mode and potential of political organizing were clearly highly differentiated, and we needed to know how' (Massey 1994: 128).

Within these different disciplinary and national traditions, and as a result of the intersections between them (see Urry 1996), a body of literature examining restructuring at a local level, but within a context of international global economic processes has emerged. The destabilization of monopoly capitalism hit third world regions first in the 1970s, rather than in the 1980s when it was felt more acutely in high-wage regions. Work carried out in third world countries foreshadowed events to come elsewhere. Research on Jamaica following IMF intervention (Bolles 1977; Kaufman 1985) and on Mexico as it attracted international capital, both in Mexico City (Beneria and Roldan 1987), and in the maquiladoras (Kopinak 1996), addressed issues that would become central concerns in other parts of the world. Several of these cases emphasize the negative effects of restructuring processes on women.

June Nash's work (1989) on Pittsfield, Massachusetts, addresses the implications for life and politics after the demise of a major employer in a context where corporate hegemony has been secure for most of the twentieth century. Her work is particularly useful for understanding the apparent political acquiescence that often accompanies a plant closure. Gaventa (1990) also addresses the issue of acquiescence, in terms of Appalachian peoples' perceptions of powerlessness in the face of international capital. Nelson and Smith (1999) examine household livelihood strategies in the context of a polarization between 'good' and 'bad' jobs with the loss of manufacturing work in rural Vermont.

Canadian studies of the local effects of capital restructuring follow the tradition of Canadian political economy observing the very different effects and outcomes for disparate local communities. Work in this tradition helps make sense of the way Canada is inserted into the global economy, taking into account the conditions for labour and capital which have arisen historically. These include post–Second World War struggles which provided entrenched legal rights for labour unions, leading to a higher rate of union membership than in the United States or Japan, but considerably lower than in most of Europe, Australia, and New Zealand (Krahn and Lowe 1998: 334–5), as well as the creation of a welfare state which guaranteed universal access to medical care and seniors' pensions, provided financial support for the unemployed and those in poverty, and regulated work places for health and safety. However, the postwar settlement protected capital's right to manage work places and to ensure continued production without fear of unanticipated strikes, while providing a well-educated and healthy labour force. Canada has also protected some of its agricultural producers through supply management agreements such as the Wheat Board and provincial milk marketing boards, and it has protected industrial jobs through such agreements as the Auto Pact with the United States. Canada's place in the global economy has also been shaped by immigration policies which have provided a ready-made labour force in a country with a limited supply.

A second purpose of work in this tradition is to assess the role that individual communities of workers play in drawing on their distinct traditions and resources in their response to global change. These include, for example, particular labour histories, the experiences of specific immigrant, visible minority, and religious community groups; and the natural resource environment in which communities have developed (see Barber 2002).

The downsizing of major employers and its effects on gender relations, labour processes, political affiliations, and forms of consciousness are examined by Corman et al. (1993; see also Leach 1998) for Stelco in Hamilton steelworkers, and by Mawhiney and Pitblado (1999) for Elliot Lake. Swift (1995) examines the changes in work organization and opportunities in Windsor, a small industrialized border city, heavily dependent on the automobile industry, and Kingston, a smaller city, with an economy more diversified around the public sector (including eight prisons and a major university) and a declining manufacturing base once dependent on large multinational corporations. Just down the highway, about forty minutes from Kingston, is Napanee, a rural town which recently welcomed a Goodyear tire factory. As historian Bryan Palmer (1994) documents the process, however, the welcome was largely constructed by the actions of the Goodyear company, which pursued a long process of courtship with the town before deciding to settle down.

Situating Canada's position in relationship to the United States and elsewhere, while looking at the specificity of the Canadian context and of individual localities, makes this study emblematic of the global–local approach which has proven to be a fruitful method for understanding how capitalism is produced and reproduced in particular places. This requires locating our specific case study in the context of broader global economic and political processes.

Globalization and the Neo-Liberal Agenda

The Asian 'meltdown' of 1997 to 1998 showed how dependent corporations have become on markets outside their host country, as stock markets in New York, Toronto, Vancouver, London, and Frankfurt witnessed serious reductions in share values for a host of their blue chip listings. In the words of the Deutsche Bank Group's chief economist the rapid slide in the Japanese economy had made it 'the number one strategic issue facing the world economy right now,' (*Globe and Mail*, 1998: A16). Canada was hit especially hard, as Japan is its number two trading partner. As a result of the 'meltdown' Canadian exports to Japan dropped almost 40 per cent in the first quarter of 1998 (McKenna 1998b: B9). Western economies such as that of British Columbia, that prospered from the Asian boom, were then rapidly sent into recession. The Canadian dollar dropped to its lowest level in decades as currency speculators took advantage of the crisis and panicky investors moved money into the United States and out of the more 'Asian vulnerable' and resource-dependent Canadian market.[1] Canada's vulnerability to external shocks in the global economy was readily apparent.

What has come to be termed 'globalization' is difficult to define. Teeple identifies four critical components to the operation of global capital: '1) It requires "freedom" from national controls or intervention; 2) has ultimately no national allegiance; 3) has interests that span the world and far exceed national jurisdictions; and 4) operates within a world economy and possesses a "global perspective" in which domestic or national markets form only one element and indeed are too small for the productive capacity it possesses' (Teeple 1995: 55). Teeple further argues that in the postwar period a number of the prerequisites for global capitalism were put into place. These included an escalation in the degree of international trade and direct foreign investment; the expansion of transnational corporations; the growth of global financial markets beyond the reach of national banks; the application of microelectronics to commodity production, distribution, and circulation; and the expansion of the labour force to include previously non-industrial regions (Teeple 1995: 56–68).

Gordon Laxer notes that much of what globalization signifies lies at the heart of the capitalist Enlightenment project over the past two hundred years. He identifies the basic assumptions which underlie it as universalism, scientism, rationality, private property rights, and individualism. But despite being couched in the language of progress, 'notably missing are [the Enlightenment's] heart and soul – popular democracy, equality and solidarity (fraternité)' (1995: 296).

We would argue that there is an emerging consensus among social scientists that the complex of factors – technological, organizational, political, and ideological – that make up this process have produced a *qualitative* shift in the way the economy is structured.[2] In Canada this shift is most evident after 1989, although elements of it had emerged earlier. This shift entails a substantial modification of what has come to be termed by political economists as the Fordist regime or model of industrial organization.[3] As Moody (1997: Chapter 5) argues, many of the changes to the organization of work entailed the adoption (in modified form) of innovations first elaborated by Japanese corporations after the Second World War in the political climate of a drastically weakened labour movement there.

Laxer challenges some of the fundamental premises of globalization: that national sovereignty is being eroded, that the level of transnational ownership is considerably higher than in the past, and that market reforms in fact enhance democracy. He points out that for both Canada and large areas of the third world, with their histories of colonialism and transnational penetration globalization is hardly a new phenomenon (Laxer 1995: 288–9). Although there is some disagreement concerning the precise form that globalization takes, Arrighi reminds us that there is a basic agreement among sociologists that globalization 'is not as unprecedented a phenomenon as most observers think and that an understanding of its meaning and prospects requires a temporal horizon that encompasses centuries, rather than decades' (Arrighi 1999: 123–4; and see also Wolf 1982 as discussed above).

What appears to be increasingly clear is that global capitalism as a functioning system will not eradicate the inequalities that were cemented by earlier stages of capitalism. As Mander and Goldsmith argue, the global economy may be new, but it is 'less so in form than in scale' (Mander and Goldsmith 1996: 4). Technologically enhanced commerce operating at tremendous speed, the shift in global power from democratically elected government, and the eradication of much regulatory control over national economies and corporate activities is new. What is not new are the ideological principles which underlie the system: the primacy of economic growth and the 'free market,' freedom from government regulation and freedom to consume (Mander and Goldsmith 1996: 4–5). Global scale is supposed to trickle benefits down to everyone, but as the essays in Mander and Goldsmith's collection show, the framework put in place shows no sign of levelling inequality. Rather, inequality is increasingly entrenched, and in certain regions such as Latin America and Africa, it has taken on alarming dimensions (see Petras and Veltmeyer, 2001; Chossudovsky, 1996). After ten years of free trade in Canada, Statistics Canada data for 1998 show a widening gap between rich and poor (Statistics Canada 2000).

In one of the most comprehensive and in-depth treatise on the phenomenon of globalization to date, Petras and Veltmeyer (2001) argue that a major divide has emerged in terms of the analysis of, and theoretical perspective on, the issue. On the one side there are those who see it as a set of interrelated processes that are inevitable and about which necessary adjustments can and should be made. Adherents of this view are to be found across much of the political spectrum. On the other hand, there are those who view globalization as a class project rather than as an inevitable process. From this perspective,

> the network of institutions that define ... the new global economic system is viewed not in structural terms, but as intentional and contingent, subject to the control of individuals who represent and seek to advance the interests of a new international capitalist class. This class, it is argued, is formed on the basis of institutions that include a complex of some 37,000 transnational corporations (TNCs), the operating units of global capitalism, [together with] the World Bank, the International Monetary Fund (IMF) and other international financial institutions that constitute the self-styled 'international financial community'... In addition, the New World Order is made up of a host of global strategic planning and policy forums such as the Group of Seven (G-7), the Trilateral Commission and

the World Economic Forum; and the state apparatuses in countries at the centre of the system that have been restructured so as to serve and respond to the interests of global capital. (2001: 12)

From this perspective 'globalization' is neither inevitable or necessary, but rather is replete with contradictions that generate forces of opposition and resistance (Seattle, Prague, Quebec, the Zapatista uprising, mobilization against the Multilateral Agreement on Investment, etc.).

In tune with this view are the arguments of those such as Patricia Marchak (1991) and John Warnock (1988) who convincingly argue that what we refer to as a globalized economy has been very much a *political* project. This political project, referred to as neo-liberalism, has had various related dimensions, perhaps the most visible being the transformation of regulatory structures of the state at its various levels. While this is usually seen as a process of deregulation leaving as it does the individual much more exposed to the whims of market forces, it has also entailed re-regulation. This re-regulation has taken place typically via treaties and agreements among and between nation states which have served as a protective shield for the reinvigoration of international corporate capital. Agreements such as NAFTA have allowed multinational capital to revitalize itself via massive acquisitions and mergers, and to exploit economic opportunities previously the privileged domain of state enterprise, as in Canada.

This neo-liberal political project has entailed another key dimension, in addition to its more visible institutional manifestations. This dimension is more clearly ideological. Proponents of the neo-liberal agenda, which in Canada coalesced around the federal Conservative Party in 1988 during the election campaign fought over the proposed Free Trade Agreement with the United States, have undertaken extraordinary steps to ensure that neo-liberalism would become the *hegemonic* discourse, in the Gramscian sense, in society. In other words, the 'common sense' understandings that shape any debate about economy and society have been decisively reshaped in Canada today so that discussion of key issues cannot take place without confronting new imperatives such as 'competitiveness' and 'efficiency.' However, the content of these imperatives is rarely examined which is what makes them crucial in shaping public discourse, or, to put it another way, hegemonic. It is necessary that critical scholarship deconstruct this hegemonic discourse.

This ideological component of the neo-liberal project has been, as Marchak (1991) has carefully detailed, assiduously nurtured by conservative think tanks, business councils, and associations for some years now. In the political realm, the neo-liberal project was initially most forcefully promoted by the Progressive Conservative Party, and later the Reform (now Alliance) Party, but it has long been favoured by elements of the federal Liberal Party as well. By the mid-1990s the Liberals had become its most avid promoters. The efforts of these forces to build an ideological consensus around the neo-liberal agenda has had remarkable success, at least until very recently. This is nowhere more true than in the area of transforming state policies.

The State and Globalization

We view the national state as the 'handmaiden' for many of the changes placed under the rubric of globalization. Yet in the postwar period the state played a different kind of role. While there is no doubt that one of the functions of the Keynesian welfare state was to provide a healthy and educated generation of workers in preparation for the labour market, it mitigated the harsher effects of capitalism by institutionalizing collective bargaining, enforcing health and safety, hours of work, and child labour regulations, and by providing subsistence for the unemployed, the aged, the sick, and the disabled (Teeple 1995: 15).

More recently, however, and aided by the reshaping of public views around the neo-liberal project, states have withdrawn from these kinds of roles, and have increasingly restricted their role as 'handmaidens' to global capital by promoting and implementing a variety of policy instruments that have become part of the daily life of citizens around the world. We use the word 'instruments' in the sense that these policies, which include privatization of the state sector, deregulation, the reduction of social citizen rights, and trade liberalization, have been used as tools to achieve very specific ends. Chief among these ends is to give private capital a much greater role than it had heretofore in organizing the affairs of society.[4] This has entailed reducing the role played by other social sectors, and the power these had through state organizations and agencies ostensibly under the democratic control of parliamentary government, however indirect this may have been.

Beyond reducing the power held by different social groups in civil society, however, this neo-liberal project has had as a main objective the reduction of the role of the state itself. For enemies of the Keynesian welfare state this objective is central because, to quote the eminent German social theorist Jürgen Habermas, 'it is the power and capacity for action of an interventionist state apparatus that ultimately determines the success of the [welfare state] project.' (1989: 55). The power of social groups beyond the corporate sector is reduced when the variety of social welfare functions are shifted from the public to the private sphere.[5]

In some societies these policy instruments associated with the neo-liberal era have more successfully replaced those previously associated with the Keynesian welfare state. It is remarkable how widespread this policy consensus has been. It has been successfully promulgated to the point that it has become the hegemonic political project – the dominant worldview in the Gramscian sense – in a number of countries.

How the state came to play such a role is not a simple story, and to some extent, individual chapters must be written for each society. There have been exceptions as well, but they are few. Where they occurred, it has taken the sustained organizational resistance of a sizeable sector of the people to turn things around, as it did during the prolonged popular protests in France in late 1996. More recently, the first attempt to put together the Multilateral Agreement on Investment was scuttled, according to one of its leading proponents, by the combined efforts of a grass-roots international organization with strong representation in Canada together with the resistance of the French, once again.

Changes in Work, Implications for Class

One dimension of the new economic model that has emerged with the globalization of capital encompasses transnational financial institutions and the formation of continental economic spaces in North America, Europe, and Asia (Friedmann, 1993: 371). But there is another dimension to this model, which entails the host of changes that are having a definite impact on the structure of employment. These include gendered impacts, different outcomes for various age groups seeking employment, for the quality of work life, and the growth of social inequality within communities and across communities. It is this dimension that is particularly germane to the processes and outcomes at the community level that form our principal concern in this book.

Underlying these changes to the structure of employment has been the incessant drive by corporations to increase their 'flexibility.' As Bluestone and Harrison argue in their well known American study *The Great U-Turn: Corporate Restructuring and the Polarizing of America* (1988), it is the desire to increase flexibility in dealing with labour that is paramount in corporate strategies to deal with new competitive pressures and achieve the unprecedented levels of profitability demanded by major institutional investors. Increasing flexibility has become a euphemism for cutting their wage bill. These corporate strategies include: (1) unremitting pressure for concessions from unionized and non-unionized workers in order to reduce their wages and overall compensation packages; (2) the introduction of a two-tiered wage structure into the workplace whereby newly hired workers are paid much less than previously hired workers doing what is basically the same job, and this lower wage rate continues for a much longer period than had previously been the case; (3) the promotion of part-time contingent work schedules which include the introduction of a growing cadre of part-time or temporary workers within the firm itself, and/or the growth of subcontracting, where workers are supplied by another, typically non-union lower wage employers; (4) promoting the strategy of 'union avoidance' whereby firms increasingly 'out-source' production to non-unionized firms and/or individuals at home or abroad, while downsizing or shutting down unionized plants. Bluestone and Harrison argued in 1988 that as a result of the success in implementing these strategies, of the one in three American workers that was represented by a trade union after the Second World War, only one in six would be so represented by 1990 (1988: 49). In summarizing the thrust of these processes, they have written: 'Altogether, almost 4 out of 5 workers displaced from manufacturing jobs found themselves skidding into unemployment, skidding completely out of the labour force, or skidding down the wage scale. For these workers to hold on to a middle class lifestyle required that there be two or more workers in the family' (1988: 64).

The disturbing pattern that Bluestone and Harrison argued was becoming a central motif of the American economy in the 1980s, is now well entrenched in the Canadian context as well. Considering this, Graham Lowe, a prominent analyst of the changing structure of employment in the Canadian context, has noted that in the increasingly polarized job structure in this country, 'The decline of permanent employment is another sign of insecurity ... Permanent jobs provide higher average wages and better benefits than non-permanent ones.

The permanent – non – permanent wage gap is $3 per hour. In 1995, two-thirds of permanent jobs had at least three of five benefits (employer-sponsored pension plan, health insurance, dental benefits, paid sick leave, paid annual vacation), compared with only 18 percent of non-permanent jobs. Only 16 percent of permanent jobs offered none of these benefits, compared with 60 percent of seasonal, temporary, or casual jobs' (2000: 69).

Not all lament the rush to flexible work organization to improve profitability, of course, and some have vigorously denied that the obvious turmoil in the job structure is real cause for concern. In fact, they would argue quite the opposite. This conservative critique has focused on the emerging service economy and the high technology electronics industry. Proponents of the 'deindustrialization' thesis like Bluestone and Harrison have been criticized for ignoring the dynamic dimension of capitalism in these new sectors, which have stimulated the growth of an impressive number of jobs in the 1980s and 1990s. Job growth is proof, they say, of the dynamic nature of 'open' market economies. While some critics do not deny the painful aspects of the transition to an information-based society, they argue it will be short-term and is a necessary evil if we are to have the dynamism that is responsible for long-term increases in living standards.[6] As one critic has put it: 'many of the country's jobs were destroyed because of the jobs that were created – that many jobs are lost simply because workers prefer other and better employment ... The interdependence of job creation and job destruction is so complete that we might just as well use the rate of job destruction as a sign of economic vitality rather than as a sign of economic distress' (McKenzie 1985: 64).

However, critics of the emerging 'service economy' point to disturbing evidence of what has been somewhat inaccurately dubbed the 'hourglass' economy because of its shrinking middle tier of managerial, and blue-collar unionized workers (Bluestone and Harrison 1988: 70). As Daniel Drache argues in the Canadian context: 'While there are better paying jobs in services in a few areas, the service economy is first and foremost a low-wage economy. This is the main reason why job growth has changed the shape of the wage pyramid right across the face of the entire economy' (1991: 262).

Interestingly, studies in the United States have argued that this is true even in metropolitan areas where leading edge high technology and financial services firms are prominent. Here, the emergence of a technical and financial elite has also brought forth a host of low-wage jobs to service the new economy, jobs disproportionately populated by women, visible minorities, and new immigrants (see Ross and Trachte 1990 and Bluestone and Harrison 1988).

Empirical evidence to support these contentions is particularly rich for the United States (see Bluestone and Harrison 1982, 1988; Noyelle 1987; Rodwin 1989; Ross and Trachte 1990). Evidence is less abundant for Canada, but a few important studies suggest the emerging pattern. Like other developed economies, the shift in the job structure towards service economy employment has accelerated and is now quite advanced. While the 'goods producing' sector, primary industries (agriculture, fishing, forestry, and mining) and manufacturing accounted for about 40 per cent of employment in 1967, this declined to 29 per cent by 1988. The decline in the primary sector has been particularly dramatic in Canada (from 10.6 per cent to 6 per cent). By the latter date, service sector employment accounted for just over 70 per cent of jobs in Canada and almost 90 per cent of job growth in Canada since 1967 (Economic Council of Canada 1990: 4–5).

What then, are the essential characteristics of this new economy that is rapidly replacing the one based on resource industries and manufacturing? There is evidence that service sector growth has contributed to the phenomenon of 'occupational skidding' noted above. The growth of contingent jobs – those jobs sometimes referred to as 'non-standard' that do not conform to full-time, full year work, have increased quite dramatically. Part-time work, which was around 4 per cent of jobs in the 1960s, had grown to 18 percent in the 1990s (OECD, cited in Moody 1997: 98), and it contributed to an average of 30 per cent of overall employment growth in Canada between 1975 and 1988 (Economic Council of Canada, 1990: 11; see also Yalnizyan et al. 1994: 27–30). Other forms of contingent labour, including short-term jobs, self-employment, and temporary help agencies have also increased substantially in the 1980s. These types of employments are known to be overwhelmingly non-unionized, and less likely to be covered by fringe benefits. Wages are likely to be substantially lower than full-time, full-year jobs (Yalnizyan et al. 1998). As Lowe argues, contingent work typically entails lower skill requirements, is more repetitive, and offers less decision-making autonomy than permanent jobs in the stable work world. In many cases, especially in the retail, personal, and consumer services sectors, such work means not using your education, skills, and abilities (Lowe 2000: 65). Moreover, even among workers normally considered to be full-time, the contemporary trend for firms to out-source more and more of the work previously done by its core labour force has exacerbated the growth of the two-tiered labour market within industries and firms. The automobile industry is a prime example of this trend (see Ip 26 October 1996: B1, B4).

Sectoral analysis of job trends indicates that these types of jobs are particularly concentrated in what has been termed the 'traditional' services (over 40 per cent of jobs there being 'non-standard'), but also prevalent in the more 'dynamic' service industries as well (Economic Council of Canada 1990: chart 7). Of course, it is precisely in these areas where most of the job growth in Canada is taking place, and where many ex-employees of the restructured manufacturing sector must seek work.[7]

It is noteworthy, however, and in keeping with the American experience, that various types of 'non-standard' employment have also seen growth in primary resource and secondary manufacturing industries, where by 1986 they were over 20 per cent of employments (ECC 1990). We return to this matter below.

What then of the longer-term economic impact of this structural change; has it led to the growth of an 'hourglass' economy with a decline in the middle tier of employments and the consequent polarization of incomes as has been persuasively argued in the United States? One major research report based on Statistics Canada data for the period 1967 to 1986 found that there has been in fact a definite decline in the middle stratum of income earners, and of this 'declining middle' nearly three-fifths were redistributed into the lower group (ECC 1991: 142). This had produced, even by 1986, a measurable increase in *income inequality* in Canada, as compared with 1967. Further studies have corroborated this growing inequality since then (see Morisette et al. 1993). The study by Yalnizyan et al. (1994: 21) indicates this trend has even accelerated in more recent years. They also present data that indicates dramatic shifts in market income among Canadian families in the period 1973 to 1991. By 1991 the top richest Canadian families with children had increased their share of market income about 14 per cent, while the income share of the poorest 10 per cent of families had plummeted 47 per cent since 1973. They note that only government transfer payments to these families have prevented a free fall into destitution (1994: 24).[8]

This relative growth in jobs at the bottom of the earnings distribution is argued by some to be mainly the result of declining relative wages among young people, a decline that is manifest in all economic sectors including manufacturing and resource industries (Picot et al. 1990: 24; and Morissette et al. 1993: 20–1; Betcherman and Morissette 1994). Wages for young men especially declined rapidly during the 1980s compared to male employees in older age groups (Lipovenko 17 September 1997). It has also been argued that there is strong evidence in Canada that a growing polarization of hours worked, especially among male workers, accounted for much of the growing earnings inequality in the 1980s (Morissette et al. 1993: 22). This was likely due to a shift for some from full-time to part-time work, but especially full-time workers having to work longer hours.[9]

In 1995 we argued that it may still be too early to conclude that the trends noted above were not of a cyclical economic nature and could possibly be reversed in the near future. We did lean towards the view of the well known study by the Economic Council of Canada that took the position, even before the vicious recession of the 1990s took hold, that the 'pervasiveness of the polarization does suggest that the changes that are taking place in the workplace and within industries are *fundamental and systemic*' (Economic Council of Canada 1990: 15, our emphasis). We believe that more recent data provide strong confirmation of this thesis, and in fact indicate that social polarization has continued throughout the 1990s. The incidence of low-paying work in Canada by the mid-1990s, for example, was second only to that of the United States, where low unemployment figures mask the existence of a vast mass of working poor (Yalnizyan 1998: 22–3).

These overall shifts are gendered in certain ways. Earlier research on restructuring suggested that while in some ways women's opportunities in the labour market would improve because of the kinds of structural shifts taking place which expand the jobs available in the service sector, it was also argued that this was offset by the fact that much of the expansion was in part-time and temporary work (Bagguley et al. 1990), which continues to leave women at a disadvantage. Later research has taken a somewhat different approach. Armstrong (1996), for example, argues that if we look at labour market indicators, there has been a feminization of the labour force as more women enter traditionally 'male' jobs, and receive similar wages to men. However, the details behind these shifts include growing levels of unemployment, part-time, and part-year work for both men and women. While women are more likely to take part-time work (though not through choice) if they are unable to find full-time jobs, increasingly men too are forced to opt for part-time employment. A major difference in the early 1990s was that in the service sector women were more likely to be employed in the lower tier service industries, where the opportunities for women have been growing, particularly for part-time work. Armstrong discusses the rise in the number of self-employed workers, noting that most of these are 'own account' workers, who do not employ others, and that most of them are women. She also notes the rise in multiple job holding, especially in the service sector. It must be reiterated that much of this is low-paid work. Indeed, Canada has the second highest incidence of low-paid work among women of all the OECD countries at 34 per cent, second only to Japan (Armstrong 1996). However, as Armstrong argues, overall men's and women's jobs are also becoming more similar because many of the good jobs traditionally dominated by men are not so good any more (42).

The major gender difference that still pertains, nevertheless, is women's responsibility for caring for dependents, both young and old. This leads women towards part-time work, especially as the state retreats from its responsibilities in relation to the old, the young and the sick, and constrains their employment options even when there are opportunities. This responsibility also leads women into highly exploitative forms of work such as homework, which are both increasingly available, and seem to be also consistent with the ideology of women's caring work and the reality of the time they must devote to it (Leach 1993, 1996, 1998; Boris 1994).

There is good evidence of the development of a generational earnings gap in Canada as well, with workers under thirty-five experiencing an increasing relative decline in earnings. While the growth of contingent work in our economy has a part to play here, what is notable is that there is evidence of a dramatic increase in the gap in generational earnings for full-time workers. This gap is not a short term phenomenon, but has been growing since the early 1980s (see Morissette, 1996). As Yalnizyan argues, the primary reason for this gap is the low wages offered to young workers: 'Hourly rates of pay for workers aged 16 to 24 fell regardless of which industry or occupation they worked at, the region of the country in which they lived, or the level of education they had completed' (Yalnizyan 1998: 24).

If the nature of employment shows definite signs of change, how then have the characteristics of *unemployment* changed, if at all? While there is not complete unanimity on this issue (see Picot and Piper 1993: 34–5), there is strong evidence in Canada of a rather substantial and disturbing increase in the proportion of unemployed individuals experiencing long-term unemployment.[10] Indeed, in 1989, even after seven years of economic 'recovery,' the incidence of long-term unemployment was 100 per cent higher than the level prevailing in 1980 (Gera 1991: 99). Moreover, there is evidence of the development of sharp interregional differences in the duration of unemployment in the most recent recession. The duration of unemployment for permanently laid-off workers in Ontario has increased by 100 per cent in the early 1990s, compared to a 25 per cent increase for the rest of Canada (Corak 1993: 2).

Older workers in recent years have fared considerably worse than was previously the case with respect to duration of unemployment (Corak 1993: 12). In fact, the gap between the incidence of re-employment of younger workers, and those over forty-five has substantially widened since the late 1970s (Gera 1991: chart 8–7). Trends in unemployment are all the more disconcerting when we appreciate, as James Rinehart reminds us, that the significance of work today goes far beyond mere survival and the size of one's pay-cheque. 'Unemployment erodes personal relationships and creates feelings of disorientation, despair and worthlessness' (Rinehart 1987: 7–8).

The implications of these shifts for working-class people, and for the analysis of class are important. Work fragmentation, exemplified by the rise of contingent work, undermines a major mechanism through which workers develop class consciousness: the shared experience of exploitation on the shop floor. Workers who work irregular, short shifts, whose co-workers during any particular shift change constantly, and who experience relatively frequent periods with little or no work at all, are unlikely to develop broadly-based forms of worker solidarity. Similarly, traditional working-class communities are fragmented by large-scale economic restructuring, the demise of manufacturing industries, population movements, and transportation systems (Scase 1992: 69). Combined with the range of ideological and organizational strategies employed by management and dominant political movements, these trends have serious consequences for labour movements and for class politics more broadly conceived. Some argue that it is the fragmentation of the working class as a result of globalization that is responsible for the emergence of social democratic political parties, with pluralistic platforms rather than radical class analyses and programmes for social transformation (see Teeple 1995: 27–33).

We examine the reshaping of the job structure with a predominant focus on the employees that have been affected by corporate restructuring in our case studies, rather than on the management agenda that motivated the widespread shift to flexible work organization. In our decision to study the consequences of employment insecurity, rather than management strategies to promote flexible work organization, we found ourselves in tune with recent work by British social scientists. We share interests on the definition and analysis of employee interests at work, how current changes in the work place are affecting those interests, in particular as insecurity at various levels of the economy becomes more pervasive; (see Heery and Salmon (2000: 18).[11]

We strongly maintain the position that since capitalism, in any form, relies on class differentiation and class exploitation for its profit-making, and ultimately for its survival, class must always be critical to an analysis of capitalist transformation. At the same time, we concur with Seccombe and Livingstone (1996) that a class-reductive approach is untenable in a world where powerful disintegrative processes are at work and that it needs to be replaced by a multidimensional approach which examines factors, some of which are addressed in the discussion above, such as gender, age, race and ethnicity, and nationality.

Bringing Globalization 'Down to Earth':
The Rural Community Context

The host of changes described above are happening in a variety of social contexts, with different impacts for people in different places. The problems of the inner city associated with these changes have probably received the most attention from media, and therefore the public is perhaps most familiar with them. The dramatic growth of homeless individuals, and the explosion in the use of food banks are two very visible signs. In the early 1990s surveys by Canada's largest food bank indicated that substantial numbers of new middle-class families and individuals were added to the food bank user population.[12] It was not coincidental that corporations were moving to eliminate a sizeable proportion of their middle-management employees, in addition to shutting down operations altogether and moving south to the United States or Mexico.[13] Our concern with the micro level of analysis will be focused on the 'working through' of these trends at the level of manufacturing rural communities in the Central Canadian context. We approach small manufacturing-based communities as a window into the changing reality of Canadian society. Examining and questioning the changes at this level can and probably should lead us to examine the society as a whole and the ways in which it is rapidly evolving.

There has been considerable academic debate around the meaning of both 'rural' and 'community.'[14] We take communities to be local social systems which are spatially organized, and within which there are both shared interests and conflicts based on class differences, as well as other factors such as gender, age, race, and ethnicity. The term 'rural' tends to have been historically associated with agriculture, but also with other forms of primary activity such as forestry. The decline of agriculture has led to a default definition in recent years, based primarily on population. Now, rural tends to refer simply to those areas with a low population or low population density (Bryden 1994: 46).

The geographic boundaries of rural communities today are increasingly hard to define as people organize their lives to draw on the resources of more than one town or village on a regular basis.[15] The spatial or territorial dimension of the communities we study is a characteristic shared with the ecological perspective to community studies, and indeed we have some interest in the interrelationship between the human community and its environment. However, this perspective has been interested primarily in the spatial consequences of social organization (Bell and Newby 1972: 33), and particularly in the urban context. We, on the other hand, are more concerned with how the wider political economy impinges on our communities over time, and what factors in the community shape the way in which external pressures are handled locally. Numerous factors complicate attempts to classify and define rural communities, such as proximity to larger centres, historical settlement patterns, and more recently the diversification of economic activities with the decline of agriculture, towards new forms of manufacturing, tourism and recreation, and social services (Bryden 1994; Fitchen 1991).

Colin Bell and Howard Newby (1972) have argued that it is possible to categorize many studies of community into two large groups: those that study community as an object in its own right and those that find the community context a useful local context or social 'laboratory' for empirical studies of broader sociological problems. In other words, in this latter approach the emphasis is on making a contribution to understanding the broader issues, rather than discovering the community and taking this as a principal focus. Although this distinction is helpful, it is too simple to capture what some studies have attempted to accomplish. Our own study has a strong emphasis on utilizing the community as a locus for examining broader issues affecting Canadian society at the end of the twentieth century, but we seek also to expand our knowledge of small rural communities dependent on manufacturing activities. In so doing, we hope that we contribute in some way to each of these communities knowing a bit more about itself. If successful, we will have helped to bridge the gap in community studies characterized above by Bell and Newby some time ago.

It is legitimate to ask, Why should we study rural communities at all in understanding the changing reality of Canadian society? This question is especially apposite if one is to believe, as some have suggested, that contemporary social processes can best be assessed through urban, industrial studies (Creed and Ching 1997). In contrast, rural communities are microcosms of change, and as such they represent a sociological entity that is a manageable unit for study and analysis. However, it might seem surprising that in a country as highly urbanized as Canada is today, a sizeable proportion of the population is classified by federal government statisticians as 'rural and small town.' Indeed, in Saskatchewan, New Brunswick, Nova Scotia, Prince Edward Island, Newfoundland, the Yukon, and the North West Territories, this group still comprises approximately 40 per cent or more of the population. In all provinces except Ontario and British Columbia, more than 20 per cent of the population are rural and small town.[16]

Aside from where people actually live now, we might also consider that a very substantial proportion of grandparents, and even parents of adult Canadians had their origins in, and spent much of their lives attached to, rural communities. In short, most Canadian families had roots in rural communities but one or two generations ago. And while many, especially more recent immigrants, have left these rural environs abroad to escape desperate economic circumstances, they brought with them, as did rural-to-urban migrants in the Canadian context itself, rural worldviews or ethics, values, and ways of doing things that had been shaped and reshaped through the centuries-old interaction of people with an environment that was basically rural in all its facets. This is an essential if not always visible aspect of Canadian heritage that present generations carry with them, that has shaped our social institutions, and that gives a distinctive flavour to our political culture. It may also hold some valuable secrets that can be put to good use as we seek to rebuild rural *and* urban environments that are more sustaining of community in the future.

The rural worldview is difficult to pin down in social science terms, yet at the same time it is probably the most reliable defining feature of rural peoples and communities. Some social scientists have argued, following extensive systematic attempts to define reliable indicators of rurality, that we should 'do away with rural' (Hoggart 1990; Halfacree 1993; Shucksmith 1994) as an analytical category. Yet, as anyone familiar with rural communities knows, 'rural' remains a meaningful category to people who live outside cities, even as restructuring renders the rural more difficult to define for analysts and residents alike. Shucksmith argues that rural is more useful seen as social representation than as a particular kind of space, in other words 'a symbolic shorthand ... something which captures what they [rural residents] feel about rurality' (Shucksmith 1994: 127). We agree that social scientists must take peoples' commonsense notions of what significant concepts or keywords seriously mean to them (Williams 1983), and not simply dismiss them as irrelevant if they are difficult to quantify.

Nevertheless, we believe that there is a particular material reality that comes with living in a rural area. This is tied to distances between communities and between points on the maps that organize people's everyday lives (in other words, from home to schools, to stores, to doctors, to child care providers, to work, to the implement dealer, to fitness classes, and back through the list to home again). It is also tied to the very real consequences of policy decisions frequently made far from rural communities and without considering their interests. Such decisions often lead to inequality of resources within rural communities compared with urban ones, including inadequate health care (the shortage of rural doctors and the closing of small-town hospitals are but two examples frequently in the Ontario news) and social service provision (the lack of rural child care spaces, and of services for abused women and children), and few job and training opportunities (it is difficult to attract and retain good quality jobs in rural areas, and training programs are often outside of commuting distance – two issues we take up in later chapters).

Shucksmith (1994) argues that in the everyday world of rural community politics, contested ideas of what rural actually means become highly charged and have significant consequences in the shaping of rural life and, in the example he provides, for the direction rural economic development takes in particular locales. This observation clearly has particular implications for lines of differentiation within communities including but not limited to class, race, and gender. Fitchen

(1991: Chapter 16) explores the 'folk' definition of rural for the people she talked to in upstate New York, and found it to include an apparent contradiction between 'a high quality of life' and a set of 'sacrifices' or 'difficulties.' Fitchen argues that quality of life is non-material whereas standard of living is material, which supports our position that we need to keep symbolic ideas about the rural closely tied to the material reality of living it, because both of these, operating together, result in a particular lived experience of rurality.

Why Manufacturing-Dependent Rural Communities?

Scholarship on rural Canadian communities has waxed and waned over the past several decades. Interest with community research in the United States in the 1950s saw its counterpart in Canada (see Hughes 1963, and Miner 1963), but for the most part the emergence of a critical social science in Canada in the late 1960s and 1970s did not rekindle a similar interest in communities. This was perhaps because previous research had tended to have more structural-functionalist, conservative overtones (but for Ontario, see Barrett 1994; Rayside 1991). More recently, scholars working within the political economy tradition have revived an interest in communities, but much of this interest has focused on understanding the social organization and crisis of fishing communities, mainly on the east coast (see Apostle and Barrett 1992; Connelly and MacDonald 1983; Davis 1991; Sinclair 1997; Felt and Sinclair 1995). There has also been a small amount of research on other resource-based communities, principally those that are agriculturally and mining-based (see Hansen and Muszynski 1990; Koch and Gartrell 1992), as well as the work by Bowles (1982) that has had a broader focus.

Although communities based on primary resource extraction lie at the heart of what typifies much of the Canadian hinterland, they do not exhaust hinterland communities. Moreover, there are other numerous rural communities, more typical of southern Quebec and Ontario, that have been sustained by diverse kinds of *manufacturing* activity for well over 100 years. Among manufacturing-dependent rural communities we find a range of situations, from those with a relatively diverse economic base, where no dominant enterprise leaves its stamp on the community, to others where a single firm has provided the community's raison d'être. While the bulk of these communities exist in the more densely populated and long-settled agricultural regions, some rural communities in the hinterland owe their existence to manufacturing activities, closely linked to the extraction of primary resources.

Manufacturing industry is popularly associated with large urban centres, although in the early part of the Industrial Revolution it had a decidedly rural character. At the beginning of the Industrial Revolution, manufacturing flourished in the still densely populated English countryside. This thriving, dispersed, small-scale rural industry produced woolen goods and cotton cloth up until the threshold of the nineteenth century, when dramatic changes to the division of labour in industry and the invention of steam power allowed nascent capitalists to concentrate production in large modern factory establishments in the larger towns (see Mantoux 1961: Chapter 1 and Thirsk 1984: Chapter 13).

Manufacturing never left rural areas entirely however. In the central Canadian countryside the decline of early domestic industry was caused by the influx of cheap manufactured goods imported from Britain (see Johnson 1971, 1973). Soon after there emerged a larger-scale rural industry tightly linked to the agrarian economy. The early grist mills and cheese factories in the countryside were supplemented with agricultural implement manufacturers, furniture factories, canneries, garment factories, and a host of other manufacturing establishments stimulated by the demand provided by the farm community prospering from wheat, initially, and later a mixed farming regime (see Jones 1946; McCallum 1980; Winson 1985). The history of these manufacturing towns and villages in Canada is still in its infancy, but the few pioneering studies we have provide some insights. In her study into the furniture and garment manufacturing towns of Hanover and Paris, Ontario, respectively, Joy Parr (1990) notes that industry began in these locations in the mid-1860s, saw its heyday in the first three decades of the twentieth century, and began to decline after the Second World War. The principal firms in each town had failed by the 1980s. The longevity of the community-based firms in Parr's study may have been an anomaly. Our own research indicates that many of these local companies had either been bought up by larger national firms or were absorbed by or bankrupted by the entrance of powerful U.S. branch plant operations by the mid-1950s. By the 1980s and early 1990s new trends in corporate capitalism, aided by federal policy decisions, resulted in the shutdown of numerous manufacturing operations in the industrial heartland of Canada.[17] In this process rural communities were often hard hit (see Winson 1993: Chapter 8, and Leach and Winson 1995).

Fitchen's study (1991) of upstate New York indicates that some rural communities are even *more* dependent on manufacturing activities than major metropolitan cities such as New York City, where large complex service sectors concentrating financial institutions and information technology have developed. The decline of manufacturing activities in the context of rural upstate New York posed special problems because service sector growth that could have ameliorated this decline has not been strong. Rural communities were also seen to be stressed by the long-term crisis of the farm sector, a crisis that dates from the high interest rates and collapse of land prices that occurred with the 1981 recession. Fitchen argues, however, that the loss of factories in rural communities has had a more pervasive and deeper impact than the decline in farms (Fitchen 1991: 74).

In other respects Fitchen's findings in rural New York State reflect much of what others have found about corporate restructuring in metropolitan areas: evidence of definite 'occupational skidding' to lower-paying, often part-time work with limited benefits. Older workers, particularly men and the less-educated, were especially disadvantaged. Moreover, it has been common for workers to experience a decline in the quality of life on the job, typically as a result of less-favourable working conditions and/or the necessity to commute farther to the new jobs (Fitchen 1991).

Despite the demise of manufacturing activity or its shift to low-wage havens offshore (see Bluestone and Harrison 1982; 1988; Healey 1993; Howland 1988) recently there has been an emergence of new types of manufacturing in some rural communities. In the United States and Canada corporations in such major sectors as automobile parts and assembly and meat-packing have sought rural 'greenfield' sites for a number of reasons (see Kenney 1993; Stull and Broadway 1990). Marsden et al. (1990: 8–9) argues that some rural areas have experienced an economic 'windfall' because they offer certain comparative advantages to the technologies and processes of flexible accumulation.[18] The major advantage rural sites offer is lower wages, and while this bears some relationship to a lower cost of living in some rural areas, it is mainly a result of local histories which tend not to include labour militancy. Indeed, as Kingsolver notes, rural workers often identify with a historical tradition as independent farmers, even long after they have left the farms (Kingsolver 1998: 12), eschewing labour organizations. Labour unions have had difficulty making inroads into rural areas, meeting with opposition from workers and others when they have tried to organize rural workers. At the same time, unions have paid little serious attention to the concerns of relatively small groups of rural industrial workers. Consequently, wages have not been driven upwards or combined with expensive benefit packages. In the current era of industrial restructuring, in which union avoidance has become a key strategy to keep costs low and profits high, the absence of an organized labour tradition, combined frequently with evident anti-union sentiment, is a valuable asset to firms seeking new locations. This should not imply, however, that the ruralization of industry is only into areas where there is an absence of wage labour in manufacturing. Rather, wage labour has tended to emerge initially as an adjunct to farm work (see Kingsolver 1998), eventually substituting for it as labour-intensive agriculture and independently owned farms decline. But the ideology of the rural independent producer continues to prevail, as we shall see in Chapter 7. Of course, these remarks apply mainly to rural areas that had a strong *agrarian* history. Where other types of economic activities prevailed, different social relations tended to emerge.

There is a growing literature on the ruralization of both the meat-packing and auto industries, a process which transforms social relations in rural communities. Kingsolver discusses how Toyota was made welcome when it set up a plant in rural Kentucky, and explores the unanticipated changes to community cohesion there. The increasing penetration of the auto industry into rural Ontario, in particular the auto parts industry, is promoted by the provincial government, and is seen by some in rural communities as a remedy for economic ills caused by the decline of traditional agriculture and manufacturing. To date, however, there has been little scholarly work on this.

By contrast, there have been a few serious studies on the impact of what Fink (1998) calls the 'new breed' of meat-packing enterprises on rural communities in the Midwest of the United States. Fink's study of an IBP factory in Perry, Iowa, is a disturbing story of brutality, prejudice, and immorality on the part of the company, met by violence, apathy, and eventually deep distress by the workers. Fink describes how the meat-packing industry, which had grown in rural areas alongside agriculture from the late nineteenth century, became urbanized and unionized during the Second World War as part of the U.S. war effort. During the 1970s the 'new breed' of firm emerged, deliberately destroying the urban industry by buying up urban companies and relocating production in rural areas where they set up non-union plants and hired women and visible minority workers. As Fink shows, the new industry built on existing rural ideas about class, gender, and race, which justified lower wages for women and non-white workers. At the same time, they appealed to the desperation felt by declining rural communities in need of employment opportunities, no matter how bad those jobs eventually turned out to be. Fink describes how IBP's threat to close the Perry facility in 1994 was met with appeals by local business community and social service community members alike.

In this industry, job turnover is astoundingly high as a result of job stress and management whim. Fink estimates turnover at IBP in Perry to be approximately 400 per cent per year (Fink 2000), which means that the local workforce is soon exhausted, and companies turn to attracting workers from more distant communities. IBP is reported to have imported groups of Mexican and refugee workers, deducting the costs of travel and rent in company-owned dormitories from their pay cheques. With the rapid turnover that continues, crime rates in meat-packing communities rise, and there is tremendous stress on the local infrastructure (Fink 1998; Grey 1998).

Lack of research on this industry in Canada hampers efforts to draw reliable conclusions here. What is clear is that the meat-packing industry has undergone tremendous restructuring over the past ten years, especially since the demise of the long-time industry leader in the meat-packing sphere, Canada Packers (see Winson 1993: Chapter 8). Numerous large urban meat-packing facilities have been closed down, while production has shifted to smaller centres as in the United States. Major employers, such as Maple Leaf Foods, which is led by the McCain family, have been able to batter down workers' wages some 40 per cent in acrimonious labour struggles, effectively using the threat of plant shutdown to their advantage.

The experience and consequences of this form of industrialization in Canadian rural communities is yet to be analysed and merits attention. Anecdotal reports from the auto sector, for example, tell of entire rural auto-parts factories staffed by visible minority immigrant workers bussed in daily from the Greater Toronto area. Clearly, labour utilization of this kind requires a rethinking of class and race in rural communities. Indeed, rural manufacturing communities are a valuable object of study because they insist on the problematization of class, in contrast to a prevailing rural ideology which posits rural communities as classless communities of small property owners.

Sustainability in the Rural Community Context

Almost since the concept of sustainability was initially propelled into the public consciousness by the Bruntland Commission Report of 1987 and other international meetings, commissions, and summits, it has proved contentious and contested. Its initial formulations have received trenchant critiques, particularly when the concept is linked, as it so often is, with the concept of development.[19]

Our own work on communities linked through manufacturing to the global economy has forced us to think about what it is that makes a community more or less vulnerable or resilient to the external forces we discuss earlier in this chapter. One of us (Winson) was forcefully confronted with this issue when he returned to a small northern Ontario town he had lived in as a child. He and his family had left because the asbestos mine that had provided employment for many townspeople closed. He had assumed that this event was the death-knell for this community of only 700. Nevertheless, almost twenty-five years later, upon his return, he found the town still there and essentially intact. Businesses in town were basically holding their own and had been for a good many years. Indeed, the town had even expanded with a new modest housing development on its periphery. Thus, even in a region noted for single-industry resource communities, with all the disadvantages and vulnerabilities this implies, it appeared that some communities defy the stereotype of resource industry decline.

However, a return to the community seven years later produced a less favourable impression. Several of the businesses in the small commercial core had closed and local inquiries, plus an interview with the township reeve, indicated that a malaise had set in. Years before, the decline of the community's resource base had been offset by the modest expansion of the public sector there, such as the opening of a Ministry of Natural Resources office, and employment provided by the provincially owned electrical utility, Ontario Hydro. Moreover, other public sector employers including a regional provincial police office had helped to give lifeblood to the community for years afterwards. It was the major cuts at the federal and especially the provincial level to the public sector that was now undermining the sustainability of this community.

This example brings to the fore the role that *economic diversity* can play in determining community stability and material well-being. Clearly, the community noted above had a more diverse employment base than was immediately apparent, despite the major role that one resource-based company served in the community. It also shows that it would be a mistake to view diversity solely as a private sector affair. For a long time public enterprise played a substantial role, if often a less visible one, in providing even small communities with good jobs, jobs that typically helped to buffer them from the greater volatility of private firms linked to the vicissitudes of the market.

The part that economic diversity plays in the life of a community is a theme that we explore in Chapter 7, through our case studies. While there is a generally held assumption that greater diversity should lead to more community stability, there is research that suggests the relationship is not as straightforward as might be expected. Diversification in some directions may indeed stabilize a community affected by volatile swings in resource commodity cycles, for example, or one with a principal economic activity characterized by highly seasonal employment demand, such as agriculture or tourism. On the other hand, diversification in another direction may even exacerbate the volatility of the local economy as some studies suggest. In this book we analyse economic diversity and its supposed relationship to community stability and ultimate sustainability, using our own research, as well as empirical research by others.

While much literature assesses the benefits provided by economic diversity, using quantitative measures of employment stability, not so much attention is paid to the *quality* of employment that local economies provide. Is it possible that a single industry resource-based community could provide jobs that according to a number of criteria are of superior quality to the majority of jobs available in a more diversified rural community? Indeed, our own research suggests that this can be the case. The implications of this are usually lost in economic studies that focus primarily, and often entirely, on quantitative measures of diversity and employment stability.

However surprisingly resilient some communities might be, they are in a perilous condition the likes of which has not been seen for several generations. The global political economy has historically had deleterious effects on the human communities it has engulfed. Indeed, while the classical liberal worldview has been preoccupied with the revolutionizing and dynamic effects of capitalism, at the level of community capitalism it has typically been a corrosive and often wholly destructive force. The characteristics of the world capitalist economy today may indeed be anathema to enduring human communities in the absence of protective countermeasures at both the local and/or national levels.

Constructing and maintaining healthy communities under this social and economic order is destined to be a continual struggle. We believe that any other view on communities today is at best naive, and at worst irresponsibly misleading. Building healthy communities is inevitably about balancing competing local interests that external forces are constantly putting askew. It is about trying to capture some degree of local control in a context where control is forever being drained away from the community and concentrated elsewhere, either by powerful economic actors (today transnational corporations) or by governments, which today increasingly see their role as handmaidens of business. The issue of sustainability, with respect to communities, cannot be disentangled from the wider political economy. Neither can it be detached from ecological concerns, although these latter concerns are much more immediate for some communities, in particular resource-dependent communities, than for others. The matter of sustainability is a complicated issue, with several overlapping and competing dimensions. Yet it must be discussed, if only because we believe that people need strong communities to thrive, and among those communities, *small, rural* communities have something very valuable to contribute to human welfare and happiness. For this reason, it is useful to envision policies that will allow these communities to reach their potential and to retain what valuable characteristics they have for us today. This policy-making is no easy task today, nor was it in the past. Community is the crucible in which globalization finally works itself out. It is where the rubber hits the road.

In this book we are particularly interested in exploring the welfare of those groups thought to be most vulnerable to changes under the rubric of 'restructuring,' in the rural community milieu. In particular, we are concerned with unskilled and semi-skilled workers, female labour, older workers and rural youth.[20] Do rural communities serve as a 'buffer' to protect the most vulnerable members of the workforce from the ravages of globalization and the neo-liberal agenda? Or do rural communities lack the economic dynamism and social solidarity needed to provide any real buffer to global pressures? The fate of the blue-collar labour force in restructuring rural manufacturing communities has been all but ignored to date. We propose to explore their condition, largely although not entirely using a comparative case study approach. The comparison of communities having different types of industrial structure will allow us to consider how significant matters such as economic diversity can be in deciding the future of this segment of rural Canadian society.

Many would agree with Gordon Laxer that people today want a sense of belonging, security, equality, respect, personal development, and freedom (1995: 308). If this book has an overarching purpose, it is to contribute, if only in a small way, to improving the chances that Canadians shall realize such goals. The powerful proponents of the now dominant 'neo-liberal' agenda, in fact, claim that our best chance in achieving these goals, given the changes in the wider world economy, are through policies that promote trade liberalization, deregulation, and privatization and policies that leave the individual ever-more exposed to raw market forces. The question rural communities, and indeed all Canadians, need to ask is, Is there good evidence to support this claim for the dominant agenda?

We may and should ask, What have the results been so far? Are the benefits hoped for materializing, and if so, are they widely available, or captured by just a few? How are rural communities likely to stand up to the new environment created by this agenda? What are their specific weaknesses, and strengths, in this new environment?

In pursuing these questions, rural communities will be participating in a wider debate that has waxed and waned in Canada for about ten years now and which will likely not go away for some time. It is a debate that, in varying forms, has transfixed other societies as well, from the Scandinavian countries to New Zealand, with deep reverberations in the developing world. The outcome of the social struggle that underlies this debate, without a doubt, will determine the kind of society Canadians will call their own until well into the twenty-first century.

CHAPTER THREE

Community Sketches, History, and Method

The villages and small towns of Ontario provide a counterpoint to urban life in the province. Like rural communities in other industrial regions, they embody and promise an unchanging, slower-paced way of life. The common experience of nurturing community and land in the face of both bias in favour of the urban experience and values and natural unpredictability obscures lines of social differentiation. It also creates local ties that are deep and highly valued. In *The Country and the City*, Raymond Williams takes the images associated with these powerful ideas, and through his systematic analysis of English history and literature, shows how they exist in tension with each other, sustaining a divide that obscures the ways in which both have been transformed by industrial capitalism. Williams observes that 'the change from admiration of cultivated country to the intense attachment to "unspoiled" places is a precise record of this persistent process and its effects at one of its most active stages' (1973: 293). Recent attention to late modernity focuses on the urban, perpetuating the idea that rural communities are not valuable culturally, socially, or economically (Creed and Ching 1996).

Small towns and villages have come and gone in Canada. Nevertheless, as a form of human settlement they do have some degree of persistence (see Hodge and Qadeer 1983: Chapter 2). Data on small towns and villages with a population of fewer than 10,000 people indicate that, after a long period of decline with rapid urbanization, smaller communities began to stabilize in the 1960s; indeed, since then about one-third of all small communities throughout Canada have remained stable with respect to population (1984: 35). As a proportion of Canada's population, small communities experienced a small decrease between 1961 and 1976, with the exception of New Brunswick where the decline was more drastic (1984: 37).

The slowing down, and even reversal in some regions of the long-standing rural-to-urban flow of population in Canada by the 1970s is certainly partly the result of the profound disillusionment with what urban life has become.[1] It would also seem to express a strong desire to capture – or recapture for some – the simplicity, tranquillity, and closer human associations that are so frequently associated in the popular mind with living in the countryside.[2] And while this transition back to the rural has not been successfully accomplished by all who have attempted it (see, Barrett 1994), it does, nevertheless, signify that for a growing number of people there is value in having a countryside, and rural communities in it, that are vibrant and vital, and sustainable over the longer term.

This chapter has two objectives, one methodological and the other historical. First, it describes the process of the research, outlining how we came to select each community, and more specifically, the workers we approached to interview in each one. It continues with a sketch of each community, together with some details about the present-day demographics, economic profile, and labour market opportunities. Contemporary sketches are followed by a relatively brief industrial history of each community. These histories are intended to demonstrate the depth of the manufacturing industry in each place. Four of the five communities we looked at have industrial roots that stretch back into the nineteenth century. At that time manufacturing enterprises were established, and grew, to service what had begun as agricultural centres. These communities are by no means 'greenfield' sites for industry, if by that term we are to understand sites where labour has not been accustomed over generations to industrial work and its rhythms. Their histories show the processes through which their cultures of work emerged. The histories provide a context for the ways in which the economic restructuring of the 1990s was experienced in these small, rural, industrial communities.

Methods of Inquiry

Our data collection followed a multiphase process between 1992 and 1999. In 1992 we interviewed workers laid off from the Canada Packers plant in Elora, a picturesque town in Wellington County, Ontario. In 1993 and 1994 we extended the study to workers in the towns of

Harriston and Mount Forest, also in Wellington County, who had experienced a recent lay-off. In 1996 we conducted follow-up interviews by telephone with thirty-four of the original sixty-eight informants in Wellington County. From this data we were able to identify some trends in the 'new employment' patterns. In all communities interviews with key informants aided in identifying these. In 1997 we received a grant that enabled us to extend our study to better illustrate the diversity of experience found in small manufacturing communities and to widen its geographic scope.

The second phase of this project began in the late spring of 1997. We analysed data on manufacturing, as well as census data, for various years, for thirty-nine small Ontario communities (found in the *Scott's Directory*). Recent British and U.S. literature convinced us to explore the extent and shape of the new rural economy in the Canadian context, and especially the role of the high technology sector (a problematic term that we discuss later in this chapter) in shaping its prospects. We interviewed workers laid off from a traditional manufacturing company in Arnprior, in the Ottawa Valley, where, because of the proximity to Ottawa, high technology companies have been locating. With its diversified economic base, Arnprior includes both older, traditional manufacturing industries, as well as several companies classified as high tech firms. These high tech firms represent the jobs of the new economy. Some analysts and policy-makers see them as the salvation for manufacturing-dependent communities that are losing their traditional industries. In Arnprior we interviewed eighteen of forty workers who had been laid off from Weavexx to see how they had fared in the local labour market. We also interviewed a variety of key informants – people with specialized knowledge because of their jobs – including a number of plant managers.

Single-industry communities have historically been a distinguishing feature of the Canadian economy, especially in hinterland areas (Lucas 1971). Sometimes, as in the case of pulp-and-paper mill towns, the economic activities qualify as 'manufacturing.' A single-industry community allows an exploration of the significance of economic diversity in an era of dramatic change. With this in mind, we then turned our attention to Iroquois Falls in northern Ontario. We were drawn to this community for two reasons. Iroquois Falls was the site for one of several 'model forest' projects across Canada that depended on federal funding to promote more sustainable forest management and socioeconomic development. Second, it was familiar to one of the authors (Winson) because it lies a short distance (in northern Canadian terms) from a small community that he had lived in many years ago, and the possibility of revisiting the area many years later was intriguing.

Our concern is displaced workers. What constitutes displaced workers in a town where (at least not yet at that time) the paper mill had not downsized through mass lay-offs? Since we know that there had been little or no new hiring for several years, we contacted young people, recently out of high school. In previous decades they would have made an effortless transition from high school student to a secure, well-paid worker at the mill. Through a random sampling of the list of 1993 high school leavers, we contacted thirty-four of these people and for financial and practical reasons, interviewed them by telephone.

In general, respondents were interviewed in person, usually at their homes, though occasionally people felt more comfortable meeting in a neutral place, such as a coffeeshop. All but a few interviews were tape-recorded and subsequently transcribed. Most people were interviewed only once, with the exception of the thirty-four individuals with whom we conducted follow-up interviews in 1996, and a handful of people with whom we sustained ongoing if relatively brief contact. For the in-depth face-to-face interviews, we obtained names in one case from a helpful office employee, in another from the former union steward. Often our only route was snowball sampling, as one worker led us to several others. Sampling was constrained mainly by our capacity to track people down. Very few of those contacted to set up an interview refused our request. Typically, interviews lasted between an hour and an hour and a half.

Throughout this process we endeavoured to obtain a representative sample, matching our sample with what we knew about the workforce as a whole at each worksite; we paid particular attention to the proportions of men and women and the age of workers. We used an interview guide containing a series of questions and probes designed to elicit information about the lost job, periods of unemployment, details about jobs when re-employed, educational achievement, employment information on other household members, and general information about lifestyle changes resulting from the lay-off, usually because of a significant drop in income. We explicitly asked about pay before and after lay-off, and details of employment-related benefits. Most people were willing to supply that information. We also asked how workers had been treated by unions and company management, how they felt about losing their job, and whether they thought it had affected their relationships with family and friends. The specific questions we used are reported in an appendix at the back of the book.

As interviews unfolded and a relationship developed between the worker and the interviewer, we discovered that conversation often moved away from the interview schedule and took interesting directions suggested by the worker. This individualizing of the process is one of the benefits of semi-structured interviews since it allows unanticipated themes and concerns to emerge, often beyond the knowledge of those designing the project and those carrying it out. One result, however, is considerable variation in the information gleaned from each interview. While this provides tremendous richness for the study, it sometimes presents difficulties in comparing data.

In the transcribed conversations (see Chapter 6) we do not always link employees with specific companies. This is necessary, as is the use of pseudonyms, to protect the identity of our respondents, which might otherwise be revealed by the particulars of their comments.

Key informant interviews involved people with particular expertise in their communities, such as high school guidance counsellors, company human resources officers, municipal community development officers, mayors, as well as individuals in the non-profit sector in organizations supporting people looking for work and in need of assistance (such as job placement agencies, food banks, and family resource centres). We also interviewed the plant managers of twelve companies in Arnprior, representing the full range of manufacturing industries there, from the most research-intensive high technology company to what had effectively become a packaging warehouse for a U.S. conglomerate. These plant managers provided information about their company's past and future, as well as data on their current workforce. During the period of research, Weavexx maintained a skeleton operation in Arnprior; its plant managers declined to be interviewed.

In Wellington Country interviews were conducted largely between 1992 and 1996, that is, beginning in the depths of the severe recession of 1990. This macroeconomic disturbance made the inevitable disruption that comes with plant shutdowns and job loss worse. Accounts in Canada's major newspapers reported that the national economy was picking up and on the road to recovery by late 1993 to 1994. Interviews conducted in 1996 and later in the 1990s show that this was a 'recovery' that would be quite different from that experienced in earlier business cycles. Indeed, something more profound was happening, affecting the very structure of Canada's economy.

Elora: The Rise and Fall of a Rural Manufacturing Community

We selected Elora because in 1991 it lost a major industry, Canada Packers' Stillmeadow agrifood-processing plant.

Elora has a dramatic geographic setting, sitting at the point where the Grand River is forced to squeeze through a narrow gorge. The beauty of the gorge, now surrounded by a conservation area, makes Elora a popular tourist destination, as does its close proximity to the cities of Guelph and Kitchener-Waterloo, both about a twenty-minute drive away. Along Mill Street, which runs beside the river on its north bank, many small boutiques and restaurants bustle during the summer tourist season. A number of bed-and-breakfast establishments occupy some of the larger Victorian homes in the village. Elora also attracts visitors to its well-established classical music festival which takes place over three weeks in the summer and to a fledgling winter film festival. Despite the ups and downs of the Ontario economy over the past decade, Elora's proximity to urban centres and its established tourist industry have enabled it to continue to prosper.

The 1996 census reported that the town had a population of 3,346, representing an increase of 1.9 per cent over the 1991 figure. Of these, 105 people (3.7 per cent) identified themselves as either visible minority or Aboriginal, and 200 (6 per cent) identified their first language as other than English. Statistics Canada reports 15.4 per cent of the population as working in manufacturing, while almost 70 per cent were working in the service sector.[3] Elora's population has increased by 43 per cent since 1971.

To some extent, Elora has become a bedroom community for cities like Guelph and Kitchener-Waterloo and even the more distant Greater Toronto.[4] New housing developments in Elora are often marketed in the newspapers of the large cities, offering less expensive housing on larger pieces of land, with the added allure of a village setting. Most of the job opportunities in the town are in the service sector. The handful of manufacturing enterprises employ only a few people, with the exception of Little Folks, a children's bedroom furniture manufacturer that employs fifty-four individuals (*Scott's Directories* 2000). At an earlier time, however, the manufacturing base in Elora was much more significant.

Elora emerged by the late nineteenth century as an impressively diversified centre of small industry. Incorporated in 1858, the average size of its small craft shop economy was four employees, although four establishments stood out with respect to size: a foundry and machine shop with thirty employees, a wagon shop with fifteen employees, a cabinet factory with ten employees, and a flour mill and distillery with nine employees that took advantage of the superb location for water power from the Grand River.

Over the following decades, considerable change to its industrial base took place, although the town retained its industrial character. The key changes are indicative of the wider process of capital concentration and centralization that characterize the Canadian economy throughout the twentieth century. One small furniture company, for example, was begun by John Mundell in 1857 and served the local market for chairs, bedsteads, and other basic furniture. Over the years it expanded and began importing and selling furniture from the United States and Europe (Thorning 1991d). Destroyed by fire in 1873, the factory was rebuilt and continued to produce up until the 1950s, when it was again destroyed by fire. At that time the firm ceased to be locally owned and was sold to outside interests, ending 105 years of local ownership. In 1965 the factory was purchased by Simmons, which built a new plant in 1970. During the 1980s the plant changed hands several times as part of corporate takeovers and downsizing, and in 1989 it was closed permanently.

Another furniture manufacturer, which has survived, was originally named the Elora Furniture Company. It began operations in 1906 and was finally sold to Simmons in 1969. Now it is owned by Little Folks and produces children's bedroom furniture.

A key firm in the community was the Elora Manufacturing Company, formed in 1873 to boost the local economy and to fill a market void as the only carpet manufacturer in Ontario. This relatively large manufacturing firm turned out to be a decidedly mixed blessing for Elora, as some of the nastier features of industrial capitalism were introduced to the relatively quiet agrarian village setting, including shift work and Sunday work, which in turn upset the traditional routines of the town. This manufacturing operation was also characterized by frequent work stoppages and lay-offs caused by the vicissitudes of distant markets. Moreover, most of the skilled and better paying jobs went to outsiders, many brought in from the United States (Thorning 1991c).

The Elora Manufacturing Company underwent several reorganizations and was ultimately a financial failure and a major liability for the town and local shareholders, who lost everything they had invested in the firm (Thorning 1991c). After some years, however, Elora was able to attract a young manufacturer of disk harrows from the nearby town of Fergus. T.E. Bissell, who began production in the old carpet factory premises in 1901, proved to be a shrewd farm implement manufacturer and for nearly thirty years ran a plant in Elora selling his highly regarded disk harrows to farmers across Canada, the United States, and even as far afield as South Africa and Ireland. By the 1920s Bissell was the town's largest industry (Thorning 1991e).

Thorning's study of T.E. Bissell and his firm provides one of the few insights into the economic, social, and cultural dimensions of manufacturing in small town Ontario during the early decades of the twentieth century. He describes an industrial entrepreneur who was keenly aware of the upstream and downstream characteristics of the market in the farm implement sector. This was a small company that depended upon national and international markets for its suppliers and for the sale of its products, even in its earliest days. In this sense the firm departs from the stereotype of local small-town business. T.E. Bissell survived because he knew how to weather the volatile markets which he depended upon, paring down his workforce, and reducing costs whenever business was slack. He was also careful not to take on debt unless absolutely necessary, typically using capital reserves from the firm for any expansion required during boom times.

While the firm was well integrated into national markets at the level of buying and selling, its management structure was extremely narrow, and vested ownership, control, and management in Bissell himself. In this absolute control exercised by the firm's owner lay the great flexibility the firm had in dealing with market fluctuations, but this also made it impossible to build up a more comprehensive company that could have expanded beyond the market niche it occupied. Bissell's corporate goals were conservative and narrow. They tended to emphasize stability and financial security, rather than short-term profit, which no doubt accounted for the firm's longevity during the turbulent economic times.

The Significance of Small Town Manufacturers

If we take the Bissell firm in Elora as emblematic of small town manufacturing at the turn of the century, it was clearly not the structure of the firm or its operations that made it distinctive as a 'small town' entity. Other firms of similar size and characteristics existed in larger cities at this time.

Thorning (1986: 29–30) argues that what made Bissell a small town manufacturer, and what constitutes his specific imprint on the social and cultural life of the community, was 'his identification of himself and his firm with the village of Elora, and the values of paternalism in the factory, the church, and the village; by the flexible and non-confrontatory relationship with his labour force; and by his agrarian liberalism and his belief that cities were inherently evil places. As the large fish in a small pond, Bissell was able to exert an influence in the community that would not have been possible in a larger center. The industrial agrarianism as exemplified by Bissell was atavistic: the values of deference and free market liberalism that it embodied became increasingly anachronistic in the 1920s. Even so, these values persisted in the factory's middle management [and] in the community.'

A distinguishing feature of the small-manufacturing towns of southern Ontario, then, was precisely the imprint given to them by this entrepreneurial class, and especially the industrialists, who gave these towns their earliest economic foundations and, as the case of T.E. Bissell demonstrated, later firmly shepherded them into the modern age of industrial capitalism by integrating their economies into the national market.

The values inculcated by this class of largely male entrepreneurs tended to emphasize paternalism, deference to authority, loyalty, the values of thrift, and most importantly a strong work ethic, typically reinforced by the extraordinary personalities of the entrepreneurs themselves. Indeed, their business was their life. It may be thought that these values had passed by the wayside by the latter part of the twentieth century, as the towns' manufacturing bases became largely absorbed by national and multinational firms. However, our research in several of these communities suggests otherwise. Indeed, these values are still alive and well, even among the blue-collar labour force engaged in small-town industrial operations that have been fully integrated into larger industrial corporations. This was despite the inroads made by industrial

unions in the meantime as well. In spite of the changing material conditions, the values of 'industrial agrarianism,' nurtured by a class of indig-
enous manufacturers many decades earlier, have proven to be most
durable, long after the conditions that gave rise to them all but vanished.

Lacking a suitable heir, Bissell sold out in 1928 to outside interests
related to the Hiram Walker–Gooderham Worts liquor business. After
the sale, the firm was able to survive the worst of the Great depression
reasonably well, and following its merger with the Fleury farm implement firm it prospered during the general economic boom that followed the Second World War. The economic expansion masked the
deeper problems that were to finish off the Bissell company when the
farm implement industry took one of its cyclical downturns. These
problems had to do with the shift in ownership and control to outside
interests who were often preoccupied with financial and other concerns completely unrelated to Bissell's operation. Management brought
in from outside during these years typically had little experience with
the farm implement industry and were often not very long in their
jobs in any case. This was a marked departure from the steady 'hands
on' management style of the original owner. When business turned
down at the end of the 1940s, the outside management believed a
solution to the problem lay in merging the firm with another company
producing electrical transformers – a completely unrelated product
line. In the end, this proved to be a confusing and inefficient management decision, and the hoped-for improvement in profitability did not
occur. The firm continued its financial free fall and went bankrupt by
1954. With the banks foreclosing on the Bissell company in that year,
over 200 jobs were lost, a significant blow to an industrial economy
the size of Elora. Thorning argues that the firm's demise marked Elora's
shift from a 100-year-old manufacturing town to that of a bedroom
community for a workforce that increasingly commute to nearby industrial centres (1991i: 6). Tellingly, the Bissell name now identifies a
bed and breakfast in the house where the family had lived.

The failure of the Bissell firm in 1954 was surely a hard blow to the
local manufacturing economy, but not all of its old manufacturing
foundations had been knocked down. Furniture making had long been
a part of Elora's industrial base and continues to be so. By the mid-
1970s its several furniture manufacturers had been bought out by a

large conglomerate corporation, Simmons Ltd., which had 310 employees in Elora in 1976. Nevertheless, these furniture plants now accounted for over three-quarters of the town's industrial workforce, a sign that the industrial diversity that had once characterized Elora was all but gone.[5] By the mid-1990s only one of its furniture plants was left, however, and the sole surviving operation employed a little over seventy people, a far cry from the 300-plus in this sub-sector fifteen years previously. As we demonstrate in the following chapter, furniture manufacturing was a sub-sector of manufacturing that was seriously affected by the Free Trade Agreement of 1989.

Around this time the town's other remaining industrial employer of any size, Canada Packers' poultry-processing operation, also shut down as a result of the foreign takeover of its parent company, and the restructuring of the new company that took place.[6] This last event decimated what was left of Elora's long industrial tradition.

Interestingly, while manufacturing activities based in Elora have declined, census surveys over the past fifteen years indicate that the proportion of individuals reporting to be employed in manufacturing who reside in the community has *not* declined, and indeed remains the most significant occupational sector in the town (Statistics Canada 1991). This may indicate that former employees of manufacturing firms once based in the community have opted to remain in Elora and commute elsewhere to industrial jobs. It also suggests that there may be more stability in terms of the social and cultural characteristics of the community than the demise of much of its manufacturing activity would otherwise suggest. Finally, the community had been able to attract a new auto parts plant by the end of the 1990s, an example of the trend towards the ruralization of auto manufacturing in Ontario. It is too early to say whether this will lead to something of a renaissance of manufacturing in Elora, but it does mean that manufacturing is not entirely out of the picture.

Mount Forest: From Diversified Agrarian Workshop to Low-Wage Fabrication Centre

The town of Mount Forest is less than an hour's drive north of Elora, situated at the point where Highway 6 from Hamilton to Owen Sound crosses the Saugeen River. Mount Forest was selected for our study because in 1994 a Westinghouse plant, which had been in the community since 1979 and had employed about 250 people in its unionized plant, completed its closure, following two years of gradual 'downsizing.' Unlike Elora, Mount Forest is further away from urban centres that could provide comparable industrial jobs: it lies about seventy kilometres from Kitchener-Waterloo, 100 kilometres from Guelph and London, and 120 kilometres from the Greater Toronto Area. These distances, as its Chamber of Commerce (1998) puts it, 'makes it easily accessible to those centres of population without the disadvantages of having developed as a bedroom community. Consequently, Mount Forest has a life of its own – independent but not isolated.' For the laid-off workers, however, the distance from urban centres made finding a new job more of a challenge. The town promotes, simultaneously, both tourism and industrial development. Local tourist attractions include outdoor recreations such as fishing and hunting, cycling and hiking, skiing and snowmobiling. There are also a number of shows and fairs held throughout the year. Mount Forest has a hospital with thirty-seven beds, three private nursing homes, and two non-profit child care centres.

The population of Mount Forest in 1996 was 4,530, up 6.2 per cent from 1991. Ninety-five people (2.3 per cent) identified themselves as Aboriginal or visible minority, and 235 (5.2 per cent) claimed a language other than English as their first. Since 1971 Mount Forest's population has increased by 33 per cent.

According to the Chamber of Commerce, in 1998 there were thirteen manufacturing plants employing 575 people. The 1996 census established that manufacturing jobs were held by 31.6 per cent of the workforce, while 56 per cent worked in the service sector. The average hourly wage rate for a production worker was $8 to $12, for a tool and die maker $12, and for a secretary $10. In 1998 the largest manufacturing employer was K-Brand, which makes sports caps, knitted items, accessories, and promotional items, employing 276. Four companies produce for the auto industry, but none of these employ more than thirty people. The second-largest manufacturer was Vintex Inc., which manufactures plasticized textiles in the building vacated by Westinghouse. We take up the discussion of many of these manufacturers in subsequent chapters.

In 1994, at the time of our fieldwork in Mount Forest, there were empty storefronts on the main street, and the sidewalks seemed quiet. During that summer McDonalds had set up a temporary vending cart in the town, presumably to test the viability of a franchise, but this never materialized in permanent form. A Tim Horton's doughnut shop opened in 1996.

Mount Forest is another town that developed with an intimate connection to the surrounding agrarian economy of the nineteenth century. The early settlement policies of Upper Canada that granted farmers sufficient land to support a family, and the preferential access producers had for their wheat to the dynamic British market gave farmers relatively high cash incomes here, compared with small agriculturalists in other countries, particularly in Europe. Relatively high farm cash incomes also made it possible for farm families to purchase all manner of consumer goods, and agricultural production goods, especially farm implements, on a wide scale (see McCallum 1980: 87, 100–2; Winson 1985: 415).[7] An acute shortage of rural labour spurred farmers' interest in labour-saving farm implements (see Jones 1946: 199). It was precisely to supply the surrounding agrarian economy that numerous manufacturing enterprises emerged in small centres such as Mount Forest and Elora.

Established at a prime mill site on the Saugeen River in 1851 and incorporated in 1879, Mount Forest's economy initially revolved around several water- and later steam-driven sawmills and grist mills built by settlers who were principally from Scotland and Ireland, and one prominent family originally from the United States.[8] The town was successful in attracting the Toronto, Grey and Bruce Railway Company, and after railway service began in 1871, Mount Forest flourished. A description in Lovell's *Gazetteer of British North America* in 1874 gives good indication of the well-diversified nature of the community by that early date: 'The village of Mount Forest possesses good water power and contains churches of seven denominations, two sawmills, three flowering and grist mills, two woollen mills, an iron foundry, an agricultural implement factory, two tanneries, two brick fields, two telegraph offices, a branch bank, several assurance and insurance agencies, two printing offices issuing weekly newspapers, five hotels and several stores. The cattle fair is held monthly' (Edwards 1979: 49).

According to the 1871 census, Mount Forest's large foundry and wagon shop, both incorporating steam power, stood out as the dominant establishments in this community in terms of employment. A few years earlier the town's foundry was turning out some 500 ploughs, 200 stoves, sixty cultivators, twenty drag saws, twenty-five straw cutters, and a number of other agricultural implements every year, with sixteen to twenty workers employed (Edwards 1979: 71). Later, the foundry evolved into a successful manufacturer of threshing machines, shipping their product to western Canadian farmers well into the 1920s.

Its location on the rail line to Owen Sound helped ensure the town's existence until the mid-twentieth century. Mount Forest saw various industries come and go, and its economic link to the surrounding farm economy became more tenuous. Among the industries in the early decades of the twentieth century was the Mount Forest Carriage Company, described as one of the leading industries of the town, which employed some seventy hands to fill orders for Manitoba and the Northwest. However, the firm did not survive the coming of the automobile.

Another company was a large wardrobe manufacturing firm, which relocated from Winnipeg in 1900 and briefly supplied major Canadian retailers before closing down. Some decades later a knitting mill was established in town which began as a manufacturer of military clothing during the Second World War (see Mount Forest *Confederate*, 16 August 1906; 4 January 1940).

In 1954 the T.S. Farley Company located in Mount Forest and began producing radio and television coils. In 1958 General Instruments Ltd. took over and changed production to automobile radio tuners. Employment had increased to eighty hands by 1962, making it one of the community's largest employers (Mount Forest *Confederate*, 17 May 1962).

By the late 1960s, however, both Canadian National and the Canadian Pacific Railway had ceased to provide rail service to the town, and about that time Mount Forest was declared an area that could be considered for assistance by the federal government's Equalization of Industrial Opportunities Program. This was an indication that Mount Forest was becoming increasingly marginal to the way in which industrial capitalism was shaping up after mid-century.[9]

For a time the government incentives had some effect. The town's casket manufacturer and a wood products firm that had once been a manufacturer of horseless carriages received government loans to expand, as did the local veneer manufacturing plant (Mount Forest *Confederate*, 29 November 1973; 18 July 1974, and 3 October 1974). Other firms attracted to Mount Forest at this time included a plastics and adhesives firm, a manufacturer of travel trailers, and the Acme Ruler Company. Employees for the latter, however, were mostly moved over from a Toronto plant the firm owned (Mount Forest *Confederate*,

2 September 1971; 21 November 1974; 2 January 1975). Soon after these firms were established, however, other significant industrial operations were shut down. First to go was the egg grading station that had been in existence for over forty years. Then in 1977 Kinney Limited closed its Mount Forest footwear plant, citing growing competition from low-wage Asian imports. Some 150 people were let go, an estimated one-third of the town's workforce at the time (Mount Forest *Confederate*, 20 January 1977). While it was not long before, a U.S. sports clothing manufacturer, K Brand of Orange City, Iowa, had taken over the footwear plant (again, with Canadian government financial incentives), it provided fewer jobs and at lower wages (Mount Forest *Confederate*, 24 March 1977; 1 June 1977). For example, that about 100 people applied for two jobs in a candy-making facility nearby is an indication of the depressed local labour market by the end of the 1970s (Mount Forest *Confederate*, 7 April 1977).

In 1980 the town was given new life when it was able to attract a large multinational, Westinghouse Electric Company, to locate in Mount Forest. Westinghouse closed its long-unionized plant in Hamilton, Ontario, and re-established its factory as a non-union operation elsewhere. Mount Forest agreed to build a water main to the plant site and changed by-laws to allow more discharge in sewage of copper, cyanide, and chromium to accommodate the firm (Mount Forest *Confederate*, 31 October 1979). Westinghouse had begun operations by 1982 and a year later employed 139 workers – which by this time had unionized as well.

Westinghouse provided a substantial number of what we have come to call in the 1990s 'good' jobs, ones that provided an hourly pay that was at least twice the minimum wage, complemented by a comprehensive benefits package. It also provided female blue-collar labourers with a rare opportunity to access semi-skilled and skilled employment in the community and the incomes that such work provides. It was a real loss to the community, then, when the parent firm in the United States decided to close the plant as part of wider efforts to pay for disastrous management decisions made in the late 1980s (see Chapter 4). Through the 1990s, however, manufacturing employment in Mount Forest did not witness a dramatic downturn, because of the expansion of the garment manufacturer, K Brand. Many of the displaced Westinghouse workers went to work for this new firm. As we shall consider in more detail later in this book, the jobs gained in the garment firm did not quite compensate for those lost at the Westinghouse plant. Starting wages were nearly one-half of those at Westinghouse, and fringe benefits were few. Those workers who could do so generally chose to commute out of the community now to find new employment.

Harriston: The Fate of a Small Agricultural-Processing Centre

At about the same time that Westinghouse left Mount Forest, the village of Harriston lost its Canada Packers dairy plant, leaving 100 people without jobs. Founded in 1878, Harriston lies about fifteen kilometres west of Mount Forest. The community's industrial base is all tied to its agricultural roots in the surrounding area. In the past couple of years Harriston joined with three neighbouring communities to form the Town of Minto. This kind of amalgamation has been promoted by the provincial government, as a measure to reduce the costs of municipal services. Harriston's municipal website states that 'its shady, tree-lined streets border an agricultural area that is one of the most fertile in Canada. This makes Harriston the centre for abundant agricultural commerce.'

The population of Harriston (without the other three Minto communities) was 2,008 in 1996, an increase of 0.7 per cent over 1991. Of these people, none identified themselves as Aboriginal or visible minority, and 3.2 per cent claimed a first language other than English. Harriston's population has increased slightly since 1971, by 11 per cent. With the loss of the Canada Packers plant, Harriston's industrial employment opportunities were halved. In 1996, 115 people, 13.5 per cent of the local labour force, were employed in manufacturing, while 73 per cent were employed in the service sector.

Like numerous other communities that emerged out of the wheat economy of Upper Canada, Harriston had a well-diversified manufacturing base.[10] With building beginning in the 1850s at the point where the Elora-Saugeen Road crossed the Maitland River, the village could count on water power to run a sawmill and grist mill. Soon it had a woollen factory, planing mill, shingle factory, and an agricultural works that produced stoves, cultivators, ploughs, and straw cutters as part of its industrial base, as well as a carriage factory and a shoe manufacturer (Tuck 1978). For a while, furniture manufacturing and the Harriston Furniture Company dominated local industry. Producing tables, sideboards, and dressers, this company employed fifty-five men by the end of the nineteenth century. However, by 1919 a serious fire destroyed much of the plant and its new owners, the Ziegler brothers of Waterloo, decided not to rebuild.

As a regional centre for processing the bounty of the surrounding farm economy, Harriston really made its mark, particularly after the railroad was built to pass through the town. Harriston's flour mill ground locally grown grain, and other agricultural-processing enterprises sprang up soon after. Among them was the Harriston Pork Packing Company, a prosperous farmer-owned cooperative, which employed more than fifty men by 1900. After some financial difficulties it passed into the hands of the Montreal-based Davies Packing Company, and flourished supplying pork and beans to Canadian troops during the First World War. The plant was closed after the war, however, and for a short time its building was converted to a broom factory before it became the Harriston Packing Company in 1937. Pork products were the only ones to surpass cheese and butter for a considerable time in Harriston. At least three cheese box factories were in production until the 1950s, when alternative methods for packing cheese closed them down.

The firm that dominated the food-processing activities in Harriston – Canada Packers – had its origins in the 1890s, when Aaron Wenger built a three-storey cold storage building for butter, which was at that time exported to Britain. The building was bought by the Gunn family, who used it to store eggs and house a pickling operation. Blocks of ice were drawn from the Maitland River in winter and pulled on sleighs by horses to the plant, which was insulated with sawdust-filled walls. This plant was further expanded during the First World War to include chicken-processing activities, and later ice cream and soft drinks as well. In 1927 the Gunns' factory was taken over by a man who was to become one of Canada's most successful food-processing capitalists, J.S. McLean, and his newly established firm, Canada Packers. Sugar restrictions during the Second World War led to the abandonment of soft drink and ice cream production in favour of an egg-exporting operation. After the war ice cream production resumed under Canada Packers' York brand, and in the late 1940s a new dairy building was constructed to specialize in such products as ice cream, butter, and powdered skim milk (Tuck 1978).

Canada Packers grew to become the principal industry in Harriston. This was partly because of the demise of most of its other processing concerns in earlier decades. Although the plant was unionized, the town's growing dependence on one firm proved disastrous. By 1979

Canada Packers passed out of the hands of the McLean family and into those of people with a very different vision of how to do business.

The new owners, Hillsdown Holdings PLC of Britain, were not interested in operating businesses that functioned within Canada's supply management system that governed such sectors of agricultural production as milk, poultry, and eggs. Canada Packers' dairy division was sold to the Ault Food dairy company, which at that time was part of the John Labatt brewing empire, itself controlled by the Bronfmann family through Brascan Holdings Incorporated (see Winson 1993: 119). Shortly afterwards, in 1991, amid allegations from the union that Labatt was importing low-cost ice cream from the United States to get around Canada's dairy regulations, it was announced that the Harriston plant would be shut down and all workers laid off (see Harriston *Review*, 16, 23 January 1991 and *Globe and Mail*, 14 January 1991).[11]

With this event the town of Harriston ceased to be an agricultural-processing centre. As we shall see in Chapters 4 and 5, the few jobs available locally for the aging workforce laid off from the Canada Packers plant were mostly low paying and in the service sector. For those who wished to stay in their community and find stable work at comparable pay, the only option was to commute. This option, as we shall see, has become more prevalent in what were once vibrant small manufacturing towns in Ontario.

Arnprior: The Long Transition from Lumber Mill Town to High-Tech Greenfield Site

The town of Arnprior in Renfrew County lies sixty-five kilometres west of Ottawa, where the Madawaska River flows into the Ottawa River. There is no bridge to the province of Quebec here, but a ferry crosses the Ottawa River during the summer season from a tiny village east of Arnprior. In winter, travel to and from Quebec means crossing the river either at Ottawa or Pembroke. In the summers of 1997 and 1998 the main street of Arnprior was busy with local people going about their daily business, but with some tourists as well, for whom the interlinked art and gift gallery, bookshop, and cafe are a particularly popular destination. A shopping mall on the edge of town is a favourite place for women with small children and the elderly to stroll, browse, eat, and drink, especially during cold Ottawa Valley winters. Close by is a cluster of fast food restaurants. It is interesting to note that the ubiquitous McDonalds is able to sustain an outlet in Arnprior (along with a combined Wendy's / Tim Horton's), but not in any of the other communities we studied. Although it is clear that some tenants of the mall stores have been there for some time, there were also a number that appeared and disappeared during the period of our fieldwork. There are a number of generic family-type restaurants in Arnprior, and two Chinese restaurants. Local businesspeople, however, lament the absence of a 'good' restaurant to which they could take business guests and clients.

The 1996 census reports Arnprior's population to be 7,113, an increase of 6.5 per cent over 1991, and 15 per cent over 1971. Of the 1996 population, almost 4 per cent state that French is their first language, while another 4 per cent identify a language other than English. Three per cent of the town's population is Aboriginal or visible minority. The manufacturing sector represents 29 per cent of employment in the town, while the service sector represents 59 per cent.

Gerald T. Bloomfield and Elizabeth Bloomfield (1989a) classify cities, towns, and villages in 1871 by their intensity of industrial employment and by the degree of diversification of their industrial structure. According to these criteria, Arnprior was less industrial than average at this time, going by the percentage of its workforce employed in industry. Arnprior was at the southern edge of a county that was still undergoing the settlement process in 1871. However, it had the advantage of a railway connection with Ottawa. Renfrew County, as a fringe county, had a mean value of industrial production about half that of the southern Ontario norm (Bloomfield 1992: 90). Arnprior's dominant industries were wood processing, textiles, leather, and the making of bricks, tiles, and pottery. Other Ontario towns of similar size with a sawmill defining their industrial landscape included Carleton Place, Port Perry, Hawkesbury, Trenton, and Orillia.

While very small craft shops were the norm for the county, this was offset by the presence of the very large McLaughlin sawmill in Arnprior itself, a mill so large that it ranked in the top 1 per cent of industrial enterprises in Ontario in terms of the number of employees, fixed capital investment, and gross value of production (Bloomfield and Bloomfield 1989b: 15). In addition to its sawmill, Arnprior had other wood-related manufacturing, including a shingle factory with nine employees, a small door and sash shop, and a furniture workshop. Other manufacturing operations were a wool factory (sixteen employ-

ees) and a factory producing ready-made clothing (thirteen employees). The majority of enterprises were, nevertheless, small craft-like
operations with three to four employees (Bloomfield 1992).

Arnprior was a clear beneficiary of the eastern Ontario timber trade
in the latter part of the nineteenth century, and its population doubled
between 1881 and 1901, to approximately 4,000 people (Census of
Canada 1881, 1901). The principal ethnic groups that settled there,
starting with the largest, were Irish, French, British, Scottish, and German (Census of Canada 1921). The dominance of Arnprior's mam-
moth McLaughlin sawmill marked it as virtually a one-industry town
up to the 1920s: 'For all intents and purposes, industrial Arnprior was
McLaughlin Brothers from 1851 to 1929' (Lavoie 1984: 59).[12]

The industrial structure of Arnprior was its essential weakness, because of the decline of the regional timber trade. Nevertheless, although it was 'virtually' a one-industry town, Arnprior did have a
small degree of diversification. Dontigny woollen mills was established in the 1850s, and its products were flannels, wool blankets, and
worsted cloth. These humble beginnings in the weaving trade were to
blossom into a more substantial textile enterprise in the 1920s, just in
time to save Arnprior from certain oblivion with the demise of the
McLaughlin Brothers mill in 1929.

The Huyck interests established a weaving plant in the 1920s, and
Arnprior was on its way to a truly diversified industrial community,
and eventually one with a substantial component of high technology
industries. For much of the twentieth century, Arnprior moved away
from dependence on wood industries through the establishment of a
couple of relatively large industrial enterprises in fairly traditional
industries. While the Huyck plant was manufacturing industrial textiles, principally felt for the pulp and paper industry, by the early
1950s the town attracted a subsidiary of the American Playtex company. By the 1970s Playtex was the leading employer in Arnprior,
with some 550 employees at its peak.

Huyck and Platex, as relatively low technology manufacturing industries, were major employers of unskilled and semi-skilled labourers.
For several decades (longer in the case of Huyck), their factories provided stable jobs for a large number of workers who had little education and few skills. Another firm that employed such a workforce was
the Special Metals Division of Noranda Metals Limited, established in
Arnprior in 1977. This plant began machining steel pipe into high
quality tubular components for steam generation and fuel contain-

ment in the emerging nuclear power industry in the United States and Canada. This operation later became a joint venture with the Sandvik Canada Corporation, and still later, a wholly-owned subsidiary of the Swedish multinational. Employment peaked in the early 1980s with over 200 employees, coincident with the boom in the construction of nuclear power plants. The decline in the nuclear power industry, and the recession in the early 1990s saw the workforce cut to about one-half. Since then product diversification has allowed the plant to continue operations, and the firm has managed to expand its market share of stainless steel seamless pipe, especially in the United States. By 1998 employment was back to the 200-plus level, with most of the production workers hired straight from high school and trained on the job.[13]

By the mid 1980s, the two main firms offering employment to relatively unskilled blue-collar labour in Arnprior were scaling down operations. Playtex, whose workforce averaged around 550 employees between 1976 and 1984, drastically cut back its large labour force, so that by the early 1990s only sixty employees were left. The Huyck factory (more recently known as Kenwood, then Weavexx) peaked at 330 employees by the mid-1980s, but in 1994 downsizing left it with one-third of its employees, and two years later it ceased production altogether.[14]

At the same time, the town was entering a third industrial phase, one in which manufacturing involving relatively sophisticated technological processes were involved. The question is whether the workforce thrown off by the decline of industries associated with Arnprior's second industrial phase were, in fact, rescued by the coming of the third phase. We examine these and related issues in Chapters 4 and 5.

The third, or high technology industrial phase of Arnprior did not occur overnight, but was inaugurated in the period when the traditional manufacturing industries were in their heyday. The term 'high technology' needs some clarification, however. There is no unanimity over what constitutes a high technology industry, or even a high technology firm. Indeed, a good case can be made that a high technology *industry* is basically a fiction, because high technology firms exist in what are usually considered low technology sectors, and vice versa (see Baldwin and Gellatly 1998). Studies that use a single measure to classify firms as high tech, such as intensity of research and development, often miss important features of firms that probably should qualify them as high technology. John Baldwin and Guy Gellatly (1998) argue for an approach that considers several measures, including emphasis on R&D, evidence of innovation, emphasis on new products and processes, emphasis on technology, and evidence of a skilled workforce and continuous on-the-job training.

Our fieldwork and interviews clearly indicate that Arnprior has become the location for several firms that fit most, if not all, of these measures of high technology. Not all are producing electronic and computer components, although some are. As it is these firms that are increasingly defining the new industrial landscape of the community, we wish to give the reader some idea of their characteristics, including the type of employment structure they entail.

A significant high technology beginning for the community of Arnprior occurred because of the availability of its Second World War era air training facility, machine shop, and airstrip. This facility proved attractive to Frank Piasecki, an early pioneer in the aerospace industry, and specifically in the development of helicopters. In the mid-1950s a contract to produce helicopters for the Royal Canadian Air Force (RCAF) gave a boost to the Piasecki operation in Arnprior, which was later taken over by the Boeing company of Seattle, Washington. In addition to building and servicing large helicopters, the Arnprior plant became integrated with the Boeing Commercial Airplane Group and began producing parts for commercial jet aircraft built by the company (Gardiner 1996: 4–14). Boeing's workforce was up to 150 employees by the early 1970s, 400 by 1987, and more than 700 by 1998, by which time it was the chief industrial employer in the community (*Scott's Directories*, various years; personal interview).

As a relatively high tech employer, Boeing offers little opportunity for unskilled labour. Shop-floor employees require at least some post-secondary training, such as in working with sheet metal. The firm actively encourages up-skilling for all its employees and will cover the cost of any training programs and courses related to the job. Shop-floor positions begin at around $11 per hour, with possibilities of doubling this hourly pay with experience and seniority and good benefits. Thus, Boeing's unionized plant offers a sizeable number of 'good jobs.' It is interesting, however, that according to management estimates less than one-third of Boeing's employees actually reside in Arnprior itself. The firm draws from a much wider area, in fact, and most of the management and research personnel commute from Ottawa.

In 1997 Boeing's workforce and the Arnprior community were worried about the plant closing down, particularly after head office in Seattle indicated that this could be the result if the Canadian federal government's contract for new search and rescue helicopter did not go to Boeing. Fears were heightened when, indeed, the contract was awarded to a British firm for a lower price than Boeing bid, but the plant was kept running (McCarthy 1997). The robust expansion in orders for passenger aircraft worldwide around this time may have saved the community from a very severe blow to its economy (see Marshall 1998).

Two other firms contributing to Arnprior's high technology development of late are KAO and West End, a developer and manufacturer of software and hardware for electronic communications.

KAO has developed with the micro-computer industry more generally, having evolved from a manufacturer of 5 1/4 inch floppy diskettes some years ago, to a producer of 3 1/2 inch diskettes today, complemented by the production of compact disks. The regular workforce was until recently a little over 200 and made up of approximately 70 per cent skilled shop-floor employees with post-secondary training, 18 per cent management and administrative employees, and 7 per cent science, engineering, and 'quality assurance' employees. In addition to its skilled workforce, KAO employed a sizeable unskilled 'casual' labour force during times of peak demand. KAO was able to secure casual labour from the community as needed, typically having on call up to 200 workers so that it can operate around the clock with two shifts during times of peak demand. These casual jobs pay just above the minimum wage in the province (\$ 6.80 per hour at that time) and do not, of course, offer any security or benefits.

The year we interviewed a member of the firm's management (1998) a development took place that illustrates the high degree of volatility that is typical of at least a substantial number of high technology firms. KAO management decided to downsize their full-time workforce by 50 per cent, while the firm looked for a buyer for its Arnprior plant (it was bought by Zomax at the end of 1998). This kind of employment volatility was characteristic of another firm we examined in the community as well.

West End is a company in the high technology sector that was spun off from a larger electronics firm – Newbridge Networks. West End develops software and manufacturing hardware for electronic communications that will offer customers a single source for all kinds of communications, from voice to data transmission and television. The firm is more typically high tech in its structure and employment characteristics than KAO. While West End does manufacture hardware components for electronic communications, production workers make up barely 10 per cent of the workforce. About 75 per cent of the employees are involved in research and development, with 15 per cent comprising management personnel. Manufacturing is, for this kind of firm, a relatively small part of its raison d'être. As might be expected in what many regard as a highly unstable sector, employment numbers in West End have fluctuated wildly since its inception in 1993. At one point employee numbers were almost double what they are today.

Arnprior's location close to Ontario's 'Silicon Valley,' west of Ottawa has definitely proven beneficial in attracting a firm such as West End. While close enough to the action in the electronics industry in nearby Kanata, West End offers its highly trained staff a quieter rural setting, less expensive real estate, smaller schools for the children of the numerous employees with young families, and other currently perceived advantages of rural places that contribute to the attraction rural communities have for urban and suburban professionals jaded with the life of big cities.[15]

As can be seen from the thumbnail sketches of several high technology companies, this sub-sector, for the most part, offers employment to a relatively highly trained workforce. To the extent that it employs unskilled or semi-skilled workers at all, it is generally only in a casual, part-time capacity. Some firms that are clearly high tech benefit from the availability of a pool of relatively unskilled, and hence 'cheap,' labour available in the community, a labour force that allows them the flexibility to organize their firm around lean production strategies including just-in-time production. Our research suggests that this pool of labour is available at least in part as a result of the decline of the traditional local manufacturing activities. The dependence on low-cost, unskilled labour by high technology firms has been documented by Ross and Trachte (1990) in the case of the State of Massachusetts. Our research suggests that at least some, if not all, high tech firms benefit from certain structural features of local labour markets that have produced such a labour force.

The absolute number of jobs created by the high technology sub-sector in small communities is rather insignificant, and cannot be expected to provide livelihoods to the majority of those workers left unemployed by the decline of traditional manufacturing activities. Moreover, even in the community that has been fortunate enough to attract more high technology firms than most, as is the case with

Arnprior, the number of jobs on offer has not been sufficient to make up for the declining jobs in more traditional manufacturing. But even the jobs that become available require a workforce with the requisite skills and experience. The question is, are the workers cast off by the declining manufacturing industries acquiring the necessary occupational attributes that would give them any real hope in competing for those high technology jobs that do come available? The fact that these firms are typically hiring their workforce from a much wider area, and not primarily from Arnprior itself, suggests that workers from the traditional industries do not meet these requirements.

Iroquois Falls: The Evolution of a Single-Industry Town

The second community we selected for the second phase was Iroquois Falls. As a single-industry pulp-and-paper mill town in the northern hinterland of Ontario, it offers some useful contrasts to the older manufacturing towns in southern Ontario that emerged out of the nineteenth-century agrarian economy. Unlike those agrarian communities, Iroquois Falls is dependent upon a renewable resource, the nearby boreal forest. Coming into Iroquois Falls from the highway, and turning onto its main commercial street, the visitor is immediately struck by the dominance of its single industry. The so-called wood pile, a massive mountain of delimbed spruce and pine trees, dominates the horizon, stretches to the north, and ends where the gigantic pulp-and-paper mill stands. The mill is an amalgam of old and new industrial plant representing successive phases in its development. Beyond the mill are the black waters of the Abitibi River, running north to James Bay and providing the hydro power that made the mill and the town possible in the first place.

Demographically, Iroquois Falls is rather different from the other communities. With a population of 5,714 in 1996, it is the only one of the five communities we studied to have sustained a net loss of population – 4.8 per cent – since 1991 and 27 per cent since 1971. It is also the only community we studied where the average male wage is above the average for Ontario. Here the Aboriginal population is almost 2 per cent of the total, while visible minorities account for less than 0.2 per cent. The First Nations reserve is close to town, but not included in the town population figures. The language patterns are quite different as well, with 42 per cent stating that French is their first language, and another 3 per cent stating that their first language is other than

English. Manufacturing jobs represent 33 per cent of the total labour force, while the service sector represents 46 per cent.

While the community of Iroquois Falls owes its existence to manufacturing, its origins and development could not have been more different from the other four communities that we have described. Situated in the clay belt region of northeastern Ontario in the midst of Canada's vast boreal forests, the community was established around a single manufacturing enterprise, and it has largely stayed so since. The first phase of the town's mill complex and power dam infrastructure was opened in 1914, approximately seventy years after much of southern Ontario was already settled. Initially, the project of an entrepreneur named Frank Anson, who had been granted cutting rights to the great black spruce stands in the Lake Abitibi region, the mill evolved as one of the country's largest pulp- and paper-making facilities.

Iroquois Falls was a quintessential company town, laid out according to preconceived plans. Alongside this community, which was largely English-speaking, another community sprang up, comprising largely French-speaking settlers. As the census figures show, this bilingual nature persists today.

Unlike many of its southern counterparts, the very limited nature of agriculture in this region meant that the community did not develop an organic relationship with numerous farm operators in its early years. Largely absent here was the small manufacturer, and with it the diversity that this class provided. Absent, too, was the strong paternalistic employer–employee relationship that pervaded communities dominated by small employers. In many respects the mill at Iroquois Falls represented the leading edge of industrial capitalism in its time, except that it was physically located in the bush many hours by train north of Toronto.

Over the course of the twentieth century the company that began in Iroquois Falls grew to be the largest pulp-and-paper producer in the world. A major step in this direction was the merging of the Abitibi Paper Company with the Price Paper Company in the 1950s. A more recent merger with Stone Consolidated further established its position as the top paper firm in the world.

While the corporation was expanding its reach in the world market, the workforce was organizing in its various mills to form a potent union. The seven-month strike in 1975 by the Canadian Papermakers Union was a desperate struggle to entrench company-wide bargaining rights for the new union. Despite the lack of strike pay and considerable hardship, which is still talked about in the community, the workers held on to win their battle and consolidate their position. As a result, the workforce achieved one of the best hourly wages with a good benefits package available for blue-collar workers in Canada.

In the 1980s, before considerable technological change transformed the industry, the mill employed over 1,000 people, with some 400 more employed in tree-harvesting operations. Some modest efforts were being made to bring more diversity to the community by establishing a few small-manufacturing operations. By the late 1990s these efforts had not borne fruit, and for all intents and purposes Iroquois Falls remained a one-industry town. In the 1990s rapid technological change and the corporate merger with Stone Consolidated brought on strong pressures to downsize the company's workforce. The workforce in the bush was drastically reduced, but the union successfully resisted downsizing pressures on the mill labour force for much of the decade. (These events are examined more closely in Chapters 3 and 6.)

Manufacturing in small Canadian communities continues today, but it bears little resemblance to earlier phases of rural industry. The earlier relationship with the agrarian economy has largely disappeared, although a few remnants remain in the form of the odd feedmill or vegetable-processing plant. As we saw in the case of Elora's manufacturing firms, the image of rural industry producing for a limited local market ceased to hold many decades ago. Locally owned firms were producing for regional, national, and even international markets by 1900, if not before. Some small communities were the locus for what soon became multinational industrial operations, as in the case of Iroquois Falls, that manufactured products for the Canadian and U.S. market from the early decades of the twentieth century.

The 1990s brought significant changes to those small Canadian communities that historically were host to manufacturing activities. Fundamentally, it was a decade of adjustment to the reshaping of the wider political economy produced by the adoption of neo-liberal economic policies in Canada and elsewhere. At the core of this adjustment has been a veritable transformation in the way work is organized, and the kinds of work that are now available. This marks the contemporary period of change as different from the 'normal' business cycle that has long affected such communities, as it has the rest of the economy. Arguably, not since the industrial transformation of the economy in the nineteenth century have there been such far-reaching structural changes in these communities. To be sure, there has been some element of a recent 're-industrialization' taking place, as capital shifted to 'greenfield' sites in some smaller communities. We see this as part of the wider response to pressures coming with the neo-liberal economic model, forcing business to source out to cheaper labour, cheaper real estate, and so on (see, Marsden et al. 1990: 8–9). Automobile assembly and parts production have perhaps been the most significant development in this direction, at least in the Canadian context, and only a few of the smaller communities have been winners in this process. For the most part, our research indicates that recent times have brought a variety of industrial dislocations to the smallest manufacturing-dependent communities, dislocations that are typically summed up with the euphemism 'restructuring.' We look at how this restructuring has been expressed in more concrete ways in the next chapter, and the differential impact this has had on the structure of employment.

CHAPTER FOUR

The New Rural Economy and the Shape of Restructuring

Darwin lives in business just as he lives in the jungle, and restructuring is an essential part of the process of renewal.

Canadian Business Magazine, November 1990

The new capitalism is an often illegible regime of power.

Richard Sennett (1998: 10)

Rural communities could not have escaped the economic restructuring that has shaken the wider economy. Nevertheless, the term 'economic restructuring' is particularly vague and less than informative. Under this term can be grouped all manner of changes, from those induced by government to those mandated by corporations. It is largely on the latter that we shall focus, as we explore some of the various faces of corporate restructuring and their manifestation in rural villages and towns that depend upon manufacturing activity.

In the previous chapter we provided the history of manufacturing in five small Canadian communities and argued that these communities have endured earlier rounds of capitalist restructuring. In this chapter we look at the nature of ·corporate restructuring in general terms and what it looks like in the communities that form our case studies. The chapter has four parts. The first reviews what restructuring has come to mean in terms of capital's strategies for the reorganization of production. The second deals with the consequences of these strategies for workers. The subsequent two parts examine these processes on the ground level through two different lenses. To begin with, we look at the restructuring in rural Ontario communities in spatial terms. We examine the shift in manufacturing employment that has taken place between 1979 and 1998, the period that includes the signing of the Free Trade Agreement (FTA) with the United States and the extension of free trade to include Mexico in the North American Free Trade Agreement (NAFTA). The purpose here is, first, to document what has happened to rural manufacturing employment in terms of particular industrial sectors, which has not been systematically examined separately from urban manufacturing employment trends; and, second, to draw some conclusions from this data about the impact of restructuring on jobs in rural communities. From this analysis we argue that the number of jobs in manufacturing employment has not been particularly vibrant in rural communities; indeed, jobs continue to suffer the fallout of the recession of the early 1990s, despite the economic growth that has characterized the Canadian economy generally. We can see that employment declines have been mainly in traditional industries such as food processing and furniture, consistent with trends associated with free trade, but the hoped-for expansions of high technology industries have not resulted in an expansion of employment opportunities. In fact, this sector accounts for a very small proportion of overall employment in small-town manufacturing. Hopes that lost traditional manufacturing jobs will be replaced by the expanding high technology sector are not being borne out in rural manufacturing communities. In the third part we examine corporate restructuring strategies in the case study communities, demonstrating the ways that different forms of restructuring are being played out. In the final section, we consider the implications of such corporate restructuring for the viability of rural communities.

Restructuring: Seven Strategies for Maximizing Profits

The major objective of the current round of economic restructuring, as we argue in Chapter 2, is to reinvent the capitalist system as a vital profit-making system. To this end, a number of processes have been brought into play. Perhaps one of the most slippery, and yet extremely effective, has been the *ideological process* of making 'market forces' appear to be natural and inevitable. The mantra of Thatcherism and Reaganomics – that the market must be allowed to operate freely without government intervention – is, in fact, an ideological strategy that distorts the ideas of Adam Smith and promotes as fact, rather than social construction, the basic tenets of liberalism: sustained economic growth, free markets, economic globalization, and international competition (Korten 1996).

The 'war on good jobs' that much restructuring constitutes is a phenomenon with temporal boundaries. It is a process that really cannot be understood apart from very significant changes in the policy environment within the Canadian and U.S. nation states. Far from being a 'natural' economic process, restructuring takes place in an environment that has been carefully engineered so that such corporate changes can take place. In Canada this policy environment had a crucial turning point in the federal election of 1988, when the victory for the Progressive Conservative Party sealed the deal on free trade with the United States. It also signalled a green light for business, both locally based and foreign based, that in Canada business could now be conducted largely without concern for the intrusion of government.[1] Subsequent Liberal governments have not only confirmed this policy environment, but have further entrenched it.

Within this context of a dominant 'free market' ideology and a set of government policies that effectively protect that ideology, and corporate profits, companies engage in a range of profit-maximizing strategies. These include corporate *mergers and consolidations*, which, as we saw in the last chapter, are not restricted to periods of restructuring, but which become especially active at such times. Strong companies often take advantage of economic recession to buy up weaker firms, resulting in fewer, but more powerful, corporate actors. Weaker companies seeking buyers try to make themselves attractive by lowering labour costs. This destabilizes the labour market as companies merge and facilities deemed unprofitable, or simply surplus to requirements are closed. Sympathetic government policies have meant that mergers and foreign takeovers of Canadian firms could proceed without fear of serious government scrutiny. Operations made redundant through takeover or merger could be more easily shut down and workers summarily laid off, even by firms that had previously accepted generous government grants intended to stimulate employment in less dynamic economic regions.

Corporate *relocations* constitute another profit-maximizing strategy. As we describe in Chapter 2, enterprises seeking to lower their wage bill may do so by shifting their business location, or parts of it, to cheaper rural regions ('greenfield' sites), to the 'right to work' states of the United States, or to low-wage regions in the 'third world,' particularly the so-called free trade zones. While this may produce local benefits (although this is by no means certain, as we point out in Chapter 2), it is usually at the expense of another region which has lost that employer. As global competition heats up, corporations in search of short-term profits turn their attention to speculative investments which, when they fail, as we will see later in this chapter, have direct consequences for the jobs of their employees.

A major strategy for maximizing profits has been the *computerization* of every facet of the market, from primary resource extraction, through manufacturing, transportation, and distribution. This has led, as Aronowitz and DiFazio contend, to 'unemployment, underemployment, decreasing skilled work, and relatively lower wages' (1994: 3). Computerization can replace machine operators with robots, or data entry clerks with computer programs; it can send and receive large amounts of information around the world instantly, and it can turn skilled work into a mindless monitoring function. Aronowitz and DiFazio argue that only a limited number of people in the world need the knowledge and technology necessary to make use of these technologies, leaving the vast majority further disadvantaged (1994: 19). Ultimately, they argue, we face a 'jobless future,' requiring new, non-employment-based policies and strategies.

A further consequence of computerization has been to put a new twist on the old issues of *credentialism*, that is, the relationship between jobs and job training, skill, and preparation. New microchip technologies require new skills for which workers must find appropriate training. The debate continues over who will provide and pay for such training: secondary educational programs, public post-secondary programs, private sector training facilities, or the companies themselves? A related issue is who will receive such training? Will it only be available to young adults, or will older, displaced workers have access to computer training courses as well? In an era where the number of workers outpaces the number of 'good' jobs, credentials play an enhanced role. In the past they segmented the labour market, lining up specific credentials with specific kinds of jobs through particular definitions of skill. Minor differences in years on the job or kinds of apprenticeship were used to justify small pay status differences. Over twenty years ago Bowles and Gintis (1976) argued that the schooling and credentials demanded for most jobs did not match the actual training needed for them. Now credentials operate effectively to exclude some people from the labour market altogether, as employers require ever-higher levels of education and training to fill even the most basic job.

These corporate strategies have led to the introduction of *lean production methods*, which include just-in-time delivery, multi-skilling, job rotation, teams, quality management, numerical and functional flexibility, and extensive out-sourcing, all designed to reduce the resources – including labour – needed to produce a product or service (Moody 1997: 87). A key ingredient of this new model is the drive to corporate strategies that enhance the *flexibility* of the firm in its dealings with upstream suppliers, but especially in its dealings with labour. Indeed, the continent-wide General Motors strike of 1998, perhaps one of the most economically significant strikes of the decade, was precisely about these issues (see Milner 1998: B1). Whether pursued under the label of 'downsizing,' 'rightsizing,' or 're-engineering,' management's desire to increase flexibility in dealing with its labour force and suppliers often lies at the root of these strategies. But, as the sociologist Richard Sennett argues in a recent book, the term 'flexibility' itself conceals some decidedly Jekyll and Hyde dimensions: 'Flexibility is used today as another way to lift the curse of oppression from capitalism. In attacking rigid bureaucracy and emphasizing risk, it is claimed, flexibility gives people more freedom to shape their lives. In fact, the new order substitutes new controls rather than simply abolishing the rules of the past – but these new controls are also hard to understand. The new capitalism is an often illegible regime of power' (1998: 10).

Sennett notes that, in this new phase of the capitalist economy, 'the most tangible sign of ... change might be the motto "No long term."' (1998: 22) As corporations seek to become flatter, less hierarchical, and less bureaucratic to maximize flexibility, they are finding that the short-term contract, or episodic labour, is the most profitable strategy. Indeed, the statements of a leading executive of one of the largest U.S. corporations, and one of the most aggressive in destroying 'good' jobs in recent times, is most instructive regarding the new direction: 'In AT&T we have to promote the whole concept of the work force being contingent, though most of the contingent workers are inside our walls. "Jobs" are being replaced by "projects" and "fields of work" ... People need to look at themselves as self-employed, as vendors who come to this company to sell their skills' (Andrews 1996: D1, D6). In 1996 AT&T moved aggressively to eliminate 40,000 jobs over the following three years.

In the drive for flexibility, the predominant view among business journalists and economists is that it is a necessary process to allow corporations to survive and prosper under market conditions that have changed in a way that is 'dramatic, immutable and irreversible' (see Francis 1993: 9). Trying to determine what is actually happening in the corporate sector, as opposed to what is said to be happening by neoliberal ideologues and corporate public relations departments (not always distinguishable entities) is a challenge. It was becoming clear by the late 1990s, however, that the massive corporate restructuring that defines the present era has frequently come at a very high cost, not only in human terms, but at a cost to those aims for which restructuring was presumably undertaken in the first place – efficiency and future profit. The experience of the world's largest aerospace firm, Boeing, with drastic downsizing and restructuring, demonstrates the high cost to efficiency and profitability that these strategies can entail (Biddle 1997).[2]

The study of corporate restructuring beyond a purely superficial level reveals that there are a host of motivating factors behind the current reorganization of the manufacturing sector in Canada, as elsewhere, and the forms this reorganization takes are by no means uniform. Our research also suggests the futility of ascribing one factor, such as technology, as primary in causing this restructuring activity. Technological changes play a role in some cases. In others, the most significant factor was a poor investment decision by upper management that put a global corporation at risk. In some cases the desire to take advantage of economies of scale may have induced a multinational company to consolidate production in a large plant south of the border and close down its smaller Canadian subsidiary operation. This latter strategy has become attractive with trade liberalization since 1989.[3] Whatever the immediate cause of industrial dislocation, in Canada as elsewhere, this social and economic change is being driven by the fundamental shifts in the political economy at the national level.

Small Manufacturing Communities in the Era of Free Trade and Restructuring

The 1980s was a period of recession and boom. The decade ended with an economic storm unleashed by the Free Trade Agreement and exacerbated by the sharp and deep recession beginning in 1990. The recession was particularly severe for the Ontario economy. Small communities in the province dependent upon manufacturing could not avoid being caught up in the general turmoil affecting manufacturing. While the FTA sparked considerable debate prior to and after its signing in January 1989, there was typically little discussion about the *locational* dimensions of the massive readjustment to manufacturing activity in Canada that some expected to take place. Would it be across the board, or would it hit large cities, or smaller centres hardest?

Our case studies clearly indicate that at least some small communities paid a high price during this extraordinary time of economic restructuring and social dislocation. But was this true of small manufacturing-dependent communities more generally? To gain some insight into this question we analysed data on manufacturing employment for towns in the province of Ontario that roughly correspond to the population dimensions of our case studies: that is, communities with between 3,000 and 7,000 inhabitants.[4]

We wanted to know how manufacturing employment in these communities fared in the years since the signing of the FTA in 1989. Figures 4.1 to 4.4 show trends in manufacturing and employment for the periods 1979, 1988, 1993, and 1998. This allows us to capture vital details in each community from the period just before the abrupt downturn in the North American economy beginning in 1981, through the period of recovery and boom in the mid- to late 1980s, the impact of free trade and the severe recession in the early 1990s, and the end of several years of recovery that followed this most recent downturn. The data also encompass the period of the onset of trade liberalization with the United States, and later Mexico, and the intense period of corporate restructuring that hit Canada during the recession in the early 1990s.

These data confirm that the economic turmoil after 1988 witnessed in the case studies was not specific to these communities, but was experienced to a greater or lesser degree by these type of manufacturing-dependent communities in the province at large. Overall, these communities saw employment in manufacturing firms remain fairly flat throughout the 1980s, suggesting that the dynamism in the provincial economy during these years was not of primary benefit to them (see Figure 4.1). After the Free Trade Agreement in 1989, and the steep recession that began a year later, manufacturing employment dropped precipitously through the early 1990s, so that by 1993 it was almost 10 per cent lower than it was in 1988. Our last data point, 1998, marks a time when the provincial economy experienced several years

Figure 4.1. Profile of employment levels (indexed) in small town Ontario, 1979–1998. Blind River and Mount Forest data were not used because they exceeded the scale limits. Missing data were completed using data from preceding and subsequent years.

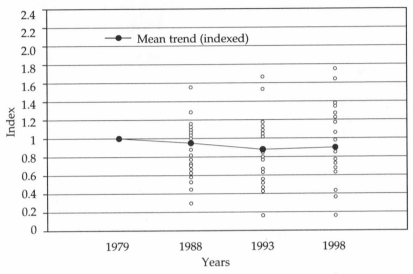

Source: Scott's Directory 1979, 1988, 1993, 1998

of recovery. Indeed, economic growth in Ontario was by this time leading most other provinces in Canada. From an employment point of view, our data suggest that for this group of communities there was little or no recovery from the turmoil of the early 1990s. This is despite the fact that *some* communities have seen manufacturing expansion. This would indicate that the overall recovery of the provincial economy has some clear locational and/or geographic dimensions that need to be addressed.

A sectoral analysis of manufacturing firms in these communities indicates that, from an employment perspective, the 1990s affected sub-sectors in different ways. The most important observation is that the two sub-sectors that are most significant in terms of absolute number of jobs, providing slightly over 50 per cent of the 26,000 manufacturing jobs in these communities in 1998, have both suffered substantial declines. In the case of the pulp-and-paper and lumber industry the decline in employment has been dramatic, at almost 40 per cent

Figure 4.2. Number of employees per sector in small town Ontario, 1979–1998.

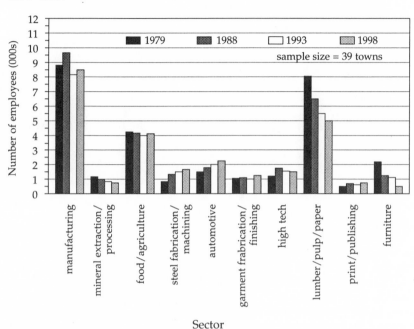

Sector

Source: Scott's Directory 1979, 1988, 1993, 1998
Missing data were completed using data from the subsequent year's directory.

(37.5 per cent).[5] Although some establishments disappeared, the decline in the overall number of facilities was relatively modest (see Figure 4.3). The decline in employment had to do with rapid technological change in this sector and some corporate consolidation. Changes to the pulp-and-paper firm in Iroquois Falls are examined in the next chapter. Data show that the change in the number of employees per firm in the industry was particularly sharp, with an average of 15 per cent fewer employees per firm in 1998 compared with 1979.

In the general manufacturing sub-sector total employment peaked in 1988. Since then there has been a decline of slightly over 10 per cent. The furniture and food-processing sectors also witnessed considerable changes. There has been, for instance, a marked decline in the number of firms operating in these communities. It is generally recognized

Figure 4.3. Number of firms per sector in small town Ontario, 1979–1998.

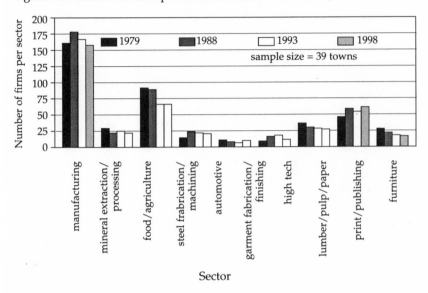

Source: Scott's Directory 1979, 1988, 1993, 1998
Missing data were completed using data from the subsequent year's directory.

that furniture manufacturing in Canada was seriously damaged by the FTA, and indeed, the decline in the number of firms was accompanied by a sharp decline in the number of employees as well, indicating that many firms disappeared for good. In the food-processing subsector, the decline in number of employees was more modest than the sharp decline in the number of food-processing establishments. This likely means that most of the firms that went out of business were small, a trend that has been under way in this industry for several decades (see Winson 1993: Chapter 6).

A couple of sub-sectors – steel fabrication and machining and automotive – experienced limited growth, although they are responsible for only a modest numbers of jobs overall. Other sectors have been essentially stable (see Figure 4.2). High technology, as representative of the so-called new economy, constitutes a very small proportion of overall employment in small-town manufacturing. Some growth occurred up to 1988, but since then employment has declined. Boeing,

Figure 4.4. Average number of employees per firm in small town Ontario, 1979–1998.

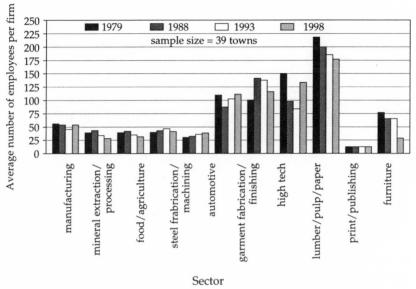

Sector

Source: Scott's Directory 1979, 1988, 1993, 1998
Missing data were completed using data from the subsequent year's directory.

based in Arnprior, accounts for about 50 per cent of the total employment in high technology in all such communities across the province. In other words, the industry touted as the cutting edge of the current economy comprises barely 5 per cent of total manufacturing employment in rural communities, shows little dynamism, and is heavily dependent upon one firm.

The experience of the high technology sub-sector in these small communities basically mirrored what was going on at the national level. Statistics Canada data on the various industries usually considered to be part of the high technology sector – aircraft and parts, communications, electronic equipment, office and business machines, pharmaceuticals, and medical and electrical equipment – witnessed *declines* in employment ranging from 6.5 per cent to 36 per cent in the period 1988 to 1994. Only the pharmaceutical and medical industries showed positive growth, and at 6 per cent this was quite modest, given the potential this sub-sector is claimed to have (see CLC, 1998: 12).

A 'Good' Jobs Disaster: Restructuring via Plant Shutdown and Lay-off in Elora, Mount Forest, and Harriston

The Free Trade Agreement, together with the vicious recession of the early 1990s, and an overvalued currency, hit the Canadian manufacturing sector with considerable force. Even before the recession's onset, published data compiled by the Canadian Labour Congress (CLC) suggest the magnitude of the impact from free trade alone. More than 400 plant closures affecting small, medium, and large firms occurred between late 1988 and June 1990 (see Barlow 1990: Appendix). Data compiled by the Canadian Centre for Policy Alternatives (CCPA) demonstrate that more than 100 of the plant shutdowns occurring in Ontario to June 1992 involved relocation of production outside Canada, largely to the United States and to a lesser extent Mexico (Healey 1993: 287–94). This process was apparently given more impetus by the signing of the North American Free Trade Agreement. Since 1994 the number of Canadian-owned duty-free maquiladora plants in Mexico has tripled to thirty from nine, employing a workforce of some 10,000 (McKenna 1998a: A1). These facts underscore the argument that many of the shutdowns taken together constitute a more or less permanent structural change to the economy and not simply temporary closures that will reopen with an upswing in the business cycle.

Four out of the five communities we studied experienced a shutdown of a substantial manufacturing operation. There was some variation in the impact each shutdown had on its host community, with the smaller towns being hit especially hard. This can be appreciated from the data presented in Table 4.1.

The Case of Canada Packers / Maple Leaf Foods

The restructuring of some of the largest Canadian-based corporations has not left smaller rural communities untouched. Some multinationals have had a presence in rural Canada for a long time, while others moved there more recently, for various reasons, union avoidance being one of them. The case of Canada Packers, renamed Maple Leaf Foods in 1990, is a good example of the former situation.

Canada Packers was a cornerstone of Canadian agribusiness for much of the twentieth century. The company that J.S. McLean cobbled together from a group of financially distressed meat-packing firms after the First World War held almost 60 per cent of the market share

Table 4.1. Workforce affected by shutdown as percentage of total manufacturing workforce by community

Community	Arnprior	Elora	Mount Forest	Harriston
Number of employees displaced by plant closure	330	130	249	110
Total manufacturing workforce in community	2,037	368	829	170
Displaced workers as % of total (A/B x 100)	16	35	30	65

Source: *Scott's Directories*, 18th ed., 1990–1.

in the Canadian beef-packing industry by the 1930s. The company evolved into a conglomerate firm producing edible oil products, canned fruit and vegetables, and dairy products, in addition to its meat division.[6]

The case of Canada Packers is illustrative of what can happen in the volatile business climate of the 1990s. The 'anything goes' market environment inaugurated by the Conservative government's 1989 Free Trade Agreement created a series of conditions that led to the dismantling of an integrated conglomerate mainstay in Canada's food business. With it, some twenty industrial plants and several thousand 'good' industrial jobs were lost (see Winson 1993: 190–7).

The FTA gave the green light for a series of major corporate mergers in Canada[7] and a new round of penetration by foreign multinationals. Among these foreign firms was Hillsdown Holdings PLC of Britain, which took over Maple Leaf Mills in 1987 as a vehicle for its attempt to have a major presence in the soon to be created North American free trade zone (*Financial Post*, 15 March 1989). By 1990 Hillsdown had completed a deal to purchase Canada Packers, which owned major national brand products and controlled a good distribution network. Together, these companies formed the new firm called Maple Leaf Foods. Not long after, Hillsdown continued its continental strategy by forming a joint venture with ConAgra Incorporated, one of North America's largest agribusiness companies (Maple Leaf, *Annual Report* 1991: 4–5).

To use an appropriate metaphor, Hillsdown's strategy with the two new firms was to appropriate the 'choicest cuts,' or the value-added processing end of their business, and discard the 'trimmings,' largely primary slaughter facilities that yielded lower profits. Hillsdown was intent on 'rationalizing' the two companies, a euphemism for widespread plant closures, lay-offs, and the radical downsizing of middle management (PDR notes, April 1989). Representing a new breed of capitalism given nourishment in Thatcherite Britain, Hillsdown executives were openly hostile to Canadian agriculture's supply management system and were not keen to continue their poultry-processing operations as a result.[8] In the end, their rationalization strategy was also fuelled by the aggressive entrance of Cargill Corporation into the Canadian market. With a new trade agreement that opened its arms to new foreign investors, and the assistance of an Alberta government grant, America's largest private company opened a new 'state of the art' beef processing facility at the end of the 1980s.[9]

The entrance of Cargill into the Canadian market had a major impact on the meat-packing industry. In Alberta its plant contributed to a lowering of wages in other unionized companies. Moreover, according to one industry analyst, 'using aggressive pricing tactics, Cargill used that plant to undercut the established players to such an extent that it was partly responsible for Maple Leaf Food Inc.'s decision to exit the beef business and leave Alberta' (*Globe and Mail*, 20 August 1992).[10] As a primary example of the new 'predatory capitalism' that characterized the Canadian economy in the 1990s, Hillsdown's two-year restructuring of Canada Packers saw the selling-off or closing of plants and even entire divisions. It sold off all its salmon farms, six of its poultry plants, and completely shut down its coast-to-coast beef-slaughtering division (PDR notes, 7 Feb. 1991). This strategy had a significant impact on its labour force, as some twenty plants were closed or sold off, and several thousand jobs were cut across Canada (Winson 1993: Table 6).

Two of the victims in this corporate rationalization were the poultry-processing operation employing 130 people in the village of Elora and the dairy-processing plant with 100 employees in the town of Harriston. After the legal minimum of eight weeks notice, the employees were laid off in 1991, after years, often decades, of service to the company.

The Case of Westinghouse Electric

Another of our case studies involves the Westinghouse Electric Company plant in the town of Mount Forest. The factory was opened in

1981, in a move that saw production shift from their Hamilton plant to this rural greenfield site. This may have been, as some workers saw it, to 'get away from the union.' Nevertheless, the company was forced by provincial labour legislation to allow a number of employees to relocate from Hamilton, and this group proved formidable in re-establishing the union in the new plant. The plant produced electrical products, including airport equipment for government, public utilities, and industry.

During the late 1980s a decision was made by top management in the United States to use Westinghouse's consumer credit division to make a foray into speculative real estate and other high-risk investments.[11] In the words of a leading U.S. business magazine, 'Westinghouse Credit Corporation, known in the company simply as Credit Corp., shovelled loans out the door with the speed and abandon of a go-go S&L [savings and loan company]. It poured money into high-risk, high-return ventures like hotels, shopping centres, junk bonds, and leveraged buyouts. Now it's paying the price' (*Fortune*, 4 November 1991, 93). Westinghouse's venture was not altogether uncommon in the era of 'casino capitalism' that typified the Reagan presidency of the 1980s.

The collapse of the North American real estate markets with the onset of the recession in 1990 proved very costly for Westinghouse. A little more than a year after Westinghouse's CEO Paul Lego had boosted his annual compensation package from $1.4 million to $1.7 million (*Fortune*, 4 November 1991, 98), the company wrote off $2.7 billion in assets (*Business Week*, 17 February 1992, 110) and began a massive restructuring to cover bad loans that involved the sale of whole corporate divisions and the lay-offs of several thousand employees (see *Business Week*, 7 December 1992, 32–4; *Globe and Mail* 24 November 1992, B9).

In 1989 the Canadian subsidiary began decentralizing, and some product lines were moved to South Carolina. In 1993 Westinghouse announced that it had sold thirty-eight of its production facilities to Eaton Yale Company, including eight in Canada. The employees at Mount Forest were told that their location was one of three in Canada to be closed. The new company had bought the capital equipment of the plant, not the building itself, and the equipment was removed and shipped to the southern United States to enhance Eaton Yale's operations.

With 250 employees at its peak in the late 1980s, Westinghouse constituted the major employer in Mount Forest and the surrounding area. Lay-offs began in October 1991 and were extended until the plant finally closed in July 1994, a drawn-out death that employees found particularly hard to cope with.

The cases of both Canada Packers and Westinghouse are illustrative of the relationship between restructuring and the permanent destruction of the 'good' jobs in what we have called the stable work world. They challenge the prevalent view that such job losses are simply the result of corporations obeying the dictates of the market and doing what is necessary (if unpleasant) to ensure a healthy and profitable company.

A 'War of Attrition on Good Jobs': Restructuring through Technological Change in Iroquois Falls

Single-industry communities dependent upon the pulp-and-paper industry represent an example of what we term the 'war of attrition on good jobs.' It does not represent a marked departure from the general trend regarding the impact of globalization on job structure, but it does have different implications for different individuals within different communities. In the case of the pulp-and-paper industry, a combination of factors are involved. Key among these is the severe cyclical downturn that occurred in this sector during the early 1990s, exacerbated by an unfavourable exchange rate before 1993 (Holmes 1997: 12). In 1991 alone the industry claimed to have lost $1.5 billion and to have shut down five mills with the loss of several thousand jobs (Madore 1992: 8). The cumulative effects of years of over cutting started to be felt as economical supplies of good quality wood were declining (1992: 8). A further pressure on Canadian pulp-and-paper firms, which has become more significant over time, has been the emergence of strong competition from lower cost firms in the United States and elsewhere abroad. This pressure becomes especially acute during slumps in the price of newsprint (Mackenzie and Norcliffe 1997: 2). Finally, as Holmes (1997: 8) argues, the high level of 'sunk' costs that pulp-and-paper mills represent (expensive mills are often combined with hydroelectric dams and equipment) means that these kinds of firms tend to favour restructuring in situ, rather than plant shutdowns and shifting production to lower cost locations.

The severity of the industry's decline in the early 1990s provided real incentives for manufacturers to reduce costs wherever possible.

With hourly wages in this industry ranking among top industrial wages, it is not surprising that severe pressures to reduce costs were met with strategies to reduce the cost of labour in the mills. Across Canada, newsprint producers have responded to this combination of global economic forces and state pressures in somewhat different ways, shaped by variations in the age of local physical plant, local market situations, and availability of the natural resource. Nevertheless, the overall trend would appear to be sizeable reductions in workforce and introduction of flexible labour practices – in other words, variants of a lean production regime (see Mackenzie and Norcliffe 1997: 3).

Together with this decidedly economic impetus was a new factor – pressure from the federal government to clean up what has historically been one of the most damaging industries from an environmental perspective. Indeed, the pulp-and-paper industry is credited with being responsible for fully one-half of all water-borne pollution in Canada. New federal standards concerning effluent from the mills were to come into effect at the end of 1992.[12]

The Case of Abitibi Consolidated

Thermomechanical pulping technology (TMP) provides pulp-andpaper manufacturers with an answer to both the problem of high labour costs, and excessive environmental damage to water ecosystems. The Abitibi Consolidated mill at Iroquois Falls has been exemplary in modernizing its operations with this process, and indeed, with respect to technological change in general.

Using mechanical methods instead of the chemical sulphite process to break down wood fibre for newsprint production, TMP was installed in the Iroquois Falls mill by Abitibi Price (now Abitibi Consolidated) in the mid-1990s. Company personnel report dramatic improvements in effluent quality with this technology.[13] As in other locations where TMP had been introduced (see Rose and Villemaire 1997: 62), the need for labour in the pulping process was dramatically reduced: the company called for an immediate reduction of 125 workers in its mill workforce.[14]

Before the introduction of TMP, there had been an earlier round of technological change – in the bush, rather than in the mill. The further mechanization of the tree-harvesting process through the introduction of high-productivity logging machines had a dramatic effect on the labour force in the bush camps. In the camp supplying the Iroquois Falls mill, the workforce of approximately 400 of the early 1980s was reduced to one-quarter of this by the late 1990s.[15]

Another strategy for reducing labour costs is corporate merger. Judging that with less competition in the industry after merger it could count on more favourable paper prices, Abitibi Price embarked on a merger with Stone Consolidated in 1997, and soon after attempted to take over Avenor Inc. The bid for Avenor lost out to a richer U.S. suitor, Bowater Inc., but the merger with Stone resulted in the formation of Abitibi Consolidated, the world's largest producer of newsprint. Another factor driving the merger was management's expectation that 'synergies' from the merger could save a further $ 200 million. Essentially, in expectation of cost savings, the directors of the new company mandated its mill managers to achieve these synergies wherever possible, and backed this up with handsome bonuses if they reached their target by mid-1999 (Abitibi Consolidated, *Annual Report*, 1997).

In addition to the impetus given to downsizing the workforce by technological change, it is very likely that the need to rationalize the new corporate merger by finding substantial cost savings also put pressure on jobs and wages. This conclusion was given more force in the 1998 contract negotiations. The company demanded a departure from its usual practice of company-wide bargaining with workers in all of its mills around a master contract. Instead, it provocatively insisted on the right to deal with each mill individually. The company's singleminded pursuit of this strategy quickly brought it to loggerheads with the union, which had once before demonstrated that the right to bargain for a single contract for its membership in all the Abitibi mills was a right that it would defend at great cost, if necessary.[16] A company-wide strike began in June 1998.

An essential factor in determining the outcome of the company's strategy to reduce labour costs in this context has been, and will continue to be, the presence of a powerful industrial union. Without the presence of the union, in this case the Communication, Energy and Papermakers Union (CEP), it is very likely that the technological change would have resulted in lay-offs. The union presence meant that the company had to settle for early retirements instead of lay-offs, and it was forced to reduce the number of jobs it initially wanted to cut.[17]

The long period of forestalling company pressure regarding lay-offs was coming to a close in 1999, however. Shortly after the end of the

1998 strike Abitibi Consolidated announced that it was planning to shut down one of its paper-making machines and lay off 140 workers in the coming months. A year later the paper machine had been shut down and over half the announced lay-offs had occurred.[18] This was a hard blow to the employees and to the community, given that the hardships of the long strike were still being felt. At the time of writing this chapter, it is still not clear how these redundancies are going to be handled. It is likely that employees taken on without job security in the 1990s, that is, those 'under waivers,' will be the first to go. To add to the anxiety, in February 2000 Abitibi Consolidated made a surprise announcement that it would merge with Donohue Paper of Quebec. The latter was touted by executives of Abitibi as a 'low-cost' producer of newsprint, one that could provide a model for the rest of the firm. It was also announced that the company now planned to withdraw some 400,000 tons of newsprint production in an effort to further boost newsprint prices (*Globe and Mail*, 10, 11 February 2000, B1). It is difficult to see how these announcements will not have negative implications for employees. Thus, the larger battle to protect the master contract with all Abitibi mills has been a partial victory, but at the local level the workforce has faced some serious job losses, after many years of protecting existing jobs. The future portends even more lay-offs.[19]

In this scenario of downsizing through attrition, existing employees are cushioned from the effects of technological change. But this is not to say that there is no impact. Rather, the impact is displaced, for the most part, to those who would in the past have constituted *new employees*, that is, the next generation of workers. These particular individuals appear to be the major victims of this process of restructuring. In this context we are speaking of a young, largely male population that in years past could count on finding a well-paying job in the mill, in their early twenties, or perhaps even before finishing high school. The downsizing that the TMP process allows essentially exacerbates a trend to reduce the mill workforce that had been under way since the late 1980s. As a result of this trend, virtually no new full-time employees have been added to the bargaining unit in ten years. The few who have been hired, have been hired as 'spares' with little formal job security.[20] The impact of this process of restructuring through attrition on youth in Iroquois Falls will be examined in more depth in the following chapters.

Upskilling and the Demise of Good Semi-skilled Jobs: Restructuring in Arnprior

The rapid introduction of technological innovations into most work-places during the 1980s and 1990s has been an extremely important factor in altering the kinds of jobs available to workers. It is now commonplace for policy-makers to identify the opportunities available in the new economy for workers with computer skills, although this claim by no means goes unchallenged. The number of jobs created as a result of microchip technology appears to have been considerably lower than was predicted a decade or so ago, at least up until the mid-1990s (see Menzies 1996: 6). One of the major reasons for this, of course, is that microchip technology has the dubious advantage of being able to eliminate jobs, even more quickly than it creates them, by speeding up complex processes and incorporating them into programs that no longer require human labour.

Yet frequently overlooked in the debate over the relationship between job creation and microchip technology is the way that this technology is profoundly affecting *all* jobs, not simply those explicitly identified as technology-related. Microchip technology creates 'McJobs,' jobs rationalized and routinized through the use of computers to perform all coordination and planning – in other words, all the thinking aspects of the job (Menzies 1996: 10). The divergent trend identified in the literature on technology concerns the new kinds of skills required of workers lucky enough to hold the manufacturing jobs in the new economy.

Rural manufacturing communities are as vulnerable as any to the effects of technology on the workforce, and our research provides compelling evidence of the polarization of skills. This distinguishes between the proliferation of unskilled McJobs in the service sector, which command low, often minimum wages, and are frequently part-time, and the remaining jobs in the manufacturing sector which increasingly require a greater degree of specialized forms of literacy, numeracy, and technical expertise.

The economically diversified community of Arnprior provides excellent examples of these more global trends. Our interviews with plant managers in companies representative of the range of manufacturing firms reveal an emergent pattern in which the more technologically sophisticated companies have increased the requirements they place on new workers. This contrasts acutely with the data from traditional manufacturing firms. These are less affected by technology and are more likely to hire workers without specific skills or education, but these are also the plants that in recent years have faced actual or likely demise.

Traditional manufacturing industries were able to hire young people straight from high school, and in most cases a high school certificate was deemed irrelevant to the kinds of work tasks to be carried out. Training could take place on the job, initially over a period of days or weeks, and as workers became more familiar with their work tasks they would devise short-cuts, improve their speed if they were paid piece rates, and along with their co-workers, build the tacit knowledge which enabled them to troubleshoot effectively. Weavexx workers in Arnprior worked for a company such as this, acquiring job-specific skills on the job, while being able to walk into the job straight from high school without formal credentials. Similarly, the plant manager at the Playtex packaging plant in Arnprior reported that high school completion was not necessary for workers there, and at Barrday, a manufacturer of protective armour clothing, no formal educational level was required to get a sewing job.

The data acquired from plant managers at the other Arnprior firms contacted are quite different. All of them stated that their basic requirements for new employees included formal educational qualifications, ranging from, minimally, a Grade 12 high school certificate for even the most basic level of production workers, to a college diploma or university degree for those filling technical positions. A couple of plant managers noted the shift that had taken place in their firms. At Pfizer Pharmaceuticals, for example, workers in earlier years did not need high school graduation, but now none would be hired without it.

There are additional trends worth noting here. One is a requirement for potential employees to undergo aptitude testing, in addition to their Grade 12 qualifications, a step that in the case of some of the workers we interviewed had eliminated them from the hiring process. Aptitude testing, from the point of view of management, is designed to assess a worker's ability to deal with text-based task instructions and the rapid changes often taking place in the workplace. As one plant manager put it: 'The jobs are changing and the jobs that we see in the future expect a lot more of the employees in particular. We have over 400 standard operating procedures people need to be familiar with. They have to have a good understanding of the regulations we have to follow. We are highly regulated and follow procedures for every step of making a product. All staff have to be trained, so when regulatory people come through they can answer questions about how they do their job. It does require good verbal skills and is getting more numerically complicated. Jobs in quality control require a college diploma of some kind, preferably university.'[21] Yet, aptitude testing effectively eliminates non-text-based forms of learning and problem-solving which may be extremely valuable to workers' capacity to successfully carry out their work.

The second trend to be noted is the adoption by managers of the idea of lifelong learning. When asked about the formal educational qualifications required for production workers, five out of nine plant managers volunteered that their companies encouraged workers to upgrade their formal skills and qualifications through taking evening courses. Support usually included paying for courses that would teach skills relevant to the company, computer skills being those most frequently mentioned. This kind of skills-building training clearly enhances the human capital available to employers facing the challenge of rapid change in their companies, while simultaneously enhancing the personal human capital of individual workers. Yet it serves to buffer a different kind of change as well, one that became clear in one of the interviews:

> We do some succession planning, career development. We try to emphasize with our employees that you should take care of your own career. We'll give you the tools and assist you in how to do that. We have a 100 percent education refund policy here, and we have some people going to university in Ottawa taking MBA courses that are being paid for, so we help that way. I think the thinking has changed a lot. The old regime thinking used to be 'well, if I work with this employer then they're gonna take care of me.' I think that thinking is done, you can expect that new people coming now, they're probably going to have 5 or 6 jobs rather than work with one employer, and as a result the emphasis is on you taking care of yourself and your career.[22]

Lifelong learning is one outcome of the volatility of the restructured economy, yet it is accessible only to those workers fortunate enough to have the means to provide it for themselves, or to work, at least for a time, for companies with upgrading policies. The ways in which '5 or 6 jobs' gets played out in the lives of workers displaced from traditional manufacturing jobs without such policies is the focus of the next chapter.

A third trend emerging from the data is the use of a variety of mechanisms to screen out the majority of job applicants. In times of fuller employment such mechanisms were not necessary for unskilled and semi-skilled manufacturing jobs, but under present economic conditions, where there are literally dozens of applicants for any apparently decent full-time job, it is not surprising that employers seek out ways to reduce the number of applicants they must consider. By far the simplest way to screen out potential employees is to 'raise the bar' on qualifications, even in circumstances where such qualifications are, arguably, of questionable value to the job. While aptitude testing provides an apparently objective means for screening applicants, another more subjective form of screening takes place in companies using casual workers alongside regular permanent employees. At KAO, in Arnprior, casual workers may be offered permanent status after being assessed on the job for their performance, capability, and work ethic.

Whatever face restructuring takes on, it has direct consequences for some, usually those in the firm, and inevitably some indirect consequences for others outside the firm – and, in fact, for the community at large. In our case studies of just five communities, the range of direct consequences is dramatic. Permanent lay-offs are one kind of reality, and early retirement with a good pension and continuing fringe benefits is quite another. In the manufacturing firms we studied we saw the full gamut of these options being played out with employees, although lay-offs have definitely been the most frequent consequence of restructuring.

Whatever form it took, however, the net effect of corporate decisions made under the rationale of necessary restructuring has been to reduce the fund of 'good' jobs available in each of these communities. Only in one of our five case studies, Arnprior, was the loss of permanent manufacturing jobs characterized by good wages compensated to some degree by the creation of more 'good' jobs by other firms.[23] Even there, however, the new jobs were not in sufficient numbers to replace the jobs lost, and the new jobs had significant qualification barriers as far as most of the workers being made redundant in the community were concerned.

Restructuring and Community Response

As 'good' jobs go, can communities remain unaffected? The simple answer to this is no, although we find it interesting how much different communities vary in their willingness to admit to the losses they experience. It was in the single-industry pulp-and-paper town of Iroquois Falls that the most open and direct discussions occurred regarding changes in employment at the mill and its effect on the community. Perhaps this was simply because the mill was practically the only game in town, and this reality encouraged a more open perspective.

In the more diversified communities of southern Ontario, where job loss had, in fact, been more dramatic, there was more reluctance to play up the effects on the community, at least in a public way. This difference arose most notably in the case of Mount Forest after the close of the Westinghouse plant there. It seemed undeniable that even to a more diversified community, the loss of the largest employer would be a significant blow. We calculated that the weekly wages lost to the town and environs were in the order of $150,000, while some $220,000 annually was lost to municipal tax coffers – this in a town with fewer than 5,000 inhabitants. Indeed, for the plant workers laid off, there was little doubt that the community would suffer, as several of them made clear to us.[24] Nevertheless, when the impact of the shutdown was reported in the regional newspaper, municipal officials publicly denied that the shutdown was a hard blow to the town, and argued instead that Mount Forest was doing very well. In fact, they demanded equal space in the newspaper to correct 'false impressions' the article had created about their community (*Kitchener-Waterloo Record*, 16 April 1998). This led us to believe that in this southern Ontario community it was much easier for town officials, and the more middle-class elements more generally, to ignore or even deny the devastation caused by the plant shutdown on the lives of many former workers. For them, Westinghouse was not the only game in town, economically speaking, even if for some time it was the largest.

For Iroquois Falls, the single-industry town built around the social relations of resource extraction, the dominant role of the capitalist labour process in community life sharpened class consciousness. A sense of class structure, and the divergence of interests that derives from that, has been historically more transparent there. This may, indeed, provide the residents with more strength on which to draw to resist capitalist restructuring, as Nash (1994) suggests for Bolivian tin workers in comparison with the laid off electrical workers she studied in Pittsfield, Massachusetts. The limited success of efforts to diversify the local economy of Iroquois Falls, a matter we return to in Chapter 7, has meant that the dependence upon the one large employer in town is a relationship that is relatively clear-cut and easy to perceive – by workers and small business owners alike.

While a strike in one of the manufacturing plants in our southern Ontario case study communities would likely have been regarded with dispassion by elements of the towns' businesspeople, in Iroquois Falls the five-month strike at Abitibi in 1998 focused the minds of all the businesspeople we talked to, from bank managers to food store and hardware store owners. All felt the impact directly on their day-to-day business operations and saw their futures as businesspeople to be directly tied with the outcome of the struggle of the striking workers in town. In fact, a few had even been millworkers themselves in the past, and this likely enhanced their empathy with production workers, to some extent.

All of these five cases demonstrate the vulnerability of rural communities that tie themselves to corporate entities based outside and which owe no particular loyalty to the community itself. During the period of long-term expansion and relative stability that characterized postwar capitalism in the developed West, a strategy of attracting multinational manufacturing plants to a rural community personified progress itself. The successful community could count on jobs that paid significantly above what small, local employers were likely to offer, and tax revenues to municipal coffers were likely to be handsome as well. Indeed, at a time when smaller firms were being absorbed by larger national and multinational corporations across North America, attracting a large corporate player to diversify the community industrial base had a powerful logic behind it.

The presence of these firms had mixed benefits from the beginning, however, depending upon one's location in the community social structure. Relatively high wages were likely to introduce elements of inequality into the local labour force that had not been there before. Indeed, in one of our case studies the local labour market was definitely divided, in the eyes of many in the community, between those who worked at the mill, and those not so fortunate who had to settle for hourly wages less than half those prevailing at the mill. On the other hand, these firms were often responsible for introducing modern labour relations, unions, and the collective bargaining process into communities previously rife with paternalistic employer-employee relationships.[25]

The host of changes associated with the neo-liberal re-orientation of the Canadian political economy and the further globalization of multinational capital brings new concerns for rural communities dependent to a greater or lesser extent upon multinational manufacturing consortiums for their economic viability. The issue of *locational commitment*, always somewhat problematic for these firms anyway, becomes more pressing as firms find added incentives to move production to lower cost jurisdictions, often offshore, or to 'rationalize' their operations, again, to reduce costs. This incessant pressure on costs may, and often does, result in the closure of plants that have been starved of investment capital for a long time. Too often in Canada these are branch plants of multinationals based elsewhere that, when push comes to shove, favour operations in their home country, or newer plants in lower wage environments.

Another danger for rural communities is the fallout that inevitably occurs from the heightened merger activity that has been given stimulus by the deregulated neo-liberal policy environment. Indeed, the current neo-liberal era is one of heightened corporate consolidation, a time when mergers of a magnitude never before seen dazzle the business community. Mergers, however, very often mean redundancies in the new corporate organization, which spells job loss above all else. It will be difficult for manufacturing-dependent communities to emerge unscathed from this trend, as our case studies demonstrate. If they do not lose production facilities, and therefore jobs, entirely from the community, they are likely to experience other types of fallout. This can range from the creation of now redundant corporate assets that have to be 'rationalized,' to the implications of merging incompatible corporate cultures and the inevitable instability this creates for employees within the new corporation. As long as it remains unfashionable for society to veto corporate mergers that can be demonstrated to harm the public good, rural communities dependent upon a relatively slim manufacturing base will remain particularly vulnerable.

CHAPTER FIVE

Skidding into the Contingent Work World

Wanted: Store Clerks, part-time, must be available to work any hours, including afternoons and evenings, Saturdays, Sundays and holidays.

Supermarket advertisement, Guelph, Ontario, September 2000

I think it's the economy in general, you've reached the point where there are reservoirs of cheap labour out there ... they can break all the rules they want, there are thirty other people standing there looking for the job. It takes away your dignity and pride, and it's very hard to deal with.

Wife of former Westinghouse worker describing the new rural economy
in Canada, 1994

Rural communities have been dramatically changed by the recent round of capitalist restructuring, much of which has taken place as a result of events and decisions made thousands of kilometres away. In this chapter we begin with a discussion of employment changes in the broader Canadian economy and with how official and media approaches to unemployment fail to capture the reality of today's work world. This serves to contextualize the micro-level realities characterizing local labour markets that our respondents were faced with in their efforts to re-establish their livelihoods. Our statistical analysis presented in this chapter is supplemented by in-depth qualitative material presented in the next chapter. By these means we hope to reveal more fully the contemporary reality of life after lay-off and restructuring for many rural people in Canada today.

What is happening in smaller communities is not always represented fairly by national statistics which are supposed to reflect the economic reality of Canada and which are used to form the basic information for social and economic policy. As we saw in Chapter 3, rural communities, especially those dependent upon manufacturing activities, have shown since 1979 worrying levels of unemployment and sluggish job creation, despite the economic prosperity of the mid-1980s in the wider economy.

The severe recession beginning in 1990 caused a dramatic rise in unemployment for most of Canada, and rural manufacturing communities were no exception. However, by 1993–4 the business press was replete with 'news' of economic recovery. While this was undoubtedly the beginning of recovery for some stockholders, as share prices rebounded into 1994, for employees still dealing with official unemployment at around 11–12 per cent, talk of recovery was just that – talk. Taking a more cautious approach, the federal government did not push the recovery theme until much later. By 1998 the first budgetary surplus in many years (Finance Canada 1998) and the creation of several hundred thousand new jobs, up 3.2 per cent from 1997 (Statistics Canada 1999: 3), led the government to speak of recovery as well.

Governments have typically used unemployment as a standard indicator of economic well-being. However, these statistics rely on an extremely narrow definition of unemployment. Statistics Canada has traditionally confined the official numbers to those people registered as unemployed and actively looking for work. Moreover, because unemployment is calculated using twelve independently measured weekly reference periods, the rate of unemployment appears lower than it would if, for example, it was measured based on labour force experience over a one-year period. If the latter method were used, in other words, if the number of people who have experienced unemployment at some time during the past year is calculated, Statistics Canada tells us that the unemployment rate would be almost twice as high.[1]

Changes to unemployment insurance policies over the past few years have reduced the number of people eligible to claim, as workers find it increasingly difficult to meet the new eligibility requirements. As a result of such changes unemployment figures appear to have improved. Indeed, after dramatic changes to the unemployment insurance scheme by the federal Liberal government, the percentage of workers losing jobs who qualify for benefits has plummeted from almost 90 in the early 1990s to approximately 45 per cent or less by the end of the decade.[2]

In a somewhat different manner job creation statistics are misleading because they fail to reveal the *kinds* of jobs that are being created. Pressure from a number of directions has led government to identify how many of the jobs created are part-time. However, little more than perfunctory attention is paid to the type or quality of jobs that are emerging in the new economy. This attitude, that 'a job is a job,' is exemplified by a Mount Forest town councillor who pointed out that a recently opened doughnut shop indicated that the town was well on its way to recovering from the closure of the Westinghouse plant. He apparently paid no attention to the disparity between the wages of a Westinghouse employee, who was paid around $14 an hour, and a doughnut shop employee paid $6.80 an hour. Nor did he mention the difference between full-time hours with benefits against part-time work without benefits.

Increasingly, analysts are pointing to the changing shape of the labour market, as it moves towards one where middle-range jobs (for example skilled and semi-skilled blue-collar jobs) are fast disappearing. The hourglass shape of the labour market in the new economy lends support to the polarization thesis. As early as 1990 the Economic Council of Canada labelled this situation a 'good jobs, bad jobs' scenario. This hollowing-out is a result of the kinds of jobs created and lost recently. For example, there has been a significant decline in full-time work, and a concomitant rise in part-time work through the 1990s, to the point where in 1997 part-time jobs constituted 19 per cent of all jobs. Similarly, there has been a tremendous increase in the number of people deemed to be self-employed.[3] By 1997, 18 per cent of the labour force were self-employed, and the vast majority of those were women (Burke and Shields 1999: 10).

The inability of standard labour force statistical categories to present an accurate picture of the labour market in the new economy has prompted Burke and Shields (1999) to reconceptualize relevant indicators. Basing their work on statistics from regular labour force surveys, they have recombined the data to provide a more nuanced picture of unemployment and employment in Canada.

Burke and Shields distinguish between workers in 'stable' jobs and those in 'flexible' jobs. 'Stable' workers are full-time (more than thirty hours per week), have permanent jobs without a predetermined termination date, and have worked at those jobs for at least two years. 'Flexible' workers are those whose terms of work in some way do not meet those criteria (Burke and Shields 1999: 16–17). Applying their definitions to the Statistics Canada data for May 1998 they conclude that at that time 45 per cent of the Canadian labour force (5.4 million people) were flexible workers. Even when workers under twenty-five years of age, who might be expected to vary from the norm of stable work, are excluded, this figure remains at 3.5 million. To illustrate one dramatic difference between stable and flexible workers, they calculate that for the over twenty-five age group, the difference between hourly wages for stable workers and those for flexible workers is $4.70. When broken down by gender, for men, stable workers average $19.23 per hour versus $14.25 for flexible workers, while stable women workers average $15.38 and flexible workers $11.89. The degree of divergence between the hourly wages of flexible female workers and stable male workers demonstrates polarization in the labour market and shows quite dramatically the way it is gendered (17–18).

The recent decline in the official unemployment figures obscures what Burke and Shields (1999: 12) term 'the broader reality of worklessness,' since unemployment statistics measure only those unemployed and actively looking for work, and even then only if they fit the government's criteria for unemployment assistance.[4] They propose an alternative way of measuring various forms of unemployment and marginal employment, providing some information about 'the number and condition of people who want work or who want more work but are unable to find it' (12). In their scheme, there are six categories, which represent 20.3 per cent of the labour force or 3.2 million people, who experience exclusion from the labour market in some way. In their descriptions, these categories are:

(1) the *unemployed*, as officially defined;
(2) *discouraged workers* who want to work but have given up looking for work because they believe no suitable employment is available;
(3) *involuntary part-time workers* who are in part-time employment because they cannot find, even though they continue to look for, full-time work;
(4) *discouraged involuntary part-time workers* who want to work full-time but have given up looking for such work;

Table 5.1. Unemployment rates

| | Total unemployment rate, 15 years + | | | Unemployment rate by sex, 15 years + | | | | | |
| | | | | Male | | | Female | | |
	1986	1991	1996	1986	1991	1996	1986	1991	1996
All Ontario	6.8	8.5	9.1	5.9	8.6	8.7	8.0	8.4	9.6
Arnprior	8.1	9.1	10.5	6.7	8.5	11.7	9.8	9.9	8.8
Harriston	6.2	4.1	6.2	7.2	5.3	7.1	3.0	2.6	3.8
Iroquois Falls	8.4	14.2	9.5	5.8	15.6	9.0	12.8	11.8	9.7
Mount Forest	7.3	6.7	9.7	6.2	5.5	10.8	8.6	7.9	9.0
Elora	7.6	7.0	6.7	7.7	6.5	5.0	7.5	8.5	9.3

Source: Adapted from Statistics Canada, Census of Canada 1986, 1991, 1996.

(5) *marginal temporary workers* whose fixed-term or short-term jobs pay them less than $10 per hour; and

(6) the *marginal own-account self-employed* who have no (paid) employees and work fewer than 35 hours per week

(Burke and Shields 1999: 13)

This conceptualization of unemployment and underemployment is particularly useful for examining the labour market outcomes for the displaced workers in our community case studies (see Table 5.1). Official monthly or annual unemployment rates were not available to us at the community level. The census data in Table 5.1 indicate what the official unemployment rate was at one point in every five-year period. These data indicate that unemployment rates have declined somewhat from the mid-1980s until 1991. This latter date comes just before the worst of the early 1990s recession took hold. By 1996 the higher rates reflect the lingering effects of this recession. The exception is Iroquois Falls, which experienced greater unemployment in 1991 because of a dramatic slowdown in the pulp-and-paper sector at that time. Female unemployment rates are also consistently higher, reflecting the persisting bias towards employing males in the resource sector. If we take Burke and Shields's analysis seriously, we would suspect the unemployment figures, which indicate unemployment rates in all the communities in 1996 to be not so very different from the provincial average. They fail to portray what is really happening in these communities. The way Statistics Canada collects unemployment data means that it may not accurately reflect what is going on in a specific community. For example, many census respondents who are recorded as employed are likely to be working *outside* the community, in nearby, or not so nearby urban communities. The census method is unable to capture the proportion of community residents who are unable to commute to work, and for whom there are few work opportunities locally.

Our research indicates that such unemployment data not only underestimate the unemployment situation but also do little to illuminate the real changes in the labour market that were under way during these years. Our data show that many people who lose access to stable full-time jobs with benefits have little option but to move towards flexible, casual, part-time forms of work, when they seek alternatives in the new rural community economy. These people move from living in a stable work world to living in a contingent work world, a difference with far broader ramifications than simply a change in work arrangements. Our findings suggest that for working-class people in rural communities, who have been displaced from stable jobs, Burke and Shields's concept of structural exclusion is particularly appropriate.

Losing a Job in the Stable Work World

Following the closure of the Canada Packers facilities in Elora and Harriston, and the Westinghouse plant in Mount Forest, laid-off workers found themselves looking for work in an economic environment that was not conducive to finding comparable work. Mount Forest had enjoyed the stable jobs provided by Westinghouse, and the spin-off jobs and economic security that accompanied it, for a mere ten years. Workers in Harriston had grown up with the earlier incarnations of Canada Packers; it was almost impossible to imagine their town without a working dairy-processing plant. Workers in the community of Elora fared little better, as manufacturing had been in decline there for decades. When these factories closed there was no stable employer waiting to occupy the factory building. Those seeking stable jobs could only look far afield for them, or if they wanted to stay in the community they could opt for jobs in the new service sector, or the low-wage manufacturing sector, and that option was only available in Mount Forest.

Table 5.2. Mount Forest: workers laid off from Westinghouse

1994	Women (n=17)	Men (n=13)
Median age	40	38
Unemployed	3	3
Retired	1	0
Working	13	10
Average pre–lay-off hourly wage	$12.98	$14.90
Average hourly wage	$ 8.29	$16.50
Unemployed more than 1 year between lay-off and 1994	8 (47%)	2 (15.4%)
1996	(n=6)	(n=9)
Average hourly wage 1995	$10.22	$12.90

Table 5.3. Harriston: workers laid off from Canada Packers

1994	Women (n=12)	Men (n=10)
Median age	55	61
Unemployed	5	0
Retired	1	5
Working	6	5
Average pre–lay-off hourly wage	$11.07	$11.77
Average hourly wage	$ 9.18	$11.03
Unemployed more than 1 year between lay-off and 1994	5 (41.7%)	0 (0%)
1996	(n=7)	(n=5)
Average hourly wage 1995	$ 8.62	$ 12.39

In 1993 and 1994, about two years after the initial lay-offs in each community, we interviewed sixty-eight workers from these plants. The data for each community are summarized in Tables 5.2, 5.3, and 5.4. At the time of the interviews fifteen (22 per cent) were not working but were seeking work, two (3 per cent) were participating in training programs, and seven (10 per cent) considered themselves retired; in other words, they were not working, nor were they looking for work.[5] Overall forty-four (65 per cent) were involved in some form of paid work when we interviewed them.

Table 5.4. Elora: workers laid off from Canada Packers

1993	Women (n=13)	Men (n=3)
Median age	36	35
Unemployed	3*	1
Retired	0	0
Working	8	2
Average pre–lay-off hourly wage	$10.93	$12.00
Average hourly wage	$ 7.90	$ 8.75
Unemployed more than 1 year		
between lay-off and 1993	11 (84.6%)	1 (33.3%)
1996	(n=2)	(n=7)
Average hourly wage 1995	$11.19	$14.00

* Excludes two women in training

At 22 per cent, unemployment among these workers was at least twice the official figure for these communities or for the province. Unemployment for women in this sample was even higher, at 26 per cent. We could easily include in this group several of those who considered themselves retired, since they had come to this conclusion only after months or even years of looking unsuccessfully for a job. Of course, had we applied the government's template for unemployment, many of the people we have included in this category would not have qualified.

Another dimension of unemployment not captured in the official statistics emerged from our interviews. This is the reality of what is officially termed 'long-term unemployment,' that is, being without work for a year or more. The number of people whose period of unemployment following initial lay-off had lasted at least a year was extremely high. For the sample as a whole, twenty-seven (40 per cent) had been unemployed for more than a year. Not only was unemployment particularly high among women who had lost their jobs, but the length of time people had spent unemployed varied by gender as well. For the twenty-six men, three had spent more than a year unemployed, while for the forty-two women, twenty-six – more than 50 per cent – had been unemployed for more than a year. In the case of the Elora shutdown, approximately 90 per cent of the female workforce had experienced long-term unemployment.

In the government's statistics these workers are excluded as soon as they become ineligible for unemployment benefits. Casualties of the restructuring economy, they are disposed of by the statisticians. Until the 1980s, postwar economic cycles indicated that economic improvement benefited all but the most marginal of workers. It was only those more or less permanently excluded from the labour market – the chronically sick or disabled, older workers, the illiterate – who remained unemployed when economies were in the middle of an upswing. Restructured economies in the late 1980s and 1990s operate differently. In fact, a prime objective in companies in recent years is to employ as few people as possible. Yet the policies developed in the postwar period have not kept pace with this change, continuing to treat unemployment as a short-term and unusual phenomenon, and displaced workers as if they have personal deficits – which might be physical, psychological, or related to their human capital – preventing them from successfully finding employment.

Hourly pay rates are a common measure that both workers and policy-makers in Canada use to assess jobs. However, using hourly pay rates *alone* as a quick way of assessing employment and re-employment, as many analysts do, can be misleading since it fails to capture other ways in which new jobs differ from old ones. In terms of pay, the average hourly wage at the Canada Packers plants, of around $12 for the thirteen men and $11 for the twenty-five women, had taken a significant tumble, dropping to about $10 for the men who were working and to about $8.50 for the women, two years after their initial lay-offs. For the seventeen women Westinghouse workers, the drop in average wage upon re-employment was particularly precipitous: it had fallen from $13 an hour to just over $8 an hour.

For the thirteen men who had worked at Westinghouse, average hourly pay had, in fact, increased from around $15 to $16.50. This might seem, at first, to contradict some of what has been said above. Apparently some workers were able to do better, economically speaking, by moving on from their old jobs and finding new work. What we learned from the conversations that took place during our face-to-face interviews, however, provides evidence to rethink this outcome. True, some respondents, mostly men, did find work at a higher hourly wage. However, for virtually all of them this increased wage came at the cost of commuting daily out of the community. It can be safely assumed for most of these individuals that once the costs of running a vehicle used for commuting were factored in, their hourly wage would be less than they had once made locally.

In addition, it must be noted that for a number of men, this higher wage did not go with full-time work. It constituted, rather, relatively high-paying *part-time work.* It was necessary for these individuals to find other jobs as well. Earning more on an hourly basis, therefore, did not necessarily mean one's take home pay at the end of the week was greater than before.

The vignette of the post lay-off experience of Jim Larker gives an idea of how difficult the new reality of contingent labour was. Jim Larker was one of several people we interviewed who began his career in farming. Like several other farmer/labourers we talked to, Larker was forced by the high interest rates that came with the federal government's monetary policy of the early 1980s to seek wage work in nearby Mount Forest in order to keep the farm. Two years after lay-off at Westinghouse, he was working two part-time jobs and making about 30 per cent less money. In addition, he was still trying to farm. His new reality of contingent work illustrates well the double bind more and more workers find themselves in. With a life of episodic work, not only was Larker unable to make anywhere near the take-home pay he had with his stable job at Westinghouse, but also because of the changes in the federal unemployment insurance scheme, he was usually unable to collect unemployment benefits.

'When I was straight days [at Westinghouse], I knew I had to get up at 6 to go to work. I knew I was going to be there Monday to Friday. I wasn't going to be laid off on Wednesday or Tuesday. I knew I was straight days. But these other jobs ... I work to 12 o'clock at night now when I am on afternoon shifts. I get home at 12:30 a.m., in bed by 1, get up at 4 to go out on the truck and maybe come home for lunch, and some days only have lunch and then go back to the other job.

'Last week, I worked Thursday night up in Walkerton, got home and was in bed by 1 a.m., and I got up at 4:30 and got into the truck at 5. I did ten and a quarter hours there, then I went in to Walkerton again ... We only worked 6 hours in Walkerton [at the processors], but then the trucking place wanted me to work again Saturday morning, and I thought, what the hell, its only three hours, so I did that again.' (Jim Larker, former Westinghouse employee)

Piecing together part-time jobs over the course of a week could prove to be an exhaustive experience. Periods of unplanned downtime interrupted by a crazy patchwork of paid labour required Larker to be at different jobs consecutively without a break. The only thing that broke the work routine was the constant driving between jobs, and between the job and home, often late at night when he was dead tired.

When we first reported these findings (Leach and Winson 1995) we were unable to determine whether the situation workers were in when we interviewed them soon after their lay-off reflected a more or less permanent condition. In other words, we did not at that time know whether a worker who had been unable to find a job since his or her lay-off would remain unemployed. It was possible, after all, that this relatively bleak picture would change as the economy picked up, that these unemployed workers would be able to find work in a more elastic labour market. To try to elicit work trajectories more fully, we reinterviewed about half of the original respondents (N=36). Respondents for this new round were randomly selected from the original list that had worked at the Canada Packers plants and at Westinghouse. Interviews took place in the autumn of 1996, some four years after the initial lay-offs. The findings at this time were instructive of emerging trends. Of these thirty-six, only two individuals were not working at the time of reinterview, and neither of these was among those who had been unemployed two years earlier. In other words, we were beginning to see what has been called in the British restructuring literature, a 'chequered pattern,' as individual workers moved from unemployment to temporary employment and back to unemployment again, over a period of a few years. As the summary tables show, average hourly wages had again shifted, but it is difficult to discern a clear pattern. These shifts seem to be attributable largely to the intersection of extremely local (that is, within a few kilometres of a specific community) labour market dynamics with gender issues, and will be discussed further in Chapter 6.

A major problem with using hourly wages pre- and post–lay-off as points of comparison is that this does not account for changes in the number of hours people are working. The implications of this have been touched upon already. Interviews indicate a major change in the lives of these workers: whereas in their old jobs they had worked forty hours a week, sometimes more because of overtime, in their new jobs they were frequently working only part-time hours. This is consistent with Burke and Shields's emphasis on the trend away from full-time hours in recent years. Thus, while the difference in average hourly wage may not appear to be that great (although we should not underestimate the difference one or two dollars an hour makes at rates of around $10 an hour), in terms of annual income, the difference between pre-lay-off and post-lay-off pay was, in fact, quite dramatic. When we returned to talk to people for the second time in 1996, we asked them to estimate their annual income for 1995. Many people at first had difficulty doing so, and this was precisely because they had been forced to work so many part-time jobs during that year or had experienced irregular periods of lay-off. By piecing together the information they were giving us about hourly rates, hours, and weeks worked, they were eventually able to come up with an approximation.

Table 5.5 shows the average annual income change by plant and by gender. These data show two types of variation, first between men and women overall, and second between the women from the Canada Packers plant in Harriston, and the women from the other two plants. Overall, men's incomes decreased by 18 per cent while women's incomes decreased by 39 per cent. The increase in average income for the men laid off from Canada Packers incorporates a large increase for two men (32 per cent and 57 per cent, respectively), and a significant drop for one, from $24,440 to $13,500 (45 per cent). At the other two plants, men's annual incomes dropped, by approximately 15 per cent. Five of the thirteen men were making more in their new jobs than in their old ones, although, as we have already noted, this was typically the result of piecing together two or more part-time jobs, enduring a very long commute each day, or both. Only two women were making more money in their new jobs than in their old ones. For one of these it was only a slight increase. This woman was commuting about eighty kilometres each day to work, and she was still subject to a cycle of lay-off and recall. The other was a woman whose pre-lay-off hourly wage had been considerably less than all the other women in the sample ($7.50 compared with about $11).

Women were affected more dramatically by the lay-off in terms of annual income, four of them experiencing a drop of between $15,000 and $20,000 per year. There is also a striking difference between women who worked in Harriston compared with those working at the other two plants. This can be accounted for, at least in part, by better access for women in Mount Forest and Elora to factory jobs relatively close by, whereas women in Harriston who were unwilling to look beyond the very local labour market found themselves with only very low paid, part-time work options.

Table 5.5. Average change in annual income before lay-off and in 1995

Employer	Men	Women
Westinghouse	(n=6)	(n=9)
Year before lay-off	$30,808	$29,088
1995	$25,500 (–17.2%)	$20,000 (–31.2%)
CP Elora	(n=7)	(n=2)
Year before lay-off	$24,232	$22,538
1995	$20,380 (–15.9%)	$15,000 (–33.4%)
CP Harriston	(n=5)	(n=7)
Year before lay-off	$24,351	$23,201
1995	$27,100 (+11.3%)	$10,200 (–56%)

The issue of women's access to the more distant labour markets where men were working is tied up with the gender division of labour in the household. The divergence between men's and women's work trajectories after lay-off is clearly a trend that needs to be investigated further (see also Leach 1999); it will be discussed further in the following chapter.

The impact of job loss on individuals was dramatic, cutting income on average by at least one-third, and in one case by two-thirds (from $27,000 to $9,000). This does not mean a fairly minor cutting back on 'extras' such as holidays. Rather, a massive drop in income such as this undermines people's capacity to meet their basic needs of food and housing; we explored with our respondents what this actually meant in terms of day-to-day living and we present their responses in the next chapter.

The shift to part-time work, well documented in the literature as a feature of corporate flexibility strategies, is starkly evident. Our interviews in 1994 revealed that 15 per cent of the men and 54 per cent of the women were employed in part-time jobs. By 1996, 25 per cent of the men and 78 per cent of the women in the sample we reinterviewed were in part-time employment. In 1996 the average part-time hourly wage for men was 80 per cent of the average full-time hourly wage. For women it was 64 per cent. The shift to part-time work is accompanied by an equally important move towards more casual work arrangements, in other words, to jobs with either limited terms, or more commonly in these communities, jobs that never become permanent, and from which workers can be summarily laid off, without notice, reason, or termination pay. These changes require workers to organize their work lives and their family lives in new, and often stressful, ways as they are forced to participate in the contingent work world.

Workers who lost their manufacturing jobs because of corporate restructuring could be interpreted as relatively isolated cases. To the extent that they may not be isolated, or at least may be similar to the experiences of other similarly situated communities, one may attribute these changes to the location of Harriston and Mount Forest at some distance from larger urban centres. Related to that, and perhaps more importantly, is the remote community's inability to replace the lost employer, at the time the dominant firm in the community, with another offering comparable wages. However, our subsequent research with laid-off workers in Arnprior, only forty minutes drive from Ottawa, and about twenty minutes from Kanata, Canada's 'silicon valley north,' tells another kind of story.

Most of the eighteen former Weavexx workers we interviewed in Arnprior lost their jobs in July 1996. We talked to them in the autumn of 1998, after they had spent two years looking for jobs. The data for these workers are summarized in Table 5.6. At the time of the 1998 interviews four respondents were not working and were looking for work. One was on social assistance and fighting for disability benefits, and another was in a training program. None of these workers identified themselves as retired. Twelve women (66 per cent – almost exactly the same proportion as in the Wellington County communities) were working at the time of interview. For the workers in Wellington County, the average hourly wage for these workers had also dropped, although only by about $1 an hour. The higher hourly rate of the Arnprior group can perhaps be accounted for by their location close to a major city, as well as the timing of our interviews, which took place later in the upturn of the Canadian economic cycle of the 1990s.

As in the other communities, the most significant change experienced by laid-off workers in Arnprior concerned the organization of their work lives, rather than the hourly pay they were receiving. In contrast to the Wellington County workers, many of whom could find only part-time jobs, in Arnprior the trend appeared to be in favour of replacing full-time permanent jobs with full-time temporary jobs. Of the twelve workers interviewed who were working, seven were in casual jobs, that is, in jobs either with fixed termination dates or with absolutely no security of tenure.

Table 5.6. Arnprior: workers laid off from Weavexx

1998	Women (n=5)	Men (n=13)
Median age	43	52
Unemployed	2*	2*
Retired	0	0
Working	2	10
Average pre-lay-off hourly wage	$14.05	$14.78
Average hourly wage 1998	$13.04	$13.40
Unemployed more than 1 year between lay-off and 1998	2 (40%)	0 (0%)

* Excludes one woman in training and one man on social assistance

It seems clear from these data that most workers had left jobs in the stable work world to find themselves eligible only for jobs in the contingent work world. In so doing they skidded into officially defined unemployment, or when no longer eligible for that, into low-paid temporary and part-time work, and low-paid self-employment, becoming part of the massive number of 3.2 million Canadian workers who would prefer more stable work but cannot find it (Burke and Shields 1999: 13). While communities like Harriston and Mount Forest carry the burden of distance from economically prosperous urban areas, people laid off from traditional manufacturing jobs in communities adjacent to flourishing cities fare only slightly better. Their prospects for full-time employment in the manufacturing segment of high tech industries may be better, and their hourly wage rates may more closely compare to pre-lay-off rates; nevertheless, they face far greater insecurity and instability in the new economy than they had known in the past.

Young People and the Quest for a Stable Work World

In Iroquois Falls the paper mill's restructuring took place through a negotiated early retirement program, rather than through traumatic lay-offs. As described in Chapters 3 and 4, this industry has been affected by technological change as well as increased global competition. Attempts to downsize the labour force through lay-offs, however, could be expected to be met with forceful resistance from the union. The most straightforward route for management, therefore, has been not to replace workers who retired, and to deal with temporary

Table 5.7. Iroquois Falls: 1993 high school leavers

1998	Women (n=17)	Men (n=17)
Working	10	16
Unemployed	4	1
Student	3	0
With post-secondary education (n)	13	14
Working at Abitibi (n)	1	3
Average wage for those at Abitibi	$19.00	$23.60
Average wage for other workers	$13.16	$16.10

increases in labour demand through overtime work by regular employees. This strategy has resulted in the maintenance of a core of workers with high seniority, who are protected by their union contracts, and a few new jobs where employees have been put 'on waivers.' In other words, the new employees are outside the unionized labour force, without job security and without membership in the permanent bargaining unit. To investigate access to stable jobs in this context, we concentrated our efforts on younger people, many of whom in earlier times would have walked out of high school and into a job at the mill. In 1998 we contacted young people who had left high school in 1993, to elicit their labour market experiences after five years in the absence of available mill jobs.

The data on youth are summarized in Table 5.7. Two major findings emerge. One is that of the thirty-four young people interviewed, only four have found work at the mill. Of these four, none were part of the bargaining unit, but rather working 'on waivers,' a situation that would provide no long term security. The second finding is that the average hourly pay for those at the mill is $6 to $7 an hour more than for those who work elsewhere.

Among the thirty-four interviewed, ten men and ten women had one or both parents who had worked at the mill. Nine of the men and six of the women had spent at least one summer working at the mill. Only one man whose parents had not worked at the mill had himself worked there during a summer. All of the four working at the mill at the time of the 1998 interviews had parents who had worked there, and as well they had all worked summers there before being offered full-time jobs.

One question that interested us was whether the loss of good jobs for young people in Iroquois Falls would lead many of them to leave the rural community in search of better opportunities elsewhere. In our sample, twelve (34 per cent, six men and six women) had left the area, and their experiences of work are certainly different from those who stayed. The average wage for men who left was $18 an hour, whereas for those who stayed it was $23.60 – if they were able to get a mill job, but only $12.50 if they were not. For women who left the area the average hourly wage was considerably lower than that of their male counterparts, at $10.50 (this figure excludes the part-time work of the three women students). This is a lower wage than that of most of the women working in Iroquois Falls, who averaged $12 an hour, and both of these are significantly lower than that of the one woman working at the mill who was making $19 an hour.

A further interesting feature concerns the number of young people who either had or were continuing to pursue post-secondary education. Table 5.7 shows that overall 76 per cent of the women and 82 per cent of the men had some kind of further education. Of those who had left the area, all had taken further studies, and three of the women were still involved in degree programs. Tellingly, all of those working at the mill had post-secondary degrees or diplomas, quite a different picture from past generations who could enter the mill without even a high school diploma. The consequences of this difference can be seen in a comparison of the average hourly wages of those with and without post-secondary education. Men with further education averaged $21.00 an hour, while men without averaged $15.50. Women with further education averaged $15 an hour, while three of the four less-educated women identified themselves as unemployed, and the fourth was receiving disability benefits. Two of these were providing casual child care services for which they charged $20 per day per child, clear examples of 'own account' work, which is effectively low paid and flexible.

As elsewhere, the average hourly wage was somewhat deceptive here as an indicator, since part-time work was a regular feature of work for some people. For those living in the Iroquois Falls area who were working (ten men and eight women), only one woman and one man were working part-time, but two men and one woman were considered casual, meaning that they could be laid off without notice at any time. Of those who had left the area, one of the three women working and one of the six men were working part-time. Among the

Figure 5.1 Sector of re-employment, north Wellington study

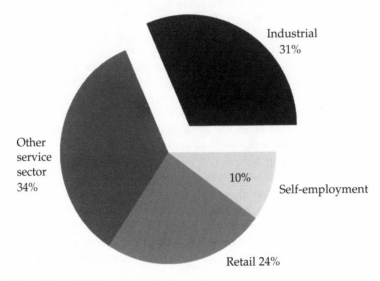

Source: Interviews, 1996.

Iroquois Falls school leavers, there was a far higher proportion of full-time workers than in the other communities (twenty-three of thirty-four or 68 per cent), and of those, only three had casual, unpredictable, work. We suggest that this can be explained by the potent combination – and it is the combination which matters here – of their relatively higher levels of post-secondary education and their youth.

Our case studies show a clear shift away from the stable work in unionized facilities that had provided earlier generations of workers with security and decent working conditions. In the 1990s workers confronted a new economy in which their most readily available work option was flexible work, at relatively low pay, especially if they wanted to continue to work in the communities where their old jobs had been. Figure 5.1 provides an indication of the industrial sectors in which Wellington County workers found new jobs, with a significant shift away from manufacturing and towards the service sector. Many people moved from semi-skilled industrial jobs into part-time jobs in restaurants, shops, and nursing homes, into unskilled factory work, into providing casual child care to neighbours, or selling vegetables in a sidewalk stall.

Table 5.8. Incidence of contingent work among those interviewed between 1996 and 1998 (N=87)

	Men	Women	All respondents
Unemployed	5 (11.6%)	11 (25.0%)	16 (18.4%)
Stable employment	20 (46.5%)	8 (18.1%)	28 (32.2%)
Contingent employment	18 (41.9%)	25 (56.9%)	43 (49.4%)
Total	43 (100%)	44 (100%)	87 (100%)

Source: Interviews 1996, 1998.

The shift to contingent work is dramatic. Half of the workers (49.4 per cent) we interviewed in all five communities (see Table 5.8) between 1996 and 1998 were in contingent work. This includes people whose work was part-time, temporary, casual, or self-employed without employees. Most of these people were not receiving benefits. If we add to this group those who were unemployed, this brings to 67.8 the percentage of our interviewees who were, in Burke and Shields's terms flexible workers, excluded from the stable labour force.

Region and gender have a considerable impact on the likelihood of becoming a contingent worker. Over half the women (56.9 per cent) interviewed in Wellington County had become contingent workers. With the high rate of unemployment among those women (25 per cent), this brings the loss of employment stability among women to 87 per cent. The incidence of contingency among the Iroquois Falls workers (41.9 per cent) indicates that it is as much a phenomenon of younger workers as it is of those displaced after many years in the labour market.

These numbers are staggering. They show the difficulties faced by rural community residents looking for work in the new economy. Those determined to find jobs comparable to the ones they lost experienced an uphill battle. This battle was frequently fought over distance, when the only comparable job was many kilometres away. Sometimes the battle was to gain the appropriate educational requirements or specific training to equip them with new skills, or to convince new employers that as workers over forty years of age, they would be able to adjust to using computers, reading technical instructions, and using rapidly evolving equipment.

At other times the battle was over the lack of public services to support the workers' search for a job or their day-to-day needs when they found one. Alongside these battles there were always the hidden enemies of sexism and ageism, which we will discuss in the next chapter – racism is only absent from this list because all of the workers we talked to were white. These have been extremely effective in keeping women and both older and younger workers out of the remaining decent jobs; and older workers were often quick to articulate their perception that age was a factor when employers passed them over. In this kind of labour market environment, such workers are forced to occupy the unstable and insecure jobs of the new economy.

We now turn to a more in-depth look at the human impact of restructuring. Here the focus is on how restructuring caused people to reorganize their family lives as well as their work lives, and how it intersects with factors such as gender and age.

CHAPTER SIX

'Forget All Your Dreams and Good Luck with Your Life': Lay-Off and the New Reality of Contingent Labour

I went into that job to pay for a car, and twenty-seven years later I was still there. But that job sort of got you because you had your health insurance there and you have a regular income and so you just kinda stayed there and it was comfortable ... And to do something that wasn't so comfortable, and going back to school, interviewing for jobs, and all those kinds of things you haven't had to worry about. In the financial area, I think about the money I was bringing back home then and how I seemed to never have any money and yet now I'm getting in a month what I got in one week, and I still don't seem to have any money. But when I think back and about the money I did have and about how carelessly I managed it.

Former Weavexx worker, Arnprior, 1998

In the previous chapter we discussed some of the trends that emerged from our case studies, in terms of the shift away from 'good jobs' towards those organized to be flexible for the employing firms and the change in income levels that accompanies this process. In this chapter we take up these trends in more detail and examine what they mean to the people experiencing them and to their families. We rely heavily on our respondents' reflections of what happened to them.

It was in these individual testimonies of our respondents that the realities of lay-off from the stable work world and the gritty, disruptive, and stress-filled entrance into the world of contingent labour began to fully emerge. In the context of the dozens of interviews we conducted over several years, a fuller picture of restructuring in the rural context took shape, one that takes us beyond the one-dimensional view given to us by statistical artefacts that typify most of the literature on the subject. Most significantly, these testimonies shed much-needed light on the hidden underbelly of the new rural economy.

We begin this chapter with an assessment, through the words of our respondents, of the reality of losing a job that may have been held for many years, and losing all the social supports, routines, and, of course, financial security that the job provided: in other words, the world after lay-off. We then turn to the changed labour market situation that these newly unemployed workers found themselves in. For most, this reality was what we call the contingent work world. In addition, we consider the situation of those most vulnerable to restructuring – the infirm, older and younger workers, and those with little formal education. Finally, we consider some local cultural factors, and the significance of attachment to place in defining the situations of our respondents.

Lay-Off and Its Aftermath

If we are to believe the standard reports in most newspapers, losing a job is mostly about short-term financial hardship, which in Canada is presumably made easier by the benefits from what used to be called unemployment insurance. While so-called reforms to unemployment insurance in the 1990s have drastically reduced the proportion of workers who would now qualify for benefits under the new rules, and thereby increased hardships for the newly unemployed, our fieldwork taught us that being laid off is about much more than tight finances.[1] For most it represented a tear in the fabric of their lives. We were to find out that for a surprisingly large proportion of our respondents, this 'tear' was to be a major one. It would not be possible to put their lives back together in any fashion that resembled their situation before lay-off.

Losing stable employment that has structured one's life for a long period is first and foremost a *psychological trauma* (Jahoda 1982; Warr 1987). This point was made clear to one of the authors as she sat talking to a woman, laid off four months earlier, in her kitchen. The woman's husband, whose job at the same company had terminated just days before, was methodically mowing the large lawn that could be seen from the window: 'I told him you were coming ... he can't bring himself to talk about it,' said his wife, with tears in her eyes as we watched him ride the mower up and down, seemingly in slow motion.

Other respondents, particularly women, were better able to verbalize their feelings about being let go. A worker of nine years at the Westinghouse plant said that her initial reaction to losing her job involved intense feelings of insecurity:

> You're losing part of something ... you've got all these people that you've kind of got to say bye to, and that's hard too. And you don't know if you're going to be able to get another job. You didn't know if you were going to be able to handle your bills and whatever. I felt pretty terrible, because you were kind of lost, unbalanced ... At times it was very frustrating and depressing, because you know you are a good worker and you know you can do the job, and nobody wants to give you a chance.

Another respondent, a man who had just turned fifty and had worked for many years at the Canada Packers plant in Harriston, had been laid off a couple of years before we interviewed him. He had not been able to find stable work in or near his community, and at the time of the interview he was on welfare. Of life after lay-off he said: 'I don't give a damn any more, and I don't have any interest any more. You lose it sitting here day in day out, that's no good for anybody ... I was a happy-go-lucky person, but ... Now, you don't look at life the same way.'

For some, it was the petty humiliations and injustices of beginning a new life with very little money and security that got them down. A former Elora plant worker gave us some indication of what she and many of her fellow employees faced: 'A couple of times you really had to embarrass yourself going to the food bank. Nobody wants to know how degrading that is when you have to walk in and say, "Can you help me?" I was so embarrassed, the first time I had gone I had done nothing but cry ... [I was thinking] I don't believe this ... You have to give a lot of credit to the Salvation Army and to the food banks around, because without them I don't know what a lot of people from Stillmeadow would have done.' A fellow plant worker voiced similar feelings when asked how he felt being forced to depend on the local food bank: 'I hate it. I'm embarrassed ... I feel like here is a great big guy standing there asking for food. That really bothers me an awful lot, but what I know is that there is another guy out there who needs it worse than I do. And I feel that I'm taking it from him.' Other respondents talked of the humiliation they felt, as adults in their thirties, having to approach ageing parents for handouts and cash to pay rent or the hydro bill.

Another part of the fallout of plant shutdown that contributed to the psychological trauma of the experience was the severe disruption of routine that so many said they had experienced. Whether it had been welcomed or not, work deeply structured the life of each of our respondents, dictating its rhythms week in and week out. Most indicated, in one way or another, that this rhythm provided by work was somehow a comfort in their life, something that they missed when the job ended. They were forced to try and find a new rhythm, but the reality of a depressed job market and limited opportunities was making this impossible for all but the fortunate few who did find stable work, usually by commuting out of the area.

Don, once an employee at the Elora plant, summed up eloquently what a surprising number of respondents felt about this matter: 'I've lost my routine ... lots of days I'll say, what day is this? I went to bed at a certain hour and woke up at a certain time. I still wake up for that time to get up and get ready to be at work for 5 o'clock ... I don't have that any more ... You're all screwed up now ... the only routine I've got is to get my cheque, and I know what I've got to do. I've got to get to the grocery store and to the bank and that sort of stuff and then the routine is finished until another few weeks ... You walk a thin line all the time on unemployment or on welfare.'

In a similar vein, Al Laramie, who worked at Westinghouse for forty-four years in Mount Forest and previous locations, explained how he felt when he lost his job: 'We were working four days a week, ten hour days, and it was the fact that now you're not there. Like you've got nothing to do. It is a routine that you get out of. After forty-four years it's a hard thing to break. That's the part that bothered me the most. Right now you're lost. Everything is wrapped around the fact that you were there [at work] from 7 a.m. Monday until 5.30 p.m. on Thursday and then you developed your life after that. You've had your life around the three days and now you've got to develop your life for seven and it's hard.'

Several of our respondents talked of feelings of boredom and lack of direction in their lives as they struggled to cope with the absence of the structure and regular activity that work had provided. Tracey Rivers talked at some length about the problem of not working, and how staying at home led to boredom and eventually to a rut: 'For a while it is great, and then you get bored being around the house ... But when the kids are in school and you're here by yourself, you get into a rut. You just get so bored ... you don't even feel like going outside the house. You were wishing you were working ... Being around the house when you're not used to it, and I wasn't busy and you just get so lazy and then you just can't snap out of it, you know. I was always so busy at work and then you come home to not being busy.'

Darlene voiced the same concerns when we talked with her, but she was also clear about how her feelings of self-worth were tied up with having her job: 'I tried to keep as busy as I could, but you really get down. You really get down and depressed when you don't have a job because when you have a job it gives you some self-worth and it gives you a routine ... It gives you something to look forward to. And then you've got money coming in, which gives you security.'

In her interview we got a picture of how some people attempt to structure activities by 'keeping busy' at home. Work is more than giving routine, however, and because it is intimately linked with self-esteem in various complex ways, the absence of work cannot be replaced with busyness at home.

All of our respondents indicated that lay-off had entailed some degree of psychological trauma. Clearly, this was far more serious for some, resulting in hospitalization for depression, than for others. Many of them did not want to belabour the point, preferring to mention only that it had been difficult, but that 'life goes on,' that 'you have to move on.' This 'grin and bear it' attitude is perhaps not a surprising response given the predominantly Anglo-Saxon Protestant culture that prevails in most of the communities we studied. As well, people reject their sense of helplessness, and try valiantly to find solutions to their predicament. For the most part the men we talked to were more reticent about going into the details of their emotional state in the period after they were laid off. The reticence of the men was mentioned several times by the women we interviewed, especially when we interviewed couples who had both been working at the same factory and who were, in their different ways, each trying to deal with the situation. Though often reluctant to elaborate in depth on their feelings, from time to time these men would drop clues that things had not always gone very well. Such was the case with one man who had indicated through the course of the interview that things were generally alright, but then let it drop that he had separated from his wife, and had spent a month in hospital because of 'the stress thing.'

It also became clear that one's marital situation often played a significant role in shaping the post–lay-off experience. In this regard, several respondents told us that the personal impact of the lay-off would have been devastating for them if it had not been for the support of their spouse at the time.

While by middle-class standards the jobs of our respondents lacked the enrichment that makes jobs interesting for some, it was nevertheless quite significant to them in providing an ongoing, dependable circle of friends and acquaintances. The role of these *friendships* in maintaining an individual's psychological balance cannot be underestimated, for once they were lost, they were clearly sorely missed. Katherine, a long-time Canada Packers worker told us that she thought about 'losing contact with all your friends that you knew for that many years, and I think that a lot of people were upset about that part of it, too. [Now] you're not available for social activities. You're not as closely in contact with your friends that you were for so many years. With working there for twelve years you made friends through that. I find that [in her new job] you work with so many different people, you are not working with the same people from one day to the next so you don't get as close a relationship with them.'

Another worker who lost her position at the chicken-processing plant in Elora compared her workmates to a family: 'Everybody seemed to be close-knit...It was more close-knit at Stillmeadow [than at her present job in a bar]. Everybody respected everybody...I don't see a lot of my friends now. I don't see a lot of people that I used to...some of them I miss; a lot of them I miss.'

A woman who worked at the Elora plant with her husband voiced similar feelings about co-workers: 'Everybody told all their family stories and you got to know the family of the people as well as just the people. If somebody's kid was sick everybody felt bad the kid was sick, and they all wanted her to get better, you know. We brought pictures of our kids; we were constantly talking about our lives. It is like, you go home and you've got a family at home, you've got a life there. But you've also got another life at work. You can't wait to get back to this life, to get back to the people at work to tell them, this is what I did today and let them know. Yes [I miss it].' In a similar vein, another woman who worked at this plant told us that she and her husband 'were in touch with a lot of people at the plant. We were really close, we all kind of worked together and then did things after work ... It was hard for a lot of people.'

Some of the former employees at the Westinghouse plant in Mount Forest voiced the same sentiments: 'You spend eight hours a day with those people, you're bound to get attached to them socially, and you spend more time with them than you do at home,' a female plant worker told us. 'It's just like another family. I miss that.'

It was not only female workers who stressed loss of workmate friendship, although female respondents were more likely to mention it. Jarrod, a former Westinghouse worker, said that apart from the income, he missed 'the people, the friendship. The worker friendship. There wasn't anyone in the end that you couldn't walk up to and talk to. You had something in common with them ... Work is social, I agree with you.'

As interviews progressed we began to see that our respondents were put in a double bind by their job loss as far as friendships were concerned. Not only did many of them feel that they had lost their job-related friendships, but the new constraints they found themselves under (financial, and lack of time for those now forced to commute to work, or work two part-time jobs) undermined the socializing they had done with other friends not related to work. As Marlene, a former worker at the Elora plant told us when asked how the job loss affected relationships with friends: '[It's] not so much the relationship but more the lack of it ... we don't go to see them ... We have no money for gas. I spend so much money on gas going back and forth to work [at her new job some distance away] that on the weekend we just stay home. Why put the gas out? We hardly ever see friends anymore.'

Even for those not so financially pressed, the effects of job loss inevitably affected their ability to maintain friendships, if only because they felt guilty putting a financial burden on others by going over to visit. A few of our respondents did say that they still socialized with former workmates, that their lives in this realm had not changed that much, but overall there was a strong sense of loss with respect to the socializing that was part of their stable work lives. This was perhaps most strongly voiced by the former workers at the Elora plant, where the workforce had been largely female, but workers in all the communities we studied indicated a sense of loss to varying degrees with respect to friendships. We had the strong sense, and particularly so in Elora, that plant shutdown was very much about the loss of community. In this case the community of workmates who had been together some time and were mutually supportive and important to the well-being of each others' lives.

Undoubtedly related to the curtailment of contact with friends, and the impossibility for many to afford the recreational activities they once had had, was the increased pressure on family relationships.

This seemed to be particularly bad for couples where both partners had been working at the plants and who were suddenly at home together, unemployed. It is worth noting that more than a dozen of our respondents were in this position. Before the lay-offs this situation provided numerous advantages for the couples and their families. Plant shutdowns brought intense discord and stress to such families as they faced the loss of two incomes. In his work with unemployed workers in London, Ontario, Burman (1988: 185) found that families could cope with one job loss, since one spouse could stimulate the other vicariously through her or his job, but when both partners were unemployed the family suffered more.

Janice and her husband both worked at the Elora plant, and after lay-off she said their relationship was 'especially hard, because you fight. You got no money to go anywhere so you are in the same place day after day. It gets on your nerves, you worry about bills constantly ... you don't ever seem to have your own space.'

Parenting suffers as well under these stressful conditions. Some found they did not have the patience needed for their children when they were consumed with their own problems. One couple worried about the effect of their strained relationship on their 3-year-old son: 'It's not fair to Billy because the pressure gets to us ... we don't have as much patience. It affects him too, because when we are fighting over bills he kind of backs away ... When the pressure is so bad on us, then we don't like doing the things we used to do with Billy. You worry when you don't want to read a storybook or go outside and throw snowballs.'

An additional strain on family relationships came when adult children, because of their own problems in the labour market, returned to live with their parents, placing even more stress, financial as well as other kinds, on an already over-extended household.

The argument that work is central to defining what is unique in human beings is hardly new; indeed, it goes at least as far back as Marx and his writings on alienated labour in capitalist society. In more recent times numerous social scientists have agreed with Kates et al. (1990) that 'work and working fill a central role in our lives meeting a multitude of emotional, social and psychological needs.' The testimonies of our respondents demonstrated that when their stable work world was disrupted, one could expect a breakdown in living routines, the deterioration or dissolving of friendships, and the emergence of new pressures on family relationships. These testimonies of laid-off plant workers provide further evidence that work remains a critical force in giving meaning to the lives of those who do it.

Losing one's job is primarily about financial stress. Given the limited and declining financial support available to those who lose work, how could it not be so? Our interviews were replete with details of the financial burden workers faced once their job ended. Everyone was affected to some extent. Even those who claimed to have been relatively unscathed financially often revealed at some point that they had done without something they were previously able to afford. Situations varied, of course, as a few found work at a good wage without much delay, some older workers had pension incomes and were more likely to have paid off their mortgages, while others were successful at getting unemployment insurance. However, as we have seen in the previous chapter, on average our respondents experienced a substantial fall in income which proved to be no short-term thing. Four years or so after lay-off their incomes averaged a full one-third less than they had been before lay-off.

The financial aspects of job loss were a constant worry, unlikely to be alleviated fully when new jobs were found. As we saw in the previous chapter, they are likely to be at a lower wage than the old jobs. Job loss led to financial distress for all but the most fortunate. Job loss and loss of income meant difficulty making ends meet, either for a short time, or in the longer term. For some, this meant adjustments, such as cutting out things like prepared food and restaurant meals. While apparently minor, these conveniences can take some pressure off working wives and mothers facing a double day of paid work and domestic tasks.

Even when working at their previous unionized job, our respondents often lived a life that many middle-class people would consider exceptionally frugal. After lay-off their spartan existence became rather grim. The wife of a couple that worked at the Elora plant provided a window into this experience: '[It has been hard] living without, like the little extras. We never went out to parties or a show or dinner but we would take a little trip up to his sister's cottage or I would go and visit my mother, but now we have to cut that out. I can't even go out for a coffee with a friend ... These are just small things ... You have to stop living almost and just have the bare necessities.'

For others it was not cutting out the small things, but more drastic changes. Ron and Joan Bassett faced financial setbacks following his job loss. Despite finding a job two and a half months after his lay-off, he missed mortgage payments and eventually, when the bank fore-closed on their mortgage, they lost their house. During this period he and his wife separated. When they were interviewed they had re-united and were living in a rented apartment. Ron remembers this particularly stressful time: 'The bank took it [their house]... Well, we did what we could to try to keep it. We were separated for a while, and I missed a couple of payments. I started making payments again, weekly payments, and I was still behind but I was maintaining it. So I borrowed money from a finance company to catch up on it. The bank manager told me I had to go back for more money but I told her that I was already at my limit. She said, you can't do this, you have to do something else. Well, I told her to go to hell and I never made another payment. I thought if this is what owning a house is all about, shove it up their ass. So eventually they put us under power of sale.'

Having their family home in jeopardy was a reality faced by work-ers in all plants, but especially the younger workers that characterized the workforces in Elora and Mount Forest. As one of the last workers to be laid off at the Westinghouse factory told us, 'there was a drastic change in my income, drastic. It was, I would say, cut in half. [What adjustments did you have to make?]... We signed the deal to build the house in October, and in February they announced they were closed.' His wife broke in, saying that 'if he doesn't find work fairly soon we'll have to sell the house. That would be the major one.'

Lucy Grinnell, a former Weavexx worker in Arnprior whose hus-band had taken early retirement shortly before she was laid off, de-scribed the adjustments they had made as follows: 'I wouldn't say [we made] a lot [of financial adjustments] until my severance money fin-ished, and my severance money is pretty much gone now. What I invested in school and what I spent going back and forth to school and regular household expenses. I would say right now we are living on a tenth of the income we were living on three or four years ago, if it would even be that.'

Darlene Shaw found the loss of income and spending power de-pressing: 'There have been a lot of times when I have been depressed at not making the money. I was, not being able to buy the things I used to buy, not being able to go where I want to go. There has been a lot of depression with the money part.'

Many experienced the reverberations of financial difficulty for a long time. The Grahams had both worked at Canada Packers for sev-eral years and enjoyed what they considered to be good wages and a comfortable lifestyle. When their unemployment benefits ran out they were forced onto social assistance. They were then living on $1000 a month compared with a combined weekly income of $700 to $800 when they had been at Canada Packers. This meant they had to move to a much smaller apartment. Job loss also meant that they had to give up the benefits that workers until recently had come to associate with a good steady job. As Liz Graham put it: 'Living on $1000 a month isn't enough, especially when you have to pay a little more than half of that out just in rent. There is no money for hydro, then we have a 3-year-old son. He needs clothes, food, medication and we just couldn't get help...We got stripped, totally. We had taken away our job, we lost our life insurance, we lost benefits, we don't have that now. Like medication is so expensive...we don't get any reimbursement for it. [Before] we had medical, we had dental. It hurts. We all need dental work...We are both fighting for our teeth right now. There is nothing we can do, we can't afford to go to a dentist. We even phoned our MPP and asked if he could do anything for us. He told us his hands were tied.' Depending on one's stage of life, the financial crunch many experienced was felt in different ways. For some older workers like Eileen Jones who worked at the Canada Packers plant in Harriston for many years, having little extra money after working so long was a great disappointment. 'I don't have the same lifestyle anymore. I think one main thing is that I don't have the spending money to buy things. I've always bought for my nieces and nephews. Even for a wedding you don't have the same money. For thirty-four years you always had your own money. It's a change. I always have to be asking for money.'

A number of the women we talked to were upset because they had fallen into a state of financial dependence on their husbands, a situation they had not known before. A former worker at the Elora plant told us: 'It doesn't make me feel good...We have always shared the bills but now you have to depend more on him to be working overtime...He [husband] doesn't like me working weekends and shift work and stuff, he doesn't like it. He would like me to find something around here that's more steady.'

Like numerous other plant workers, Kerry experienced severe financial hardship, but together with the money she lost her place on the job hierarchy that she had struggled to achieve over many years. She told us: 'It is depressing and it is a big setback because you work so long all your life, the part-time jobs since you were thirteen and getting full-time and you work so hard to get that position [as] lead-hand. You work so hard while you are there and to try to get up to management and all of a sudden one day somebody turns around and says, "guess what? We're leaving, we're going." Forget all of your dreams, forget anything you wanted and good luck with your life.'

For the fortunate few who were able to find another job at a comparable salary soon after receiving their termination notices, the post lay-off experience was one of short-term belt tightening, perhaps getting used to a life of commuting to work, and perhaps a sense of loss for the work-place friends that were no more. For the majority it was altogether a more serious affair. Being put out of work in the midst of the sharp recession of the early 1990s, especially in predominantly rural areas with limited employment opportunities, this meant considerable suffering. This suffering took the form of depression, rapid financial decline and turmoil, strong feelings of loss with respect to friendships at work and outside of work, real disruption of family and personal routines, increased marital discord and accompanying stress. Lay-off was about much more than financial loss then, whether short or long term. It was, for many, a frontal assault on their long established daily existence, and the beginnings of what was to prove a difficult struggle to rebuild.

Despite this reality, and perhaps because of a stoicism and resilience imbued in the character of the people from earlier agrarian times, there was a refusal to tolerate feelings of helplessness. In numerous conversations with our respondents there emerged a strong desire to move on, to put the painful past behind them, and to find in their current situation some reason to hope. As one woman, a single mother with two children who was able to supplement her welfare cheque with only a few hours paid labour, told us: 'I guess there is hope. There is life after Westinghouse, you just have to find it. Don't let it get you down. That's the main thing. Don't dwell on what's happened, think about the future. Don't think about the past. It's the only way.'

'You Work Day by Day': The World of Contingent Labour

Looking back on the 1990s almost ten years after the initial lay-offs affecting our respondents began, it is possible to see that their job losses represented the cusp of momentous change in the way work is organized in Canada. In following their lives for some four years after the initial lay-offs, we were provided with a window into the new world of work rapidly taking shape throughout the economy. We witnessed the elaboration of the new regime of contingent labour in the rural milieu. This labour regime was in many respects no different from what has come to characterize jobs in urban centres, although there were certain consequences for our respondents in rural communities that urban workers would likely not have faced. A key one was the severe restriction in economic opportunities for those not able to commute to a major urban centre. The economic recession that began in 1990 clearly exacerbated the traditionally limited opportunities present in rural labour markets and increased the sense of desperation felt by the unemployed there. Many of our respondents told us that beyond a few jobs available at minimum wage there was simply 'nothing out there' as far as employment was concerned. Another factor faced by many of these rural residents was the need to overcome distance to reach the few jobs available. Given the almost total absence of public transportation, the barrier of geographical space could only be passed by commuting via automobile. Many who we interviewed were forced to resort to this, although it was more likely men who accepted commuting as a feature of their new job. For working couples

---

Two Jobs, Three Kids, No Let Up

Fran Hatcher considered herself fortunate to find another job before she was laid off from Canada Packers. In her new job she was a part-time nurse's aide at a nursing home in a nearby town. Though her hourly wage had increased slightly, she had to find another part-time job so that she and her husband could make ends meet. This second job was also in a nursing home, but in yet another town. Fran maintained a very hectic pace between her jobs, which both involved shift rotation, running a household, and raising three teenage children. Many weeks she had to work six days doing double shifts with little sleep and no time for herself. After a year of this pace the stress became too great and her health began to suffer. Eventually she had a complete breakdown. Fran attributes her health problems to the strain of working all the time, financial worries, and trying to keep everything under control. She eventually needed extensive medical care. Some years later she was feeling better having quit both of her jobs, divorced her husband, and managed to obtain short-term disability benefits.

---

this meant having two cars to continue working, as previously they had typically worked at the same factory. Given the severe financial pressure felt by most respondents, overcoming the barrier of geographical space presented by rural living was a formidable task. Not having access to a car in good operating order was seen as a major issue by several of our respondents. It is worth noting that these findings are quite similar to those of an extensive round of studies of the new rural economy in Britain, which noted that transportation issues have emerged as a major barrier to social inclusion in rural areas. Specifically, 'people without a car, or without access to one, have more difficulty finding a job or accessing services' (Shucksmith 2000).

The jobs now available in the contingent work world are quite different from the jobs those people left, or those they might have hoped to obtain on leaving school. Instead, the jobs of the new economy are overwhelmingly part-time, fixed term, and casual. Competitive manufacturing industries have found it more cost efficient to maintain at least part, and sometimes all, of their workforce in a position where they can be 'let go' without financial penalty to the company, by calling them 'casual' employees or hiring them only on a short-term contract. In both cases workers are not subject to any but the most minimal provisions of standard labour legislation.

It was clear to us that workers could distinguish the different reality that characterizes what we call the contingent work world. A pay cut that was in several cases, more than 50 per cent, was not all they noticed. A woman who had recently entered the world of lean production in a local garment factory told us:

[At her new job] you can't sit down wherever you feel like it because you're tired. Plus they don't like people like people standing around talking, I mean, you just don't do that there. You're there to work. We've been spoiled [at the old job] ... You're afraid even to say anything to the boss if you don't agree with them, because I'm still on probation ... Even working with a lot of women, it's very competitive. It's competition and you gotta watch who you talk to and what you talk about. You don't know whether to be friendly or not to be friendly ... I liked working at Westinghouse better. At Westinghouse you could have a coffee whenever you wanted to. That was freedom.

We found this new reality of contingent labour was characteristic of even the most dynamic communities we examined, where elements of the 'new rural economy' were taking shape via the development of high technology manufacturing, research, and development. During our fieldwork, for example, we noted that new jobs created at Zomax (formerly KAO) in Arnprior, one of the community's main high technology firms, were likely to be contingent, in other words casual without security or benefits. As the journalist covering the job announcement remarked: 'No-one in the company would comment on if these new jobs would be full-time permanent positions, or if they would be hired through the employment agency in Kanata, used by Zomax for much of their production staff' (*Arnprior Chronicle Guide*, May 1999: 1). As we saw in Chapter 3, many of the jobs in this high technology firm were already casual, and indeed the firm seemed to depend on its ability to tap into the local labour market and utilize casual labour as needed.

In all of the communities we studied, workers who were able to replace old factory jobs with new ones were rarely recruited into permanent full-time positions. When they were, for the Wellington County workers we interviewed in 1994 and 1996, it was almost always at a considerable distance from the community in which they lived. In Arnprior jobs at companies like Pfizer, BASF, and Boeing were highly coveted, but difficult to get, as we discussed in Chapter 4. Those finding manufacturing jobs more easily tended to find them in one of two kinds of companies. The first are companies whose foothold in the marketplace is more insecure, and they employ only casual or contract workers. A number of women laid off from Westinghouse in Mount Forest were able to move relatively quickly to jobs at a garment factory in the town, called at the time K-Brand (later No.1 Apparel), and operating in a highly competitive sector of the garment industry. Their work trajectories afterwards were anything but smooth, as the company laid them off after a few months, sometimes rehired them, and sometimes laid them off again. Moreover this was a non-union environment with limited benefits and a starting wage that was about half what they had earned before.

The second kind of company likely to hire laid-off workers is the larger one which will take them on as casual temporary workers alongside permanent employees. In Arnprior, for example, a number of people worked at KAO, although they had been hired, as the cited quote indicates, through an Ottawa employment agency. Similar to the situation that Nelson and Smith (1999: 78) describe in their study, these people worked *at* but not *for* KAO. The significant difference between these two groups of workers was that the casual group were paid considerably less, received no benefits, and could find themselves without hours assigned when they were not needed. While providing tremendous flexibility for the company, this kind of strategy creates a two-tier labour force, with permanent, better paid workers eligible for benefits (the stable workforce) working alongside insecure, low paid workers, often doing exactly the same work. Contingent workers were also often on-call for work, even if they were not actually at work. If they had not worked for some time, or very much at all, call-ins like this were potentially an important source of income. This meant people sat at home unwilling to take the risk of missing the call, making it extremely difficult to engage in other kinds of activities, including looking for a more secure job. This kind of temporary work provided flexibility for the employer but insecurity and unpredictability for the workers, who found that a few months, sometimes only weeks of work, were followed by an unpredictable period of unemployment.

The growing service sector also utilizes casual workers, as well as being largely responsible for the huge surge in part-time employment, and it is here that workers were most likely to encounter part-time work as the only available option. Part-time work is found mainly, though not exclusively, in the retail and restaurant sector, particularly in the proliferating fast food sector at pizza, doughnut, and hamburger outlets, offering short hours to workers who must be available seven days a week, from early in the morning until late at night. Rural communities have also seen a large growth in that segment of the

Community Connections, a non-profit centre in the Ottawa Valley assisting displaced workers such as the Weavexx workers, told us that their major challenge was to convince people that they will never make $20 an hour again, and to live with that reality. They discovered that many people are underemployed, working few hours, and being offered extra work which they have to take, no matter how short the notice. They noted that this creates immense difficulties for those who need childcare. They see lots of contract work now, and very little of what they call 'T4' work. As well, they see a lot of 'under the table' work in smaller businesses, which creates problems because people are not building Employment Insurance credits.

service sector which provides residential care to the elderly. Jobs here are usually with private companies, and again it is part-time work that is available, this time on a twenty-four-hour per day basis. While this kind of work may be more secure over time, workers we talked to found that their schedules were very unpredictable and often subject to change with little notice and without compensation. Some women working in such facilities told of internal tensions as workers did whatever they could to ensure they worked 'good' hours (see Leach 1999).

The contrast between the predictable routine people had and the disruption of that routine after job loss was a common theme in our interviews. With regular work hours people organize their lives around the certainty of their schedules. Unemployment is the first break with routine for many workers. Frances Boucher in Arnprior described the physical effects of shift work: 'Now mind you it took me a year for my body to get used to not working shift work. My work set at home, I would find myself filling in the day hours not doing anything really and I'd find myself working at night as I'd always been working. So I'd find myself making jam at 8 p.m. when I had actually had all day to do it but because I hadn't had those day hours for so many years it took a long time to actually get back working at home during those day hours. I was so used to having that other pattern of doing things.'

With jobs in the new economy, there is no return to the old kind of routine. Fran Hatcher, who could find only two part-time jobs, was presented with new problems. Her old job had allowed her to organize her life, taking care of herself and her domestic and family re-

'You are not sleeping the same or eating the same. You're not socializing the way you would. You would have your meal planned, you would have the meat taken out in the morning or whatever you wanted for supper ... or if you had an appointment at the school at night then you were available to go. You could plan your whole day around it, weeks and months ahead. Now you can't do that, anybody working part-time can't do that ... It makes me feel down sometimes because the loss of security of a full-time job of doing what you are so accustomed to doing every day of the week. Now you can't get yourself in any kind of routine really. You might get a phone call to go in to work and you're on the go and you rush around to go into work.' (Former Canada Packers worker, Harriston 1994)

sponsibilities. With her new part-time work arrangements her work schedule was always uncertain, and these changes reverberated through all aspects of her life. Many women felt that their domestic responsibilities suffered following job loss, because their daily routines and structures were disrupted. With unemployment, training, or even a new part-time job, women found it hard to re-establish their personal life routines. This led to a sense of loss of control over their lives and a loss of well-being.

Margie James explained how she managed her personal responsibilities when working full-time, when she felt able to extend herself and happy to do so: 'Well, when I was working before I used to put my time between my mother, my kids, his [her husband's] parents, anybody else that needed me in a crunch or people who just wanted to talk, I would make myself available ... Now I don't answer the phone in case somebody wants me to do something or I don't want to hear about their problems ... I had myself where I was going all the time and just going on four maybe five hours sleep a night. I was a much better person, I was a happier person.' Both job loss and the stress of new and different jobs placed a strain on marital and family relationships. One woman said her relationship with her husband suffered at times: 'You are constantly fighting, you don't want to be bothered. There are some nights when you think, don't even look at me and especially don't touch me.'

Some found their new jobs particularly demanding and required that they work longer hours. This ultimately cut into family time. Jimmy Jones found he had to work longer to make the same money: 'Another thing about money is that you are trying harder to work longer hours to get the same. And that does cut the time you could be with your wife. Whereas if you are making a good wage working forty hours a week, then come the weekend you have the time to be with your family and enjoy things that you want to instead of what you can afford. That is what I see a lot of people working overtime, not because they want to, they are doing it just to keep up.'

Pete and Rose Reid both worked at Canada Packers and had worked out a system whereby they worked opposing shifts to allow them to care for their large family. In their new jobs, however, they worked at the same time, and found it harder to juggle family responsibilities: 'When Pete and I started [new jobs together] we both had to be there at 7 a.m. We had to get the older kids up at 6:30 a.m. so they were up with the younger ones to get them off to school. So there was a lot of worrying: are they going to be alright? Was there going to be a fire? When it first started there was a lot of fighting among them and I would get calls at work "Mom, so and so is beating me up."'

Vulnerable Workers in the New Economy

From the quotes above it is clear that living in the new economy provides different kinds of challenges and unwelcome disruptions in peoples lives. However, while these changes confront everyone to some degree in the new economy, we argue that some kinds of workers are more vulnerable. By this we mean that their structural location in the labour market makes it extremely difficult for them to find a feasible solution to the problem of making a living. At the same time, it means that these particular workers are doubly disadvantaged when governments cut back on the services they previously offered. Workers who are infirm, have young, old, or sick dependants, or whose educational levels are insufficient for the emerging labour market, could all make use of social services, in the form of extended hospital care, child care, and retraining programs. Yet, rather than providing additional assistance to those needing help in adapting to the contingent work world, all of these have been made *less* available as governments have attempted to cut their costs.

The young are also a vulnerable group in the new economy, especially if they have few educational attainments. A study of young people five years after leaving school in New York state indicated that they had not been able to stabilize their employment situations, with unemployment over 10 per cent within the group, and 72 per cent of them expecting to change jobs within the following two years. Their earnings were low overall, and even lower for women, 53 per cent of whom were earning less than $15,000 per year (Fitchen 1991: 81–2).

Older Workers

The research strategy pursued in this study led us to a disproportionate number of older workers. The fate of these workers in the new economy is a critical concern for policy-makers, since these people experience particular difficulties in finding new jobs, and those who are unable become dependent on state assistance earlier. Among the Wellington County workers, ten men and fifteen women (27 per cent of the total sample) were over fifty when we first interviewed them.

Among the Arnprior sample five men and four women (50 per cent) were over fifty, this proportion reflecting earlier rounds of layoffs which would have affected those with less seniority.

The Canada Packers plant in Harriston was especially notable for the high proportion of older employees, with the mean age of our sample being fifty-five at time of interview. It was particularly discouraging to see that this was also the community that had probably the least number of economic opportunities available to newly unemployed workers, due to its relatively small size. After decades of stable work in many cases, people who felt they were too young to retire had to scrounge around for one of the few poorly paid part-time jobs that might be available.

Among the thirty-four in the over-fifty age group, twelve were unemployed and looking for work when interviewed, seven (all of whom were over sixty) considered themselves effectively retired, one was on social assistance and one involved in a training programme. Of the remaining thirteen who were working, all but two were in flexible kinds of work, either part-time or short-term contract. It is quite clear that older workers are more likely to find themselves involved in flexible, contingent work than are their younger co-workers. One of

Older Workers, Financial Stress, and Insecurity

Gerry Bates was fifty-one years old when he lost his job at Canada Packers, and he had difficulty both finding and holding new jobs. Since his lay-off he had had two jobs at packing plants and had lost both of them. When he was first interviewed he was collecting social assistance, and had this to say about the impact of his loss of income: 'you have to cut back. We don't have the money to do anything, enjoyment or entertainment, or even if it's a necessity.' Gerry and his wife had to leave their rented house outside town and move to a small one bedroom apartment. Here they had to give up many of their belongings, including his wife's craft materials which allowed her to make a little money. Being unemployed and at home all the time makes the apartment feel even smaller: 'This place is driving me nuts, it's so small. For fifteen hours a day or more you get tired of looking at the walls, because with unemployment you don't get money to go anywhere, to go visit family or anything like that, you haven't got any extra money.'

the twelve unemployed workers, after two years of near total unemployment, was continuing to take a position that she would not consider low paid temporary or part-time work. For June Evans this was clearly becoming a difficult position for her to sustain, and she broke down as she talked about her quest for a job. One potential employer had asked her to leave after four days' work, saying that he thought the work was too hard for her. She thought it was because of 'my age, I guess, I probably wasn't fast enough.'

A few older workers admitted to us that the lay-off had in some ways been a bit of relief for them. After years of doing a physically strenuous job their bodies were wearing out under the constant strain. It was, nevertheless, a mixed blessing, because with relief from the daily grind came feelings of anxiety gnawing away at them due to financial insecurity.

Contingent work has specific implications for older workers, since casual, short-term, and often part-time work are frequently devoid of the employee benefits available in the stable sector, and to which these workers were accustomed. It is not only older workers who suffer from the absence of such benefits, but as their health begins to deteriorate with age they will not have paid sick days, drug plans, or access to preventive programs they may well need.

The physical health of aging workers looking for new jobs is also an issue of concern. It becomes increasingly difficult for older workers to carry out physically demanding jobs, or to obtain new jobs if their bodies are already ailing. Consequently health was an issue raised by about half of the people we interviewed in Wellington County and Arnprior. After both he and his wife were laid off from Canada Packers, John Butler took a job at a local feed store. In his new job he suffered problems with his legs, which required corrective shoes, and with his shoulders, both of which were exacerbated by the heavy lifting required of the job. His wife argued: 'For sure it is related [to his job] ... he didn't have shoulder problems when he was working at Canada Packers. But at his age, when he has to be lugging seed, unloading tractor-trailers of peat moss.'

Health becomes an issue for many workers as they search for new jobs or try to sustain those they have. Irene and Frank Robinson were laid off from Westinghouse at the same time, Frank after twenty years, Irene after a couple of much shorter stints. To make ends meet Irene worked at a grocery store, as she had for some ten years, while raising five children and completing her Grade 12. She described herself as poorly paid. Her ironic comment on conditions characterizing contingent work is insightful. As she said: 'The less you make, the harder you have to work.' She found the work extremely hard, and felt that her health had suffered as a result: 'My health has been deteriorating over the years, we don't know why and we are still trying to find out why. It might be the time of life, but I'm also doing extremely physical work, and I'm not young any more and it's starting to wear on me.'

These issues come to be of particular concern as workers lose stable jobs, where not only did they have access to benefits, but could have expected some accommodations to be made if they became ill or injured, and where they were protected by the provisions of their union contracts. With contingent labour there is no such safety net. Workers with less than excellent health can expect no quarter from employers in highly competitive industries.

Younger Workers

Young workers trying to enter the labour force in some ways resemble the elderly workers trying to remain in it. Young workers in flexible jobs will also feel the absence of employment benefits. Among the youth of Iroquois Falls, only nine out of seventeen men and five out of seventeen women had jobs that provided employment-related benefits five years after leaving high school. The absence of sick leave, for example, could potentially lead to more serious health problems, or to other consequences of financial loss if days are taken without pay.

Workers in Wellington County and Arnprior frequently told us that employers would rather employ younger workers rather than people such as themselves. Our research in Iroquois Falls allows us to consider, if fairly briefly, the fate of younger workers in the new rural economy. It is worth noting again, however, the features of the labour market in Iroquois Falls that make the findings there quite specific to that community, although there are similarities with other communities. We found, for example, that in a town dominated by a single major employer, the employer often provides valuable summer employment for young people. This had been the case in the communities in Wellington County, where Westinghouse, and especially Canada Packers had provided such work, and as well in Iroquois Falls, where young people have been able to depend on a summer job at the mill. In Harriston and Elora, the closure of the Canada Packers plants closed off summer opportunities for many students, making post-secondary education a more difficult option financially. Between permanent jobs for their parents, often both mother and father, and summer jobs for young people, as one man put it: 'Canada Packers basically put those kids through school.' Now in Iroquois Falls summer jobs are restricted to students whose parents work at the mill. Exactly half of our sample (10/17 men and 7/17 women) had spent summers working at the mill, and of all of those only four had gone on to find permanent work there.

The employment of a parent at the mill had traditionally played a part in smoothing young peoples' routes into work there. However, earlier informal family traditions of work in the mill were replaced within the past decade, according to the human resources manager, by new policies at the mill which ensured that only young people whose parents worked there would be considered for a part-time position. In our sample ten out of seventeen men and ten out of seventeen women had a parent who had worked at the mill.

In what was essentially a one-industry town, jobs at the mill had for decades been the ticket for those who wanted to stay in the north, and close to home. This had been especially so for those who had limited or no post-secondary education. Local public sector jobs did, of course, provide some employment for those with similar aspirations who might have secured post-secondary education, typically in southern Ontario. There was also a strong social class dimension determining whether one went into the mill or came back as a teacher, nurse, or administrator of some kind. The new economy facing young people offers few opportunities regardless of social class, however, for government cutbacks and public sector downsizing have gone hand in hand with declining employment at the mill. The mood among young people interviewed was, understandably, rather gloomy concerning the possibility of their being able to make a life in the community they had been raised in.

Three young people, nevertheless (two men and one woman), specifically stated that they were staying in Iroquois Falls hoping to get a mill job sooner or later. One woman who had left the town expressed considerable bitterness about her chance of getting a job at the mill, and another said she would return if she were offered a job. Another whose parents had worked at the mill and who had spent six summers working there himself said he always thought he would be working at the mill, and remarked wistfully, 'I still hope for Abitibi.'

A salient issue in this northern community is the stark lack of opportunities for young women. Increasingly raised with the expectations that they could be equal partners with men in the labour force, young women in this community are faced with the local historical pattern of most of the better paying jobs available traditionally going to men, and the current reality that even the men cannot find these jobs anymore. Outside the shrinking public sector attractive employment opportunities for women are virtually non-existent. In our interviews we found that those young women who lacked post-secondary education were almost always relegated to very low paying and extremely casual employment in the retail businesses as store clerks or working at the supermarket checkout.[2] There were not enough of these jobs, however, and for some the only possibility to make money was providing informal child care to those parents with work.

While there has been some pressure at Abitibi to open up what were traditionally male jobs – those in the mill as opposed to the office – interviews with union officials and our own observations while touring the mill during the day shift demonstrated that very few women had come to occupy production jobs so far.[3] The company strategy of downsizing through attrition that prevailed through much of the 1990s precluded much change in this situation for young women. This was in marked contrast to factory employment in the southern Ontario communities we studied, where women occupied a substantial minority, or even a majority of all production jobs.

It was in the northern community that the combination of the destruction of good, stable jobs in the manufacturing sector and the 1990s obsession with downsizing the public sector presented potent structural barriers to advancing the participation of women in the labour force, and establishing women in non-traditional employment roles. Indeed, our research strongly suggested that such northern communities would have great difficulty in retaining young women at all if present trends are not reversed.

Less-Educated Workers

Education is frequently linked to positive outcomes in the labour market. This is one of the major arguments made for public investment in education, and is also invoked by policy-makers attempting to match education with labour market needs. On the other hand, Burke and Shields (1999: 2) found that: 'while higher levels of education are positively related to a better individual positioning in the job market, overall the *education effect* represents only a minor influence.' They found other factors, particularly gender, single-mother status, and age to be more significant factors in the quality of employment an individual is able to find.

Our findings indicate that education may be important in terms of perception by employers and employees, or potential employees. Technological change in most work places has brought with it an increased need for workers to be conversant with computers and other kinds of equipment often operated by computers, and to be able to decipher technical documents and instructions. To assure themselves that new workers have this capacity, it is increasingly common for employers to require Grade 12 or Grade 13 as the lowest acceptable level of academic achievement. This creeping credentialism is evident at the paper mill in Iroquois Falls, where in the early 1980s it became necessary to have Grade 12, and by 1994 potential applicants required post-secondary education. One of the interesting findings of our survey of Iroquois Falls high school leavers is that of the twenty-two people who now have post-secondary education fifteen were living in Iroquois Falls, while twelve have moved away.

> Jack Smyth worked at Weavexx for twenty-seven years before being laid off shortly before his fiftieth birthday. Since losing his job he had been working three part-time jobs: for a building contractor, with a snow removal team during the winter season, and in his own small engine repair business. He said he makes somewhere between $50 and $200 a week, all of it 'under the table.' Although he continues to apply for jobs in local factories he is not optimistic that he will be called in because he does not have his Grade 12.

As noted in Chapter 4, employers in the new economy frequently require applicants to take an aptitude test before being offered a job. Among laid-off workers over 40 years old it is extremely common for workers, who expected to be able to pursue factory work their whole working lives, to have completed less than Grade 12. Among the former

Weavexx workers in our study only five of the thirteen men and three of the five women had completed at least Grade 12. The absence of the formal document makes it more likely that they will be asked to complete an aptitude test, often with disappointing results.

Laid-off workers often seemed intimidated by these aptitude tests, which they also saw as largely irrelevant in terms of the work they would be required to do once they were hired (a perceptive insight on their part, which is probably quite accurate, as discussed in Chapter 4). Older workers are also often intimidated by the notion of retraining, especially when it involved new technologies, although some older workers, like Iris Robertson, relish the opportunity to try out new things as much as younger ones: 'I was always interested in computers. In fact, like I said, I asked for the computer training in the first place because I had used a computer at work for some of the stuff that I did, but I never had any formal training. You just feel around and try to find what button to press and when to press it.'

On one occasion, sitting in a park in Arnprior with former Weavexx workers, there was discussion about the training that a couple of them were actively pursuing. The division in the group was less between older and younger workers, since one of those undergoing retraining was a fifty-eight-year-old woman, but rather appeared to separate those workers who were willing to accept the challenge of new training, and those who felt they would not be able to learn about new technologies: 'If you're in a job for twenty-one years, you don't know anything about testing. The first few tests that I did, I am lucky if I passed through half of those. Then you get confidence and say, oh yeah, I can do that now.'

Women, Men, and Family Responsibilities

One feature of the new economy which is apparent to even the most casual observer is the existence of 'fly-by-night' companies, in other words, those that appear on the industrial and retail landscape, only to disappear after a few months, leaving their erstwhile employees yet again looking for work. In Arnprior a company called The Grange was open in 1992 for about six months. This company specialized in packaging commodities such as soap and pot pourri. One of the more interesting features of this firm, however, is that they operated what was explicitly called a 'Mom shift,' from 4 p.m. to midnight.

Families with children face particular constraints to their participation in the labour force. Short school days, including a lunch break,

March Break, and long summer holidays, as well as occasional acute childhood illnesses, all present challenges to families who need both adults in the labour force or, indeed, for those families with only one adult member. 'Mom shifts' assume two-parent families, where mom can leave for work when dad gets home from work to take over 'minding' the children. As we have described already, families where both parents work devise routines for dealing with these issues, but these routines are thrown into disarray when jobs are lost, and when parents are forced to seek alternative work. New jobs may be without a predictable schedule, without holiday pay, and with such insecurity that staying away, for no matter how genuine a reason, may be tantamount to quitting. An Arnprior man describes the change he experienced: 'Well, I had four weeks holidays, at 8 per cent, but I always took one month off in the summer to be with the kids. So it was kind of luxury for me. And then all of a sudden they close it up, and then you've got to start from scratch again, no holidays.'

Traditionally, women have been primarily responsible for childcare, although in dual earner households, this tradition had in some ways been compromised long ago, as the quote above suggests. Yet despite this, when men lost jobs they found adjusting to being at home and losing their role as breadwinner extremely difficult, and they also encountered more expectations to share familial and domestic responsibilities. Rich Williams had always worked and had always received a higher income. Clare Williams talked about her husband's feeling when she found work: 'It was even harder when I found work and he didn't. It really bothered Rich knowing that I was going out to work and he was staying home with Brett.' Rich responded: 'Well, maybe I'm a bit old fashioned, but I believe that in order for us to make it nowadays we'll both have to work ... I was glad when Clare finally got a job, and we finally got a little bit of breathing room. And then too, it's all of her money, you know what I mean. All I had was my unemployment insurance, but her money was paying the bills and that was hard too because I get so bored sitting around doing nothing.'

Despite the possibility for greater equality in gender relations in dual earner households, especially when in some of these men and women were doing very similar jobs and making similar incomes, as they were, for example, in our Wellington County sample, Leach (1999) has argued that after lay-offs decisions about entering the labour market of the new economy tend to revive old ideas about gendered work, in the home and outside of it. For example, while several of the women laid off from Westinghouse in Mount Forest were happy to find work at K-Brand, since it was close by in the community, men were unwilling even to consider sewing work at minimum wage, and would often take months to find what they considered to be suitable work, despite the fact that it might be at least an hour's drive from home. Women's larger income drop is in part due to different priorities in their decision-making process. Women make their labour market decisions taking into consideration the needs of children, and as they get older, the needs of aging parents, or other potentially dependent adults, who live in the vicinity, as well. The possibility of jobs at the K-Brand factory in Mount Forest explains at least in part the lower prevalence of part-time work for laid-off women Westinghouse workers, in comparison to other communities. This puts women at a considerable disadvantage in the labour market, and more vulnerable to exploitation in the flexible, bad jobs of the new economy, as we can see from the incidence of contingent work among women, at 57 per cent (see Table 5.8, Chapter 5).

Finding appropriate childcare when one's own work schedule is unpredictable is difficult. It could be argued that the economy then generates its own solution to this problem, since some of the women laid off from factory jobs began to provide child care in their homes to their neighbours. Several women in our study had chosen this as an alternative to finding jobs for themselves outside the home. However, at the same time that it is promoted as a form of self-employment, our research indicates that it provides only a very low level of income (about $20 per day per child), and is itself very precarious. One woman who had been a child care provider for some years while her husband worked at Canada Packers, found that when the plant closed not only did they lose his income, but they lost hers as well, since many of the children she cared for had parents who had worked there.

Local Culture and Attachment to Place

As Redclift and Whatmore (1990) have argued, restructuring is not simply received into communities; existing community structures, values, and practices affect the ways in which it is dealt with. Cultural factors affect how restructuring processes are apprehended in communities, how people respond to new opportunities on the basis of how things are usually done.

Local cultural practices are linked to place attachment. People feel comfortable living in a place where they understand local culture and where peoples' actions in general follow common sense understandings of how people should behave. These include, for example, gendered ideas about work and family life which have been shaped in the rural context. McDowell and Massey (1984) have argued that the stability of rural communities over generations is linked closely to the conservative nature of village life, and of gender relations in rural areas. Many researchers have concluded that gender relations in Ontario tend to be based on relatively conservative ideas (Carbert 1995; Ireland 1983; Leach 1999), although this is tempered to some extent by the proliferation of rural women's organizations (MacKenzie 1995; Shortall 1994).

While ideologies sustain the idea that women's primary work will be carried out in the home, it is clear from our study, along with those in other rural places (Little 1994; McKinley Wright 1995; Sachs 1996; Fink 1998), that large numbers of rural women do work outside the home. This compromises the ideology and contributes to how women respond to losing their factory jobs (Leach 1999). The contradictions between ideology and practice, thinking and action, which go more or less unnoticed on a day-to-day basis and are a common part of women's experiences, become more starkly apparent as they try to negotiate their daily lives with the added stress of job loss. For the women in Wellington County and Arnprior, the loss of a factory job was frequently experienced as a difficult adjustment to loss of self-sufficiency and forced dependence on others, usually husbands.

For Jen Burroughs, job loss and unemployed status meant a loss of the independence and control that had taken many years to achieve. It was tough to compromise that independence: 'I guess it's harder for me because I'm such an independent person and I don't like relying on anybody, I don't even like relying on my husband. I like that independence. It took me ten years to get that ... now I have to ask him for money. It's very degrading having to depend on someone else after you've survived for so long on your own. I mean I survived for ten years before I remarried, with two kids to raise and I didn't have to ask anybody for anything. Now I'm married and my kids are grown up and I'm having to depend on somebody. It's mind-boggling.'

For women for whom working outside the home injected meaning and significance into their lives, losing the job left them feeling: 'Overwhelmed, sad. There was something, as if you're losing part of yourself. You had to get up in the morning and had something to look forward to, and all of a sudden it's been taken away from you and there's a big void in you. You had a routine to go through. It made me feel important there.'

Most women found becoming 'only a housewife' difficult. Usually the family had relied on their income, and sometimes they were sole supporters. Many had always worked outside the home, and as Jayne Burch put it: 'I felt pressured into being a housewife when I was at home. I had never been a housewife before because I always worked. I really don't like it.' In this case, then, access to factory work had shifted women's role within their families. Restructuring had the unwelcome effect of returning them to a more traditional position. Employment counsellors in the communities we studied reported that women were less upwardly mobile than men, despite having good skills. Women often played down their skills to get hired, otherwise they were over-qualified for the jobs available.

Despite the shifts that restructuring has brought, attachments to a particular locality can be extremely strong, and lead to a reluctance to move to 'where the jobs are.' This has the effect of maintaining a workforce which is in many ways ultimately compliant to the changes facing them because of their strong desire to remain in the place they value. Faced with the choice between work in the contingent work world locally, or moving to another area for better work, attachment to the place of origin can operate to resolve the dilemma. In the past many of those who did not want to move out of a particular area were unlikely to seek out higher educational qualifications if they knew that the local labour market would have little use for certain kinds of skills. Our findings, that people frequently want to continue to live in the rural communities in which they grew up, suggest that this represents a resource that can be utilized by communities. At the same time, it represents a liability, since it can make workers more vulnerable to low paying, insecure jobs if this is the only way they can ensure that they can stay in the preferred area.

One of the questions guiding our research was to determine what factors motivated some people to leave rural communities to seek work elsewhere, while others seemed determined to stay despite changing job opportunities. The Iroquois Falls students not long out of high school held very strong opinions regarding this issue, showing a fairly serious division between those who have left and those who wish to stay. When asked directly whether they would want to stay if there were work, the answers were rarely equivocal.

All of the six men and six women who had left considered it the only practical choice in terms of work opportunities, although for a couple of them there was bitterness about having to leave. Interestingly of the twenty-two remaining residents in Iroquois Falls, only three indicated a desire to leave, often tempered by family ties, and two others said they would go wherever the work is. Those wanting to leave or who had already left said: 'There's no way I would go back, there are no jobs, just lay-offs'; 'no, there's nothing there'; 'the town's too small, there's nothing there for me'; 'I always hated the town, I like Nova Scotia better'; 'it's too small and gossipy.'

On the other side of the debate, people were equally sure of their reasons for staying, even when they were in marginal kinds of jobs. From these people we heard comments such as: 'it's a quality of life issue, I like hunting and fishing'; 'I'm happy here, and I don't care if jobs are limited'; 'I love it here, and I'm hoping for a job at Abitibi'; 'I like it here, it's not like the city, it's safe and friendly.'

The desire to stay in the community, or equally to leave it, can therefore be a major factor when people are looking for jobs. Those willing to move have access to far distant labour markets, while those who want to stay must rely on opportunities within easy access.

Place attachment is a locally recognized phenomenon in the Ottawa Valley, in which Arnprior lies. When we asked about people's likelihood of relocating to seek work, we were told repeatedly that Valley people want to stay, or if they leave, they will try to come back. Local professionals, including teachers, lawyers, dentists, and doctors, often grew up in the town or surrounding area, left to train, and then returned as soon as they could, either to where they were originally from, or close by. Often young people are reluctant to move for work because they are closely connected to family in the area. One man said he was determined to stay in Arnprior: 'because my roots and my family are in Arnprior, and so is her family in Arnprior mostly, like her children, so I didn't really want to leave Arnprior. I don't like the cities, you know, I like the small town, because I know a lot of people. It's better when you know lots of people, you don't have to try and make new friends and everything else.' The decision to stay is also a pragmatic choice because family members can provide various forms of support, and we saw evidence of this in all the communities, both in financial terms and others, including, for example, casual child care arrangements.

Another aspect of local culture concerns the family networks that have historically operated inside Arnprior firms. For example, company management at BASF told us that there is explicit local policy to hire the family members of existing employees when there are job openings. Thus, individual firms contain local networks based on kinship relationships. As Frank Jenkins told us: 'I'd sooner be back at Weavexx, probably because of familiarity, you knew the people, you knew what button to push, you knew who didn't, you knew who was related to who, and what to say, whereas at Pfizer, you don't know anybody.'

Family and community are important sources of support locally, offering cooperation in times of crisis, at work as well as elsewhere. Local employers have traditionally allowed time off to deal with family issues, and locally based company management maintained personal relationships with their staff, knowing families and family situations well. This led to positive relationships between local company management and employees. As a former Weavexx worker described it: 'They treated their people well. They'd think nothing of coming to your home, have a snack, have a barbeque. Go down to his place. You'd all have a barbeque. Christmas time, you'd be sitting here maybe after the party, a knock come to your door, it'd be Joe Jones [manager], and his wife, Sue. "Hey Joe, come on in," you know. And they knew that I would help them out at anytime that they needed help.'

However, there are negative consequences to living and working in such a close-knit community. A single household may comprise extended families of three (or four) generations. Older sons often live at home because they are not making enough to live alone, and daughters often live there as well with their children. In this way family units are tied together for economic reasons as well as emotional ones, and lack of privacy, especially in small houses in towns and villages, may become a problem.

The cost of real estate may also be a factor in people's decisions to stay or leave. Property in rural communities, especially at some distance from the larger cities, is usually valued at considerably less than similar properties in larger communities. When major employers pull out of a community and families are trying to leave, the glut of real estate on the market further pushes prices down, making it increasingly difficult to bring about the move to a more expensive property market. Margaret Thatcher's admonishment to unemployed workers in the north of England to 'get on their bikes' is thus as unrealistic in the Ontario context as it was in the British.

As well, expectations of family closeness operate to discourage young people from moving away for jobs or education. The increasing cost of education is, of course, also a factor here and exacerbated by job market instability. It is often difficult to commute to university or college from rural communities, yet prohibitively expensive to move away. Those who want to stay in the community choose to forego better paying work, or the potential for it, to stay local and close to their families. For these people, the only jobs readily available are low paid jobs in the service sector. At the same time, some of those working with young people in rural communities identify evidence of greater aspirations towards entrepreneurial work among younger people than in previous generations. One high school guidance counsellor told us that she sees many more young men and women setting up their own small businesses rather than being employed. This seems to be consistent with the desire to live locally in the absence of available factory work.

Small, close-knit communities also mean that it can be difficult for a person to break with his or her past. This might be a past mistake which led to losing a job, a last name with particular associations, or union activity in another company. In the Arnprior area alcohol consumption has been a large part of recreational activities, such as hunting and fishing, boating, and snowmobiling, (although this is seen to be slowly changing, assisted by the emergence of health clubs and employer-sponsored health activities). A history of alcohol dependency is often a factor in people's search for a new job. In the Ottawa Valley there is also a local practice of women using their birth and married names interchangeably to protect their privacy. Local employment counsellors advise people not to identify their union activity on their resumes or in interview because it is viewed negatively in the Valley. Of course, often this information will already be known.

On the positive side close-knit rural communities tend to generate a lot of networking between community organizations to assist people in need, but much of this assistance is done secretively to protect people's dignity and privacy. In Arnprior this has taken on its own character in the way that the local food bank is practically impossible to discover without local knowledge. Similarly, a local business operates an annual, and extremely successful, snowsuit drive which discretely redistributes used snowsuits for children whose parents are unable to buy new ones.

While some local practices are resilient in the face of change, in certain ways others are changing as restructuring takes place. Companies are less likely to hire management from the immediate locality. As one man said: 'Companies do not want their manager to be local, see. Why? So that when you lay off, "You won't like it here buster, way you go. I have nothing to do with you." But maybe if it was somebody who was local, you know that person for all their life. You know their families, and they know your family, and they know everything. You can't have that, you know. We can't have one another knowing each other.'

People also identified a shift in what a sense of community means to companies. When Boeing lobbied the Canadian government to maintain its contract with them for Search and Rescue helicopters, the company called on everyone in the community to support their bid as a community effort. According to some former Weavexx workers, Weavexx did support Boeing in this fight. However, when Weavexx announced it was closing its production line, the workers were disappointed to find no reciprocal assistance. Former workers told us that Weavexx had offered $1000 to any company that would take on its laid-off workers within a certain time, but no one knew of any company that had taken them up on the offer: 'Well when Weavexx closed, I thought that they [Boeing] should have given everybody a chance, if you put in a resume and you're from Weavexx, at least give them an interview. I'm not saying to hire them. Not asking to hire them. But I'm asking for at least an interview. And they never did that. I put in three or four resumes, and I've got warehouse experience with lift trucks, and I like working in a warehouse, but anyways, they had a job, I guess it was in spring, and I was laid off, and they interviewed my nephew, right out of high school.'

At this point in the process, laid-off Weavexx workers had to compete with younger workers and take aptitude tests, contrary to the ethic of community caring that had prevailed in earlier times: 'That's how it used to operate in this town, if one plant closed, the other plant would try to take them and help them along. Now people are commuting from Ottawa and Pembroke and wherever.'

Instead, workers face a new culture of competition at the work place. The following exchange with James McNally, a former Weavvex worker, shows the change workers face in the contingent work world:

JMcN: And then when I got on Pfizer that time, they hired seven of us, and I just found that, the way they worked it there, I found it over-whelming. Cause they got us hired at the same time, and if somebody knew something they wouldn't help the other person out, there'd be like a competition. Like 'I know more than you,' Like we started at the same time, but if they experienced something, they wouldn't tell me or anybody else to help them out. It was like their secret so they have an edge on the other person. It's hard. It's super hard when you get another job, because it's like starting all over again. It's not the same experience like if you're on a job for twenty-one years, you know. Step into a new market where you're competing against some guy next to you who's eighteen years old. You know, and you've got to compete to have his job, cause you know, they start downsizing at all, somebody's got to go.
Interviewer: Is it really competitive?
JMcN: It's very competitive, very, very competitive.

This chapter has demonstrated the ways in which altered work arrangements that come with being forced into the contingent work world shift family rhythms, options, and activities significantly. The loss of regular and reliable work patterns, and the loss of permanent reliable jobs, has deleterious effects on working families, and specifically on those workers who already face certain kinds of disadvantages in the labour market.

It is clear that corporate flexibility means household uncertainty, a situation which may have a number of negative effects. As Burke and Shields argue, there are associated effects on the larger social health of Canada when large numbers of workers are excluded from economic well-being: 'marginalized, detached and disposable workers become alienated citizens' (Burke and Shields 1999: 25). Operating alongside restructuring processes, however, are longstanding understandings about how things should be done in the community. Sometimes these parallel processes are in contradiction with each other, at other times, they are mutually reinforcing. It is somewhat ironic that the strong sense of community attachment that is often felt in rural communities operates to sustain a vulnerable and exploitable labour force, for whom work in the contingent work world is preferable to venturing to places less well known. Of course, as workers are well aware, there are few promises of stable work, even in the large urban centres. Indeed, for those who have had some experience in what Maritimers call 'going down the road,' returning to their communities of origin may be the rational thing to do. If going away to the city means working for $8 an hour, then why not go back home to more or less the same wage, but also have at hand all the social and economic supports that family and friends can provide in a small community setting.[4] In the following chapter we consider what we have learned from our case studies in terms of commonly held ideas about economic diversity, labour organization, and political futures for rural communities in Canada.

CHAPTER SEVEN

Economic Diversity, Sustainability, and Manufacturing Communities

The fallout for community members, and blue-collar workers in particular, when companies restructure, downsize, or shut down entirely can vary significantly in small communities. In this chapter we explore why this might be so and what it is that fosters resilience in face of the new external pressures of global capitalism that corrode the sense of community today.

To the extent that social science has confronted issues related to the question of resilience, it has tended to be through a concern with what is usually termed 'community stability,' and the debate has been the domain of economists and regional scientists who have examined the relationship between economic diversity and economic stability, usually measured in terms of employment and income. Regional economists and planners have long viewed increased *economic diversity* as the best path to increased regional income per capita, lower unemployment rates, and more stability in terms of employment and income more generally (Attaran and Zwick 1987: 38, Conroy 1974: 31). Nevertheless, research on the nature of the relationship between diversity and stability has remained inconclusive. Malizia and Ke (1993: 221) argue that this is because the underlying theory explaining the influence of diversity on stability is not well developed, and because of the use of inappropriate measures (of diversity in particular), units of analysis, and weak empirical tests. Ashton and Pickens (1995) argue, based on work in forestry-dependent communities, that diversification is likely to be helpful only if new industries counter the cyclical downturns of established industries. Smith's (1990) work on smaller rural communities in the United States questions the usefulness of macro-analysis at the national or state level for rural communities, noting that employment stability is highly region-specific. He counsels communities to examine the past performance of specific firms they wish to attract to their area, rather than rely on any general diversification strategy.

Given the inconclusive nature of this literature, and the questioning of the suitability of macro-analyses, which are often based on larger metropolitan areas, for the problems of small rural communities, there is some value in considering this issue using an in-depth qualitative community case study approach. As we shall argue, economic diversity has its value, but it does not alone ensure good employment and a decent standard of living, while factors of a more social organizational nature can play a significant role in producing such outcomes.

Variation in Our Case Studies

The communities we studied were chosen in part to reflect the economic diversity that characterizes small manufacturing communities. The southern Ontario pattern is for communities to have a more diverse range of industrial employers, while communities dependent upon a single manufacturing plant are usually, but not always, found in the resource hinterland, in this case northern Ontario. Figure 7.1 shows the diversity of manufacturing among our five communities.

Mount Forest lost its largest industrial employer in the early 1990s, but it had several other small manufacturing plants to bolster its economic base. By the late 1990s, one of these, a garment manufacturer, had expanded considerably, and there were an additional five manufacturing firms with fifty employees or more (*Scott's Directory* 1998). In Arnprior, the downsizing and eventual closure of a significant manufacturer, Weavexx, was traumatic for employees, but less so for the community at large. There remained six other industrial employers each with more than fifty employees, and three with more than 100 each (*Scott's Directory* 1998).

Downsizing employee numbers in the pulp-and-paper mill at Iroquois Falls, however, in the late 1980s and especially the 1990s, looked like a recipe for disaster, for both the community and the workforce affected. There were simply no other employers locally of any size to offer the displaced workers the possibility of similar work. Moreover, the fiscal crisis of the provincial government in the recession of the early 1990s, and later the dramatic policy turn towards downsizing and retrenchment of the government under the Conservatives after 1995 made it unlikely that workers would find jobs in the

Figure 7.1. Manufacturing in Mount Forest, 2001 (number of employees by manufacturer's product)

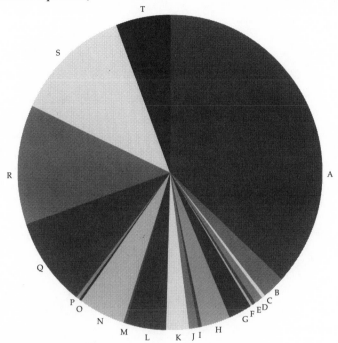

A   Caps, jackets, clothing (300)
B   Wood products, chalkboards, office supplies (20)
C   Garlic, sauces (3)
D   Antennas, actuators, recreational vehicle parts and accessories (7)
E   Signs (3)
F   Prefabricated log cabins (2)
G   Machining, metal fabricating (20)
H   Laminated boards (25)
I   Furniture components, wood components (3)
J   Newspapers, printing (8)
K   Poultry and domestic animal feeds (20)
L   Veneer, plywood (35)
M Bags, jackets, coats, t-shirts, shirts (sports) (2)
N   Caskets (40)
O   Musical instruments (2)
P   Embroidering (3)
Q   Sanders, plows, harnesses, snow-handling equipment (75)
R   Coated fabrics (100)
S   Furniture components (100)
T   Wood containers, paper products, plastic products (47)

Source: Scott's Directory, 2001

Figure 7.2. Manufacturing in Arnprior, 2001 (number of employees by manufacturer's product)

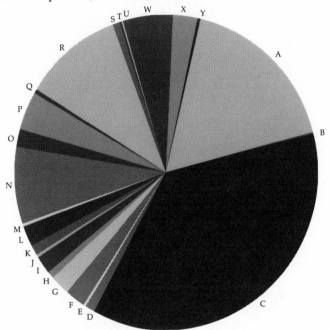

A Synthetic fibres and polymers (BASF) (327)
B Machine shop, machinery (custom) (3)
C Aircraft parts and components (Boeing) (700)
D Moulds (plastic), plastic products, machine parts, tools (19)
E Concrete (ready-mixed) (5)
F Metal tubing (GE Canada) (41)
G Reels (4)
H Printing (14)
I Industrial controls, instruments, motors, data recorders, valves (35)
J Feeds (domesticated animals) (6)
K Millwork (20)
L Metal pipe & tubing, titanium pipe, metal fabricating (40)
M Pneumatic and industrial process controls (6)
N Pharmaceutical products, veterinary pharmaceutical products (Pfizer) (150)
O Computer hardware, communication switches & components, interface cards (35)
P Rubber gloves, tampons, hair care & suncare products, cleaning compounds (75)
Q Publishing (newspaper) (8)
R Steel products, tubing (metal and stainless steel), metal coils (200)
S Windows (PVC), doors (patio) (15)
T Signs, logos (4)
U Publishing (book and magazine) (2)
V Moulding (wood), wood turnings (2)
W CD-ROM (multimedia) (100)
X Paper products, bullet-proof vests, blankets, clothing (protective) (50)
Y Vehicles (for disabled persons) (6)

Source: Scott's Directory, 2001

Figure 7.3. Manufacturing in Iroquois Falls, 2001 (number of employees by manufacturer's product)

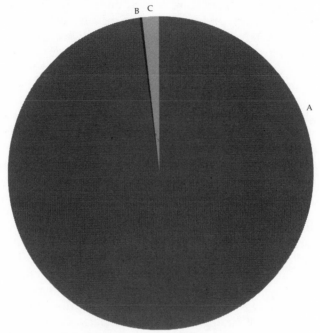

A   Pulp mill, paper products (Abitibi-Consolidated) (600)
B   Chemicals (industrial inorganic) (1)
C   Publishing (newspaper) (7)

Source: Scott's Directory, 2001

public sector, even if they should have the requisite skills. In fact, public sector employment played a significant role in providing good jobs in this community.

The Limits of Economic Diversity

Looked at from the relatively simple perspective of potential alternatives, the more diversified communities certainly seemed to offer better prospects for displaced workers. Our fieldwork in the communities challenges any simple conclusions, however, and points to some real weaknesses of a purely quantitative approach to economic diversity and community stability.

The post-lay-off experience in Wellington County showed that, despite the historical diversity of the area's manufacturing economy, very few displaced workers were able to find comparable work – in terms of wages, benefits, and the quality of the job – without having to commute some distance. The jobs available locally were either manufacturing positions requiring relatively low skill levels and offering slightly more than minimum wage, or they were part-time service sector positions, which were equally low paying with the additional disadvantages of shorter hours and instability.

Although there remained other manufacturing establishments in Mount Forest, with one exception they were typically much smaller than the Westinghouse operation used to be, and they showed no real tendencies towards expansion during the course of this study. The one firm that has shown a strong tendency to expand in the town is a garment factory producing sports-related products formerly known as K Brand.[1] This is a non-union company that often does contract work for retail firms. It has been in Mount Forest since the mid-1970s, changing ownership since then from Canadian hands to those of American venture capitalists. The firm has long made use of the pool of available cheap local labour, including employing a number of the wives of local farmers eager to supplement farm incomes, and perhaps their own industrial wage, with a second income. In the 1990s the firm adopted a number of strategies that are associated with 'lean production.' Workers' knowledge has been appropriated through efforts to formally document it, for example, the knowledge of the skilled sewers, and to have workers participate in the research department to help design strategies to improve product quality. The company also uses work cells, the so-called Toyota sewing system, designed to increase efficiency for the firm as well as teach workers strategies to maintain production when faced with staff shortages. Moves to a more just-in-time regime have been taken, and lead times for production of new products have been cut in half.

Producing in a competitive industrial sector with relatively low margins, this company offers entry level wages at just above the provincial minimum of $6.80 per hour. A minority of workers have jobs as sewers, who start at $8.67 per hour and with experience can earn $11 to $12 per hour. However, most of the workers we studied who moved to this plant after the Westinghouse closure would have started at the bottom hourly rate. This meant a dramatic cut in their wages as we discussed in Chapter 5. Consequently, many former Westinghouse employees, especially the men who had higher skill levels, gendered ideas about garment work, and greater possibilities to commute, preferred to look for other employment which meant in more distant, urban areas.

What of the other southern Ontario communities we studied? In the case of Elora, by the mid-1990s, the general decline in manufacturing had left only one firm of note, and thus, Elora could no longer be called a diversified manufacturing community. Since then an auto parts manufacturing plant that supplies Honda's Alliston plant has established itself. With over 100 jobs, this plant is a significant addition to the local economy, but it is premature to conclude that the community is on its way back to becoming one with significant manufacturing activity.

Arnprior is unique in that it *has* experienced the growth of what has been called the 'new rural economy' with its high technology characteristics. Furthermore, it still retains some of its traditional manufacturing establishments. Nevertheless, our interviews with the displaced Weavexx workers indicate that while continuing diversity of manufacturing activities may at least improve one's chances of finding work relatively soon after lay-off, it does *not* provide much benefit when it comes to offering wage work comparable to the jobs that were lost. To be sure, casual labour was to be had – at least as long as the economy was reasonably buoyant. But this was work not substantially above minimum wage, with few if any benefits, and of fixed, usually short, duration. Just-in-time production, as we saw with the KAO diskette manufacturing firm, means that the pace of production orders is the prime determinant dictating the ebb and flow of casual work.

In addition to the 'casualization' of labour, which would appear to be an integral part of certain kinds of high technology enterprise, one must also consider *volatility*. In our brief examination of manufacturing in Arnprior, one of its major high tech firms (KAO, later Zomax) downsized by approximately 50 per cent while its management was looking for a buyer for the plant. Our interviews with key informants revealed the volatility of this sector and that town officials were keen to develop a diversification strategy that would not leave the community overly dependent upon just high technology firms. Indeed, one key informant, a development officer in a community nearby, told us that town's negative experiences with high tech firms that left as soon as government grants ended had largely soured its interest in pursuing high tech firms as a development strategy. Its efforts to recover from the downturn of the early 1990s focused largely on attracting firms not usually considered high technology.[2]

The Role of Regional Political Cultures

If the economic base of small manufacturing towns can vary significantly, so too can their political culture. Our case studies represent important variations at this level. The communities of southern Ontario were embedded in long-standing agricultural regions that have evolved as politically conservative in nature. Indeed, in recent provincial elections the shift to decidedly right wing Conservative Party governments in the province has, in part, been made possible by strong support from small rural communities and the farming population across much of the southern part of Ontario.

Southern England embraced Margaret Thatcher's 'enterprise culture' with its emphasis on individualism, minimalist privatized social welfare, entrepreneurship, and self-help, while the de-industrializing north did not (Peck 1996: 104). Rural and suburban southern Ontario embrace a remarkably similar neo-liberal ideology – propounded by provincial Conservatives in the 1990s. Support for this ideology has had decidedly geographic dimensions, and it resonates particularly well where the values of the old agrarian society linger on.

The same cannot be said about the northern region of the province. There the economy was not based historically on agriculture and family farms. In the north, the economy is of more recent origins and based on the exploitation of minerals and forests; national and multinational corporations built large mills and processing plants that dwarfed many of the industrial enterprises in small southern communities. The distinctiveness of northern single-industry communities is noted by Lucas: 'Canadian communities of one industry are twentieth century products of an age of industry and technology. They are communities of today, relevant, with few past memories. Their inhabitants have no lingering myths of days gone by' (1971: 19–20).

The massive industrial enterprises of northern Ontario, employing large numbers of semi-skilled and skilled blue-collar workers, provided ideal conditions for union organization, and indeed many remote mill towns came to have a workforce organized by what were the more militant and combatant unions of the labour movement. Some observers argue that residents of small single-industry communities are more likely to be passive and fatalistic than their urban counterparts, more likely to have weak labour unions, and more likely, generally, to show little consciousness of themselves as a 'we group' with similar interests (Himelfarb 1982: 26–7). These generalizations are not well grounded empirically, however, and on the contrary, some of the most memorable – and militant – events in Canadian labour history occurred in single-industry contexts. The examples of the struggles of Cape Breton coalminers come to mind, as does the pivotal Asbestos strike of 1949 in Quebec. More recent empirical scholarship has demonstrated that class divisions can be quite sharply defined during labour struggles in such communities, with a relatively high degree of social solidarity being present among the community's working population (see, e.g., Koch and Gartrell 1992).

The organizational relationships springing from the way in which the production process was typically organized in the north have produced a distinctive political culture; this culture is more progressive than is the case for much of the southern and more populous parts of Ontario, and it is manifested in consistent electoral support for social democracy as represented both provincially and federally by the New Democratic Party. This political culture legitimizes and nurtures strong labour organizations that can have an important role in securing for the local community a greater part of the surplus generated from the exploitation of natural resources. Strong labour organizations can also be key in softening the blow from devastating downturns in commodity cycles and, in more recent years, in deflecting away from the workforce management's strong pressures to move to lean production regimes.

Economic restructuring and downsizing had a more dramatic and negative impact on employees and communities in southern Ontario. There downsizing meant plant shutdowns and lay-offs. Some differences were observed among our four communities in terms of the severance packages workers received, with the most problems for workers occurring where a union was absent, or where the union was not very strong. But even in the case where workers were represented by what, at the national level, was a strong union, at the local level the union's existence was contentious and worker solidarity weak. We believe that this could only have hindered the ability of the workforce to get the best deal, in economic terms, from the dire situation they faced. Perhaps more importantly, it meant that workers were left feeling more devastated and 'on their own' than could have been the case had the cultural and political climate been more conducive to worker and community solidarity.

The absence of a strong union presence in rural southern Ontario among the industrial workplaces we examined itself needs to be explained. In part it is no doubt due to the different material existence of workers in the southern Ontario communities we studied. There is a broad geographical dispersion of the workforce, with some employees locally based but many commuting from other small communities, and from nearby farms. Indeed, among the Westinghouse workforce in Mount Forest, a group of workers had moved from another Westinghouse facility that closed in Hamilton to take jobs in the plant. Solidarity, bonds of friendship and loyalty, are more difficult to build in these more diversified communities, and indeed our interviews of displaced workers confirmed this impression.

Our interviews with laid-off plant workers in this context did point out what we believe to be another significant factor, however. This was the ambivalent and hostile attitudes towards unions that characterized a sizeable minority of the workforce. We present evidence elsewhere that a small town and farm ideology emphasizing hard work, a reluctance to question the prerogatives of management, and an ambivalent if not hostile attitude towards union organizations, dominates the rural communities of this region (see Winson 1997). Indeed, there is research to support the contention that such values are typical of other rural communities in this part of Canada (Barrett 1994), and other agriculturally dominated regions of North America as well (see Naples 1994).

Such attitudes were not universal among the workforce we studied, of course, and indeed some workers, particularly those who were transplants from an urban environment and experienced in working in a unionized shop tended to believe more strongly in unions, and were more critical of the decisions made by management (Winson 1997: 439–42). Nevertheless, if anything the lay-off seemed to have polarized the views of the affected workers, with some tending to blame the union for the plant shutdown. The possibility of solidarity in dealing with the situation was diminished in these plants by the lack of any clear consensus, and a propensity by a significant number in some plants to be more sympathetic to the management than their own union (1997: 439–42).

Economic Diversity Is Conditioned by Social Context

In both diversified and non-diversified communities, the social institutional context is an important determinant of outcomes for workers and by extension the community at large. We had expected that if the workforce in more diversified towns fared poorly as firms restructured, then a single industry community, particularly a geographically isolated one, such as the forest-dependent community of Iroquois Falls, would be disastrous for its working population. We were forced to revise our assumptions.

In Iroquois Falls, as elsewhere, there had been pressures to downsize the workforce, which came to the fore in the 1990s as stiff competition from lower-cost American paper companies in particular provided strong incentives for Canadian companies to reduce costs as well. These cost reductions were pursued through a combination of technological changes, most notably in the pulping process, and increased flexibility in management's dealings with labour (see Holmes 1997).

Management's strategy to reduce costs by downsizing its labour force at Abitibi's Iroquois Falls operations were most successful in the tree-harvesting operations, where the further mechanization of harvesting with the introduction of heavy machinery, together with the different wood fibre requirements of thermo-mechanical pulping technology, reduced the workforce from over 400 loggers to around 150 in less than ten years.[3]

In the mill there was also pressure to downsize, driven by the introduction of thermo-mechanical pulping technology but also by head office directives, demanding significant cost savings on labour.[4] These directives appeared to be motivated more recently by the firm's desire to demonstrate to shareholders that significant 'synergies' would be had from the merger of Abitibi Price and Stone Consolidated (see Chapter 4). What is remarkable is that despite these ongoing, and indeed intensifying pressures over the years, *no* permanent lay-offs had occurred through 1998. In fact, the union had made the issue of job security a central one in its bargaining for some time, and as the pace of technological change increased in the 1990s it was able to negotiate early retirement packages for all those positions made redundant.[5]

The Union Can Make a Community Strong

Indeed, it is the role of the union, the Communications, Energy, and Papermakers Union in this case, and the solidarity of the workforce engendered by the Union and by the nature of the community itself, that would seem to be the most important explanatory factors in producing what, from the workforce's point of view, was the most equitable and benign sort of downsizing process.[6] The strength of this particular union, and not just its existence *per se*, is what we would like to highlight. This matter needs some further comment.

What has upheld the substantial benefits of mill workers is a master agreement that includes mill workers at all Abitibi mills across the country. This agreement was attacked early on by the Company in the famous seven-month strike of 1975, which occurred shortly after the mill workers had transferred their allegiance from an international union to the Canadian Papermakers Union. With virtually no strike pay through the duration of this long and bitter strike, mill workers were very hard pressed to hold on against the company's demand to go back to mill by mill bargaining (Noland 1975). Though some local businessmen were less than sympathetic to the strikers, much of the community rallied to their support and helped them sustain the fight.[7] The victory they won was substantial, and paved the way for them to be among the highest paid industrial workers in the country, with one of the strongest benefit packages as well.[8] This achievement for the workforce proved to be durable, and would not be challenged seriously again until 1998, when another long strike over substantially the same issue erupted.[9] Despite a trend towards the breakdown of industry wide 'pattern' bargaining in Canada, and especially in the United States in the 1990s, the paper workers were able to maintain their master contract once again.

Whatever one's views on unions may be, we believe that unions can be important mechanisms in society for redistributing income that would otherwise be appropriated by the owners of capital and their management. In fact, other studies have attributed the high degree of labour organization in some forest industry contexts to the relative prosperity and low rates of poverty in associated communities (see Marchak 1983 and Nord 1994: 214). Others have noticed the importance of union strength in limiting the extent to which automobile companies have out-sourced production to lower wage companies in Canada and the United States (*Globe and Mail*, 26 October 1996: B1, B4). The presence of a union, especially one that has demonstrated its solidary nature, and thereby its strength, is an important mechanism to ensure that more of the surplus generated by industry stays in the community and the surrounding region. This factor is particularly important when so much of manufacturing is owned and controlled by global manufacturing firms with no particular loyalty to place.

We might also ask whether it is precisely the dependence upon a single company that makes many one-industry communities especially solidary and thereby enhances the possibility of a strong union organization to arise in the first place. Certainly the feeling that 'we are all in this together' is much more prevalent there than in the more diversified communities in the southern part of the province. It is not lost on the community, nor even on the small business class (that might in other contexts be less than sympathetic to union presence in the community), that as the success of the union in bargaining goes, so goes the local economy.[10] Solidarity is strengthened by the great majority of mill workers who are local residents, who not only work together but have grown up together, attended the same educational institution, played in the same sports leagues, and attended the same churches. Gender, too, has likely played a role in fostering solidarity, for the great majority of the labour force is male, and the role played by the bonds built up among the male employees over years of working together cannot be discounted. Finally, and in contrast to many of the plant workers we interviewed in rural southern Ontario, workers in Iroquois Falls were more likely to come from households that had experienced a history of trade unionism.

A constellation of factors that are constituted locally – common experience of place, geographical isolation, shared history and employment situation, and gender uniformity – is important in producing the solidarity at the community level. These are vital building blocks in the formation of a strong national labour organization, one that can serve as at least a partial balance to the massive corporate entities that in the 1990s became even further engorged through large-scale mergers.

The 'good' jobs in this community, and the durability of these jobs, were as much as anything a product of a social institution – the union – which has both a local as well as a national manifestation. This institution not only had much to do with the constitution of 'good' jobs in the community historically, but helped ensure the longevity of these jobs once a situation developed that put them in peril. Our research then, supports the notion developed long ago by political economists such as Karl Marx and Karl Polanyi, and more recently by economic sociologists, that local labour markets must be conceived as realities embedded in existing social and political arrangements.[11] We believe that their characteristics cannot be fully explained without taking *local* social arrangements into account. Ironically, comparison with the communities we studied to the south suggests that in one sense, the *lack* of economic diversity in Iroquois Falls, actually enhanced the ability of the union to resist the Company's preferred downsizing strategy for much of the decade. The absence of diversity may be seen, then, as a factor promoting the maintenance of what we have called the stable work world, and thereby a more sustainable local economy. Unfortunately, this stable work world built up in the community over many decades is now under assault.

The Limits of Single-Industry Towns Today

One undeniable weakness of single-industry communities, particularly those dependent upon primary resources, is that depletion of a non-renewable resource, or unwise exploitation of a renewable one, typically results sooner or later in the catastrophic decline of the community. The history of Canada is replete with examples to illustrate this kind of weakness.

Single-industry communities today would appear to be exposed to other dangers, however, even when their resource base is secure. The case of Iroquois Falls illustrates this quite well. Even while the natural resource the town depends upon may be harvested on a more sustainable basis today than previously, because of the relatively innovative logging practices of Abitibi Consolidated, the sustainability of the community is under real threat nevertheless.[12] This threat has been building for some time, as it has in other forest industry dependent towns as companies turn to lean production regimes to boost their profits and compete with lower cost producers outside Canada.

Current employees at the mill had been protected from the downsizing pressures throughout most of the 1990s, to be sure, and this is no small miracle in today's mean and lean economy. But the same cannot be said for those younger people who have been entering the local workforce. Younger workers, those under thirty years of age, are less than 10 per cent of the workforce at the mill. The few that have been hired have been put 'on waivers,' and therefore have little security as the company pushes through current downsizing policy with the shut down of a paper machine in 1999. As a local union representative told one of the authors, the union has had no new full-time members in over fifteen years, and when younger people ask what their chances are in being hired at the mill, he has to say 'just about nil.'[13]

This situation will likely produce greater social cleavages within the community as a younger generation of workers who stay in the community is forced to accept substantially lower wages than those prevailing at the mill. The high cost of local housing is a reflection of the historically high wages in the community which punishes the workforce outside the mill in particular, and reinforces the two-tier labour market.

Since 1998 it has become clear that even the security of the permanent 'good' jobs in the mill is more and more in doubt. The company shut down a paper machine in March 1999 and laid off about 80 of a planned 140 workers by February, 2000. By the later date it had also announced another merger, this time with Donohue Incorporated of Quebec. Touted as a 'low cost' newsprint manufacturer, it appeared to us that Abitibi management was viewing the firm they had merged with as a model for how the larger company might become a more profitable operation, after enduring losses in the recent past. Then, in early 2001 the company announced it was intent on shutting down another paper machine in the mill by the following September, in an effort to restrict the supply of paper in the market and force up prices. The various unions representing workers at the mill took up negotiations to try and save the machine, and as many jobs as possible. By early summer three unions had accepted a revised company plan to keep the machine running with fewer jobs but with most of those losing employment protected by an early retirement package. The largest union, CEP local 90, did not accept the plan and continued negotiating. Win or lose, one outcome appeared certain. Within the next year the workforce at the mill would be reduced to roughly one-third of the approximately 1000 workers who were employed there ten years earlier.[14]

Contingent Work as a Threat to Sustainability

It was in the context of our fieldwork in the single-industry forestry community that a less visible but perhaps more insidious threat to the viability of the wider community came to light. Conversations with a local community activist turned to a discussion of what was happening to local service organizations in town, which had until the past few years been viewed as quite vibrant and effective. We were told that such organizations were now shutting down, and that this was viewed with some alarm by the community. When asked why this was happening, our respondent, who was involved with community affairs, attributed this change to the lack of participation of younger members in the community. This declining participation in service organizations can be attributed to contingent labour, the situation of young people who require two jobs and more time to make a living.

Moreover, younger people have little disposable income to devote to such charitable causes, as compared to an earlier generation that could count on good wages from the mill.[15] This growing prevalence of contingent labour is closely related, of course, to the implementation of 'lean production methods' by Abitibi.

Community organizations are understood to be an essential part of the social fabric of any community. They also reinforce community by breaking down the class affiliation of the union. While they are presumably in existence to help mend the human damage that comes from economic restructuring these organizations are also vulnerable to such restructuring. When service organizations are weakened, the community's social fabric is also affected. When such organizations actually cease to function, community must also suffer, unless some other entity comes forward to take its place. Our community fieldwork did not lead to the discovery of new mechanisms arising to take the place of the old, though we cannot say for certain that this was not occurring. This weakening of service organizations is not only an outcome of restructuring in northern communities; in the southern Ontario towns, lay-offs and unemployment led to the decline of community service organizations.

As the stable work world is replaced with the contingent work world, especially among young people, demographic distortions in the community are increasingly likely. Younger people are more likely to leave the community on graduation because there are no jobs available. In the past a proportion of students who went on to further their education after high school returned to the community as teachers, nurses, social workers, and so on. However, the down-sizing of the public sector has put this option in jeopardy. The key informants that we interviewed believe that nowadays once young people leave they will not be coming back.

These changes in Iroquois Falls are coming at a time when the pressures to downsize appear to be vanquishing what has been a powerful counterbalancing force to the company for many years – the union of the mill-workers. As 1999 progressed, real lay-offs, rather than early retirements, began to occur for the first time outside of a strike situation, and a heightened apprehension was palpable in the community.

Other Impacts of Lean Production

While much of the literature on the significance of adoption of lean production methods by industry is focused on labour and/or the firm itself, there are other community dimensions to this phenomenon that need more attention. Our interviews with small-business people in Iroquois Falls served to highlight some of these.[16] As part of its campaign to continually reduce costs, the company has moved to what they refer to as a 'preferred supplier initiative' in sourcing all manner of hardware and equipment supplies. For decades local hardware stores had secured an important part of company business, but with the new corporate model 'loyalty to the community goes out the window,' as one of our respondents in the hardware business remarked. Much business that was previously done locally had been lost to a larger hardware and equipment supplier in Timmins some thirty miles away. Because of their larger size they were able to supply the company with cheaper materials than could local businesses.

Such local businesses are an important source of employment for those unable to get jobs with the company, which is the great majority of job seekers these days. A hardware store can employ ten full-time and a couple of part-time workers, a grocery store up to ten full-time and twenty-four part-time employees (there were three stores in town at the time interviews were conducted). While changes in company purchasing-policies have caused businesses to retrench, the company's push to break the tradition of pattern bargaining that had prevailed for decades, a further effort to drive down its costs, provoked a five-month strike in 1998 that had even more serious effects for small business in the community. Despite the existence of weekly strike pay, striking employees drastically pared down expenditures and postponed any household projects. The results were fairly immediate for small businesses, whether they were in the hardware, food supply, or hospitality sectors. Nearly all small-business owners we talked to were forced to lay off half or more of their workforce, or drastically reduce employee hours for months as the strike dragged on.

It was in this forestry town that the complex and contradictory dimensions of sustainability became apparent. It is both fascinating and disturbing that while the Company dramatically cleaned up the environment with thermo-mechanical pulping and effluent control technologies and while it was moving to replace clear-cut harvesting with more benign harvesting system, yet the *human* community of Iroquois Falls was increasingly imperiled.

Sustainability cannot be understood outside the political economy within which the biophysical world and the socioeconomic world meet. Clear-cut logging, which represented over 90 per cent of the forest harvested in Ontario in the mid-1990s, has far exceeded the acreage replanted, with far-reaching effects to the nation's boreal forest.[17] This pending crisis of the bio-physical environment that supports community can be attenuated, or even reversed, through changes in the productive process. The federal state may impose effluent controls. A proactive forest company may avoid future confrontations with militant environmental groups (as in the case of clear-cut logging in British Columbia).[18] Nevertheless, the wider political economy that determines that labour is a cost to the corporation like any other, has dictated that labour costs be reduced. This cost reduction imperative is accomplished through the introduction of labour displacing technologies, and it is given further impetus by the desire of management to find cost savings that would justify the corporate merger they had recently completed (see Chapter 4). Whatever the motivation, the end result is 'good' jobs that have sustained the community for seven decades are being destroyed.

Sustaining the community, as well as the environment, should be possible. But we doubt whether it will succeed without a counterbalance to the forces that produce merger activity in the corporate sector and without change in the present reward structure where corporations offer positive incentives to management to decimate their labour forces and eliminate 'good' jobs. At present, government initiatives around the issue of sustainability are narrowly focused on the biophysical dimension, at least with regards to forestry communities.[19]

A more holistic approach to community sustainability must be embraced, one that incorporates the lessons learned from a previous generation of rural development policies that sought to improve the lot of disadvantaged regions. The top-down initiatives of the past were disconnected with local realities. A well-rounded government approach to community sustainability, must from the onset, incorporate mechanisms to ensure local grass roots input and on-going participation.

Embracing Economic Diversity?

It is naive to say that more diversity brings a higher quality of life and more stability to communities. The rapid replacement of 'good' jobs in Canada's resource industries by capital-intensive technologies forces communities to embrace a drive for diversification or face slowly withering away. In Iroquois Falls a clear sign that all is not well is a slow but steady decline in population. Other signs abound, whether it be the lethargy of small business, the persistent and increasing out-migration of youth, or the failure of new commercial ventures to prosper.

Numerous residents of Iroquois Falls explained that as long as there were 'good' jobs at the mill there was limited interest in developing other enterprises in town. While other neighbouring communities made great strides in expanding ventures such as winter tourism, the citizens of Iroquois Falls feel trapped in the 'dependent mentality,' of a long-time, single-industry town. Nearby Cochrane is notably perceived by entrepreneurs in the Iroquois Falls hospitality industry as a successful example of a community that has broken the resource industry mould, dramatically expanding snowmobile tourism by exploiting its location and natural beauty.[20] In a recent town council meeting the people of Iroquois Falls showed a new openness toward diversification. The inability of the union to protect the community from the Company's drive for lay-offs has created a great deal of apprehension.[21] Out of this may come real interest in economic alternatives to ensure the town's survival. It needs to be stressed, however, that the jobs any tourist-related development is likely to provide will be substantially inferior, in terms of pay, benefits, and even security compared to the 'good' manufacturing jobs being eliminated by technological change and Company downsizing.

CHAPTER EIGHT

Some Concluding Thoughts

In writing about what they have termed 'the age of insecurity,' Larry Elliot and Dan Atkinson remind us about what, for most people, are 'things which really matter.' It is the case that 'people still want a steady job, decent pay, a healthy environment, personal freedom and somebody to rely on if the going gets a bit tough. In short, they want security' (1998: 247). We agree with this assessment, and it does match what pollsters today tell us that Canadians rate as among their top priorities. Nevertheless, what most people want and what the economic system has to offer these days are increasingly at odds. To quote Elliot and Atkinson again: 'Security is the one thing the modern system cannot deliver. Indeed, it seems almost proud of the fact that it cannot offer security. Security is bad. It stands in the way of the great god of international competitiveness, the economic imperative that dominates the West's business culture and justifies everything from downsizing of bank clerks to the chopping down of rainforests' (1998: 247). To those still sceptical of such statements, we would suggest reviewing the justification given by AT&T executives for the firing of some 40,000 in the late 1990s (see Chapter 4).

Our own study of people who still perform the work of industrial labour, and about the small communities where they have lived all their lives, has also brought to the fore the dialectic of security and insecurity, of stability and instability. Our discussion of what we saw as a significant shift in the lives of our respondents from a stable work world to a contingent work world gives some idea of how the industrial labour force is being reshaped in the rural milieu. As Janet Fitchen (1991) argued some years ago, manufacturing-dependent rural communities are now even more dependent on industrial employment than large cities, where financial services and high technology companies have expanded dramatically. The fallout from restructuring in the industrial sector is particularly acute in these communities.

As a rebound in the growth rate of Canada's GNP took place in the latter half of the 1990s, there has been a real effort in the mainstream media to sell the idea that 'we're growing and everything is going to be all right.' If the texture of people's lives and their state of well-being – material and psychological – were a direct reflection of the change in GNP, then we would agree. However, many hours of face-to-face interviews with working people, together with the opportunity we had to return to many of them later in their struggle to rebuild lives damaged by the shutdown of their workplace, point to the contemporary 'disconnect' between the economic numbers in our society and the lives lived by its more ordinary citizens. It also alerts us to the barriers faced by people living in the context of a rural, small community.

Our research attests that social class remains an important variable in defining outcomes for people in the restructuring of local economies. Working people in small industrial communities bear the brunt of social dislocation occasioned by plant shutdowns and corporate downsizing. Other elements of the community are also affected, of course, but none so profoundly as the labourers we studied. With little to cushion the shock that went with the loss of their employment, and with the vacuum of good jobs in the economy of the early 1990s, the modest lives of these people were often seriously, at times brutally, traumatized.

If the turmoil of economic restructuring has results clearly defined by social class, there are some important differences in outcomes that are dictated by non-class factors – gender and age being key. The picture we saw for most of the semi-skilled older labourers we talked to, is one of forced early retirement, perhaps followed by some part-time work at low pay to make up for lost income. The rapid decline in their standard of living, together with meagre alternative income opportunities, was a depressing turn of events for those who had worked hard for many years. For women, especially those with obligations to family, and perhaps lacking adequate transportation, local re-employment usually has meant low-wage and often intermittent employment or part-time employment and perhaps multiple jobs. For many of the people we talked to, restructuring has meant the end of semi-skilled work that had given them self-esteem and a strong sense of being self-sufficient. Much of the psychological trauma some women have faced is related to the state of dependency on spouses that restructuring forced them into – a state they had either never experienced before or at least not for a good many years.

For the majority of our respondents, the end of the 'good' jobs that they once held has meant a significantly lower income, even four years after their initial lay-offs. The years since have often involved multiple jobs, and for some, particularly the men who were able to find work at an hourly wage comparable to what they once had, it has resulted in a new life of commuting to multiple jobs: a potent recipe for stress. For some with multiple jobs, the commute to work is extraordinarily long, hard work, fragmenting days and nights, driving in the dark, often in dangerous winter weather, while too often feeling physically exhausted. The extra efforts made to stave off a collapse of income are exacting a high price.

We have also seen that the restructuring of manufacturing firms in the 1990s has had a deleterious impact on rural youth: the new generation about to enter the workforce. The erosion of summer employment opportunities for youth in small communities is one dimension of this. No summer jobs place such youth at an even greater disadvantage *vis-à-vis* urban youth when it comes to furthering their education in the hope of securing stable work in the future. Given the importance of higher education and training as prerequisites for most of the better jobs in the new economy, further disadvantaging rural youth at this time is an especially disturbing outcome of restructuring.

The decline in good jobs for unskilled and semi-skilled rural workers undermines the ability of many of these towns and villages to sustain themselves in the coming years. People who formed the bedrock of the local labour force have experienced a major trauma in their work lives, and the prospects for their children to remain in the community and lead satisfactory lives with an acceptable standard of living have become more remote in the new rural economy. High technology industry has a very limited presence in small communities, in general,[1] and it is likely not the panacea for these problems, if our examination of Arnprior has a lesson for us. New, permanent rural employment there may be for the few communities who benefit from high technology, but it will likely be largely for outsiders, many of whom will choose to continue to live in other, often more urban, places. For local workers without the specialized skills required by such firms, casual work may be the only employment they can expect from the relatively volatile high technology firms. Many of the workers displaced from the round of restructuring in the 1990s fall into this group, and we do have to ask what is happening to these people, and what are the consequences for their communities?

The disintegration of the stable work world is not just an issue of income and material well-being, as we are now coming to appreciate. As Donald Levine argues, human beings attempt to make sense of the world they experience by interpreting their actions as part of a coherent life story: 'Much research in psychology supports the proposition that life changes that disrupt one's ability to maintain a plausible autobiography tend to increase inner tension, ultimately leading to feelings of emptiness or fragmentation' (1995: 9). The sociologist Richard Sennett, on the other hand, focuses more specifically on the new reality that we have termed the 'contingent work world.' In the context of the new work regime, the emphasis is on the short time-frame, casualization, and the rise of conditions that make a mockery of such virtues as loyalty and commitment, Sennett (1998: 26) poses some important questions. How can long-term purposes be pursued in a short-term society, and how can durable social relationships be maintained? Moreover, how can human beings develop a narrative of identity and life history – a coherent life story in Levine's words – in a society where episodic and fragmented work experiences are becoming the norm?

We need to consider, in other words, how major disruptions in people's lives, and the shift to contingent labour more generally, may have serious repercussions for individuals maintaining a stable personality structure, and how they affect, to quote Sennett, 'those qualities of character which bind human beings to one another and furnish each with a sustainable self.'

Our study suggests additional psychological impacts of the restructuring of work in contemporary capitalism. The lay-off experience was a psychological trauma, in part, because it took people away from the comfortable day-to-day interaction with workmates that in itself was important in maintaining the psychological well-being of these employees. Moreover, the lay-off experience produced, in a number of respondents, the desire to withdraw from much of the other routine human contact they had previously maintained. This was because they felt that their loss of income made it impossible for them to reciprocate in an appropriate manner when friends invited them over for, say, a drink or supper. The loss of a job held for years, even decades in some cases, undermined the desire to interact regularly with others: feeling depressed, some people withdrew socially.

Eventually, most respondents moved on to some other form of employment, often to what we call contingent employment. This brought with it other repercussions of a psychological and social nature. In general, it left them with less time in their lives to do the social things that they once had done. Having to work two, and in some cases three jobs, and having to commute significant distances, affected respondents' previous routine visits with friends and family. All together there appeared to be real signs of what can only be described as social *disintegration*, a weakening of the social fabric of these individuals' lives. This, in turn, leads us to question the general health of the community in the face of these changes.

We know that residents of small communities are disadvantaged in a number of ways, including isolation, less developed or non-existent public transit, lower levels of social services, higher illiteracy rates, lower average family incomes, less diverse employment opportunities, less than adequate access to good health care, and so on. Nevertheless, people choose to continue to live there, and indeed people have chosen to relocate to them from cities, because small communities are perceived to offer a higher degree of personal safety, sociability, and personal day-to-day human contact. In short, they yearn for a communal life that many can not find in contemporary urban agglomerations. We wonder whether the psychological and social effects on individuals of economic restructuring undermine the very qualities that make these communities so desirable as places to live. We might add that we found evidence that the shift to contingent labour is undercutting the ability and willingness of people to participate in the myriad of volunteer activities that others have argued is a notable characteristic of smaller towns and villages (see Bollman 1992: 39). Will the shift to contingent labour so negatively affect people's ability to participate in community affairs that it critically undermines the specific advantages still to be found in such communities?

Our case study approach to work and community in the new rural economy provides some insights, through comparative analysis, into global and local dynamics. In Chapter 2 we drew attention to the macroeconomic and political forces that provide the necessary context for any real understanding of what is happening in manufacturing-dependent communities today. In each of the communities we found evidence of the emergence of a contingent work regime as an ever more significant element of local economies. This was true whether communities were characterized predominantly by the industries of the old economy or those of the new.

Beyond this commonality of experience, geography, and local social and cultural arrangements do play a role in defining outcomes for people in these communities when restructuring takes place. Here, the north/south divide in our study stood out as particularly salient. Our southern Ontario case studies (with the partial exception of Arnprior) share common roots in the earlier agrarian social and economic order that once dominated this part of Canada. We argue that because of this residents of these particular communities share strong cultural traditions that revolve around a strong work ethic, individual resourcefulness and self-reliance, a strong respect for the rights of employers, and at least some ambivalence over the matter of employee rights, together with a suspicion of institutional arrangements associated with urban life. We note the suspicion and distrust of trade union organizations, in particular. These value orientations were not dissimilar to those found among respondents interviewed by Nelson and Smith (1999) in their study of the changing world of work in rural Vermont.[2]

This deeply entrenched culture intersects with particular geographic and structural factors. These communities were notable for their proximity to urban labour markets and the diverse opportunities offered by them to at least the more mobile of the displaced workers. This circumstance could not help but lessen the sentiment, after lay-off, that all are in the same situation facing common problems. In structural terms, the relatively diverse nature of the local manufacturing sector in these towns tended to insulate the labour force within individual small enterprises and hinder a stronger class solidarity within the community, while encouraging a lack of engagement and concern on the part of other citizens when employees at one enterprise were thrown off work.

In contrast, the northern resource community of Iroquois Falls was without the weight of this agrarian ethos, and its geographic isolation helps to ensure a commonality of economic circumstances, and particularly few employment alternatives, other than migration out of the region entirely. Added to this is the fact that mill towns such as Iroquois Falls have been dominated by large single corporate enterprises, typically for many decades. By concentrating a large number of workers in a single enterprise, the classical conditions for the formation of strong industrial unions were provided, but outside the urban context. The heavy investment of fixed capital required by pulp-and-paper firms, together with the dependence upon the natural resource, greatly lessens any threat by management to pack up and move production elsewhere.[3]

In the communities in the south we studied, plant closure was often a viable part of their restructuring strategies because of the different nature of the enterprise itself, with firms often being able to literally load up industrial equipment into trucks and quickly re-establish production in some other place – often south of the border where conditions were more propitious for easy profits.

In Iroquois Falls the impact of externally driven economic pressures was mediated by the mill workers' union, and, thus, the blow to the workforce that downsizing and a push to a lean production regime would typically signify was softened. The exit of older workers through an early retirement package that provided a decent post-work livelihood is certainly a better outcome for the workforce and the community than lay-offs of younger workers (not protected by seniority) who would have their severance pay, and then nothing. This outcome was only possible because of a strong, locally constituted source of resistance to corporate pressures that favoured mass lay-offs as the preferred way to reduce costs.

Nevertheless, we must resist being too optimistic about the prospects for such communities today in view of the power that mergers in the 1990s have given to forestry multinationals to play off workers in one community against those in another. We must also recognize that the competition with corporations in the United States and elsewhere operating in jurisdictions with lax environmental regimes and extremely weak labour laws that have barely emerged from the nineteenth century gives strong impetus to Canadian corporations to implement lean production regimes and eliminate the 'good' jobs that for decades characterized this sector of the economy. To summarize this discussion, the response to restructuring in small manufacturing-dependent communities has been shaped by geography and industrial structure, which in turn has moulded local social institutions, and especially the form and strength of worker organizations. In some areas, cultural values formed during a pre-existing agrarian order continue to weigh heavily on the present.

Another issue that we have only touched on in this book, but one that must be addressed in future research, has to do with gaining a better understanding of the combined influence of private *and* public sector restructuring and downsizing in this context. This was not a focus of our research, but it is clear from the interviews we conducted with key informants that the removal of stable public sector jobs from communities with a limited economic base to begin with is a serious matter and perhaps even more serious than it has been in large urban areas. There is good evidence that a strong public sector has been a key ingredient in the past in protecting communities from being decimated by the vagaries of foreign-owned multinational enterprise, and the ups and downs of resource economies. It has also been a most significant, though less visible, leg upon which small towns have survived as they were being increasingly bypassed by ever more concentrated industrial and commercial enterprise. As business-oriented politicians reshape the public sphere to mirror the private sector in terms of consolidation and centralization, all in the interests of short-term savings, small communities in particular are being made extremely vulnerable.

Research in other countries such as Sweden, which has some strong similarities to Canada, has found that cuts to general social welfare programs have had a particularly negative impact on rural areas, and that the effects of these cuts have been greater than the loss of programs specifically targeted to rural regions. We would expect that federal and provincial actions in the 1990s to restrict access to unemployment insurance and welfare, and cuts to welfare rates, to mention only the most obvious, are having similar deleterious effects in rural Canada.

Throughout this book our discussion has oscillated between the individuals coping with restructured corporate enterprises and the small communities that hosted these same enterprises. Some readers may well have wished for more of a focus on one or the other. We tried to balance the exploration of individual struggles and community outcomes. Nevertheless, the weight of our concern has been with the former. We would never argue that a community is basically little more than the sum of its individuals. Clearly, community is more than this. However, we do believe that wherever a substantial group of individuals within a community are adversely affected by events, community is also a victim, even though some members of it may refuse to recognize the injury.

Too many discussions of community have lost their anchor in the actual experiences of members of the various social classes that comprise practically any community and the differences and tensions among them. Community is thereby reified, and discussion of 'community' risks becoming a well-meaning romanticization of something that does not really exist anywhere except in the writer's mind. It is our hope that the balance between individual experiences and community that we have struck in this book has helped us avoid this pitfall.

We do not wish to conclude this book without at least some discussion of policy issues that could confront both the more specific problems we have explored and the trends that appear to be remaking small manufacturing communities today. Perhaps most obvious is the observation that there is a broad class of residents – unskilled and semi-skilled blue-collar workers – who have been disadvantaged by the private sector restructuring of the 1990s. So far, little has been done to secure the future of these people. A more serious, targeted effort must be made to allow this segment of the small community labour force to retrain for the industries that might be attracted to such communities in future. This is particularly important given the very low quality of service sector employment we found in all of our case studies.

As we complete this book, the Task Force on Rural Economic Renewal has just released its final report to the premier of Ontario (OMAFRA 2001). The report identifies the absence of a vision and strategy for rural economic renewal, and the bureaucratic and infrastructural impediments to developing this, a finding that echoes recent academic research (e.g., Douglas and Chadwick 2000). The task force points to many of the issues we highlight here, but with significant omissions, many of which arise from the absence of a class analysis in their discussion.

The plight of older displaced workers is serious. Yet, there is nothing in the task force report to address this issue. Initiatives might include special incentives to employers to take on workers in older age categories, or income supplements for older labourers should their incomes fall beyond a certain level. Targeted retraining initiatives should be looked at. Older workers must be seen as disadvantaged workers in the present political-economic environment, which devalues the job-related experience and skills they have acquired over decades. Older workers have particular health care needs, and these have not been well served by the recent spate of rural hospital closures; the task force does suggest a more cautious approach to rural health care restructuring than has occurred in the past.

Until better economic opportunities can be fostered in small manufacturing towns, governments must devise programs to provide employment for young people so that they may develop employment-related skills, while being able to save money for further education. Education beyond high school will be essential for most people wishing to secure decent livelihoods in a rapidly shifting economic environment; rapidly escalating tuition costs and diminished summer job prospects combine to prejudice small-town youth in particular. The task force does recognize the need for youth training programs, but fails to address the specific training needs of older workers. As well, it fails to address the lack of flexibility in training programs which often discourage prospective students, both young and older.

Serious efforts must be made to nurture local enterprise – private and public sector, cooperatives – that offer good jobs to women. Women today want semi-skilled and skilled work. Such work affords them job satisfaction and self-esteem, not to mention a good income. Too often these have been primarily available only to men. Canadians need to examine programs in other countries that retain and attract women to smaller and more isolated communities and reduces the flow of young women, in particular, to the urban areas.[4] The task force identifies the need for a rural child care program. Such a policy initiative would help meet the needs of many of the people we interviewed and would especially address the needs of single mothers.

We identified transportation as a major issue. Poor access to transportation is a serious impediment for rural community residents in finding work, and a major recommendation of the task force is for an improvement in road access across the province, as a way to improve business access. While this would alleviate some of the problems of rural residents, who tend to rely heavily on private forms of transportation, attention also needs to be paid to forms of public transportation in and between some of the larger rural communities.

It is not likely that these objectives can be achieved for the long term unless the benefits of the new economy are brought to the level of the small community. But to date any positive impact of the new economy on the rural community has been minimal. As a society we need to examine why this is so, and move quickly to rectify it. The task force made an important point in noting that the private sector is unwilling to invest in improved infrastructural services, such as high speed Internet connections, as well as hydroelectricity and natural gas, in communities that will be less profitable for it. This leaves rural communities at a significant disadvantage in attracting new industry of any kind. Moreover, attracting volatile high technology firms financed by government grants and watching them leave when the grants run out is probably not the way to go. Respondents in the Ottawa Valley told of such experiences, and the subsequent damage to small local economies. Assistance from provincial and federal governments to promote the real advantages of small community life to prospective employers – including tranquillity and personal safety, a low-stress environment, life on a more human scale, employee loyalty, and dogged commitment to a deeply held work ethic – would, however, be a good place to start.

Communities themselves would be well advised to think twice about a policy to attract industry that does not take into account the *quality* of the employment it will create. Considerable social science research shows that communities that are indiscriminate in their efforts to attract industry may well find themselves host to rogue corporations seeking lax labour and environmental standards in locations where unions are scarce and labour is conditioned to accept little. Such companies will not build up communities. More likely they will turn them into further class-divided, low-wage ghettoes in the countryside, while possibly creating a host of new environmental nightmares to deal with as well. The recent history of the relocation of the meat-packing industry to rural small town greenfield sites in the United States is instructive in this regard (see Gray 1999; Fink 1998). The Ontario task force on rural economic renewal recommends that communities enter into partnerships with private enterprise, as has apparently been successfully accomplished in some rural regions. Optimistically, this kind of collaborative approach might enhance the commitment of companies to the communities in which they locate.

One initiative in need of consideration is a well thought-out program for reinvestment in the public sector, with a concerted effort to decentralize administrative offices to small communities. Reversing the current provincial trend to overcentralize public services, from the police and education to health care, in the name of short-term cost-cutting would be an especially important achievement. The gains made from such centralizing policies do not take into account the damage they have caused across the province at the level of the small community, both in terms of what was lost to the local economy and the real decline in services experienced by residents in these communities when services are centralized elsewhere.

As far as the politicians and big business are concerned, the inhabitants of the small industrial communities, as typified by those we studied, may play a relatively insignificant part in shaping these processes in the future. However, their value to us as a society probably lies elsewhere. Such communities may well provide a highly urbanized society like Canada with an important other dimension from which to view itself – even if the viewers never actively participate or live in that dimension. For many, of course, they offer attractive choices as living conditions in our largest cities deteriorate under the onslaught of an ever more degraded environment, and a myriad of factors that add up to high levels of stress. Small rural communities will continue to embody what large urban agglomerations are not, and in so doing they and their citizens will preserve for the city dweller valuable alternatives to the not altogether successful dominant arrangements of society today. For this reason alone the integrity of our small communities and the livelihoods of their townsfolk must become a much higher national priority.

Notes

1. Introduction

1 This was reported by Michael Adams, president of Environics Research Group, writing in the *Globe and Mail*, 27 December 1999.

2 It appears to be the macro-level economic and business information which is used by policy-makers, rather than the more qualitative information provided through studies such as ours, which tends to be dismissed as 'anecdotal.'

3 This is in contrast to, for example, Nelson and Smith's (1999) considerable attention to self-provisioning.

4 We refer to non-white workers, who will have experienced the recent changes in the economy that we talk about here in quite different ways from the workers dealt with in this book. To the best of our knowledge all the workers in our sample, from all of the communities, are white. This derives from the historical patterns of settlement in rural communities in Ontario. Census figures show us quite clearly that the proportion of visible minority residents in all of these communities is extremely small. Thus, our sample reflects the present demographic picture fairly accurately in this respect. It is worth noting, however, that since our research was completed Mount Forest has experienced the relocation of a company from the greater Toronto area, which has brought with it workers and their families who are primarily of South Asian origin. We have not investigated this development, but clearly it is worth attention by researchers in the future.

2. The Global and the Local: Understanding Globalization through Community Research

1 By July 1998 the extent of the Asian fallout was becoming apparent in the

business pages of North American and European newspapers. Indeed, the anticipated recovery of the European economies was thought to be in some jeopardy because of the deep recession of the Asian countries. Japan, Hong Kong, Taiwan, and China now rank among the top ten of the European Union's trade partners (Cook 1998: B2. See also B4; Bray 1998: B11; Hardy 1998: B11).

2 We have argued this in more detail elsewhere: see Leach and Winson 1995.

3 As Mahon notes, the essence of Fordism 'was based on mass production of standardized goods, by semi-skilled workers using dedicated equipment. The mass markets for which these goods were destined, in turn, were sus-tained by collective bargaining and the Keynesian welfare state' (1993: 7).

4 While some would say that debt reduction has driven these policies, we would argue that such a view confuses the *justification* for a given policy with the objective of the policy itself. The national debt has indeed provided a powerful justification for all manner of state policy initiatives, yet in earlier times even higher levels of public debt did not provoke such policy responses. Cogent arguments have been made for choosing a whole different spectrum of policies to deal with the debt than those that the government has chosen (see Cameron 1991). The specific types of policies chosen point to a different underlying motivation than debt reduction alone. Analyses that point to the long-term crisis of profitability of private capital beginning in the 1970s and the success of the political right in the electoral realm (see Warnock 1988; Marchak 1991), among other elements, are factors that we believe have been more fundamental in bringing about the rise of the neo-liberal model than rising debt, the existence of which must itself be explained.

5 As Habermas noted, 'the displacement of jurisdiction onto the neo-corporate gray areas withdraws more and more social matters from a decision-making process that is obligated by constitutional norms to give equal consideration to all who are concerned in any specific matter' (1989: 61).

6 The interventions by Charles Schulze and Robert Lawrence have been especially influential here. See 'Do We Need an Industrial Policy?' (1985) and Rodwin (1989).

7 According to the Economic Council of Canada, by 1986 'over 40 percent of those separating from goods-industry employment found their next job in services' (1990: 16).

8 It might be asked whether this sectoral shift to service industry employment is the cause of the increasing income inequality. While it is undoubtedly a big factor, the evidence seems clear that there has been a change in

the structure of jobs in all sectors of the economy, including areas that once were the domains of unionized, stable, and relatively well-paid employment (EEC 1990: 153, and Picot, Myles, and Wannell 1990: 23–4). It might also be asked whether this job structure change, particularly the growth of low-paying employment, is simply the necessary consequence of such demographic changes as the influx of younger wage-earners into the economy and the growth of female wage labour. However, recent studies have demonstrated that such demographic variables explain little of the observed changes in the recent period (i.e. after 1980). See Picot et al., 1990: 13–15, and EEC 1991: 150–2).

9 The data are less clear for women, according to Morissette, Myles, and Picot (1993: 19). Here, some growth in income inequality is evident for women working full-time, as with men. However, women working part-time saw their hours expand considerably, reducing inequalities somewhat between part-time and full-time female earners.

10 One major Canadian study of this phenomenon defines long-term unemployment as 'continuous unemployment lasting 12 months or more' (Gera 1991: 99).

11 As Heery and Salmon (2000: 12) argue, insecurity can be seen at different levels, including 'as a property of jobs, understood in terms of increased risk of involuntary job loss and unpredictability of earnings which can be measured through a combination of indicators, including job tenure, compulsory redundancy, the incidence of contingent contracts, and the use of variable pay. Second, it can be viewed as a property of the environment in which jobs exist, understood in terms of the penalties associated with job loss and the degree of protective regulation of the labour market through employment law, trade unionism, and welfare support for workers who lose their employment. Third, it can be viewed as a property of the subjective experience of employees, understood in terms of cognitive and affective attitudes towards security of employment.'

12 According to the Daily Bread Food Bank's survey of users, completed in 1996, four out of ten users indicated they had been laid off from their jobs, with 44 per cent having lost their jobs within a year of the survey. In addition, over half of food recipients were high school graduates, a third had some post-secondary education, and 16 per cent were university graduates. It was notable that 71 per cent of recipients were in their most productive working years, between twenty and forty-four years old (1996: 25, 27–8).

13 Data compiled by the Canadian Centre for Policy Alternatives show that more than a hundred of the plant shutdowns occurring in Ontario until June 1992 involved relocation of production outside of Canada, princi-

pally to the United States and, to some extent, Mexico (Healey 1993: 287–94). Since the North American Free Trade Agreement came into effect in 1994, the movement of Canadian firms to Mexico's duty free maquiladora zone has become more pronounced. The number of Canadian plants there is reported to have tripled, from 9 to 30 by 1998, offering employment to some 10,000 Mexicans (McKenna 1998a).

14 The 'what is a community' question is one of those perennial issues that crop up in social science investigation across numerous disciplines. We believe that if there is anything to be learned from this literature, it is that 'community,' as a concept, escapes any precise and rigorous definition that would engender widespread agreement (see Wilkinson 1986; Das Gupta 1996). Indeed, Hillery (1955) found some ninety-four different definitions of community back in the 1950s, and no doubt many more have since appeared. Das Gupta's extensive and more recent review of the literature has distinguished several main 'approaches' to the study of community, including the ecological, ethnographic, holistic, structural, functional, and typological approaches, as well as an approach which he broadly refers to as the 'conflict perspective' on community (see Das Gupta 1996: ch. 1). Similarly, 'what is rural' has been extensively debated, and is perhaps even more tricky since definitions here inevitably have policy consequences. Policy-makers frequently use a population-based definition, although as Bryden (1994) notes, there is no common definition across the OECD countries. Given the state of both concepts, we find it more useful to indicate to the reader the nature of our approach to the subject, and then proceed with other matters, rather than become tied up with a lengthy definitional discussion of community that will inevitably fail to satisfy.

15 See Anthony Fuller (1998) and his concept of the 'arena society' to conceptualize this development.

16 Information on the rural/urban distribution of Canada's population can be found in Statistics Canada (1991), Part B; Cat. No. 93–340.

17 The combined effect of trade liberalization via the Free Trade Agreement of 1989, a steep rise in the value of Canadian currency compared to the U.S. dollar (from around 72 cents to a peak of 88 cents between 1987 and 1991) and the deep recession of the early 1990s took a serious toll on the manufacturing sector. Published data compiled by the Canadian Labour Congress indicate that more than 400 plants closed between 1988 and June 1990 (see Barlow 1990: Appendix).

18 Few studies exist in the Canadian context, where this phenomenon has seen the construction of auto assembly and parts plants in what were,

until the 1980s, corn and potato fields adjacent to smaller towns and cities of southern Ontario. It has been Japanese and Japanese-American joint venture capital that has led the way here. Much of the highly urbanized meat-packing complex of the former Canada Packers has been dismantled, and new packing capacity has been created in smaller urban centres such as Guelph, Ontario, and more recently Brandon, Manitoba.

19 Wolfgang Sachs's critique in *Global Ecology* (1993) represents one of the most forceful arguments of late.

20 The literature on rural issues is rich and varied. For views on women (particularly farm women) in rural areas of Canada, see: Carbert 1995; Cohen 1985; Ghorayshi 1989; Keating and Munro 1988; Mackenzie 1995; Parr 1990; Shortall 1993; Smith 1992; Wiebe 1995. For Europe and the United States see: Brandth 1994; Fink 1992; Little 1994; Little and Austin 1996; McKinley Wright 1995; O'Hara 1994; Sachs 1996; van der Plas and Fonte 1994; Whatmore 1990; Whatmore, Marsden, and Lowe 1994. For gender and restructuring in rural areas see Fink 1998; Nelson and Smith 1999; Popaleni 1989; Redclift and Whatmore 1990.

3. Community Sketches, History, and Method

1 For a discussion of the data on internal migration in Canada, see Bollman (1992: ch. 1). A poll of Canadians in 1989 in both rural and urban locations indicates that the majority of those living in the urban core would prefer to move to a less urbanized area. This level of dissatisfaction with place of residence is much less prevalent among the rural population (14).

2 Is there in fact more community spirit in small-town and rural Canada? To the extent that an involvement in volunteer and community work indicates community spirit, data support the contention that there *is* more community spirit in these rural areas (see Bollman 1992: Fig. 29).

3 It is important to note that Statistics Canada data for specific communities refer to the characteristics of individual residents. This means that statistics for manufacturing employment refer to the number of residents in the community reporting manufacturing jobs, regardless of whether such employment is in that community, or in some other one. Thus, it is misleading to correlate Statistics Canada census data with the number of manufacturing jobs existing within a community.

4 The idea of a 'bedroom community' has to be considered with care since it tends to have class implications which overlook the forms of work that are available locally, while privileging those situated elsewhere. This may well be significant if such communities are seen to be providing a labour

force for high-wage manufacturing at some distance (whose workers can afford the commute), while overlooking the lower wage jobs which service those commuters, as well as local manufacturing jobs.

4. The New Rural Economy and the Shape of Restructuring

1 The dismantling of the Foreign Investment Review Agency (FIRA) by the Mulroney government served to confirm the new 'hands-off' policy of the Canadian federal government, as did their wholesale privatization of prominent public enterprise, including Petro Canada, which was much loathed by the private oil companies.

2 According to Biddle (1997), Boeing's switch to 'lean' production methods has played a major role in its $2.6 billion in expected losses in 1997. 'Boeing is now finding its doesn't have flexibility to find alternative sources for parts, largely as a result of cutting back on the number of its suppliers as part of its push toward "lean" manufacturing practices.' The Boeing case does challenge the view that 'lean' production is a rational strategy even if one restricts the criteria for judging its success to basic profit maximization in the short term! Aside from the disastrous effects it can have on employees, families, communities, and the social fabric of society more generally, to the extent that lean production strategies undermine such fundamentals of longer term corporate profitability as employee morale and loyalty, it can also be challenged on economic grounds.

3 This last corporate strategy as a response to the then impending Free Trade Agreement first became evident to one of the authors during his interviews with American fruit and vegetable processors during the late 1980s.

4 Data were obtained from various issues of *Scott's Directories*, a directory of manufacturing firms that has information on manufacturing establishments and employment in manufacturing organized by the *community* within which they reside. This community focus makes the directory particularly valuable for our purposes. A defect of the *Scott's Directory* is that it occasionally leaves out firms in a community which it reports in previous years, and which continue to operate in the community. In order to increase the accuracy of our data analysis, we have gone to considerable length to ascertain whether companies which do not appear in a given year have indeed closed down. In most cases this was done by checking subsequent years of the directory to confirm that the firm had indeed closed its plant. If a firm had been left out by mistake, we have

used data from the subsequent year of the directory regarding employment numbers. While the data reported contain some inaccuracies (as
most, if not all, data sets do) we have attempted to minimize these as
much as possible. We believe the trends we highlight give as good an
indication as any yet available concerning developments in small manufacturing communities in Ontario.

5 Calculated from *Scott's Directories* (1998).

6 More details about this firm and its metamorphosis into Maple Leaf Foods
in the 1990s can be found in Winson (1993: chs. 5 and 8).

7 Three of the largest occurred immediately after the agreement was signed.
These were the takeovers of Texaco Canada by Imperial Oil (Exxon),
Molson Breweries' takeover of O'Keefe Breweries, and Pacific Western
Airlines' takeover of Canadian Airlines.

8 This orientation is indicated in the company's annual reports for the early
1990s. For a discussion of the differences of the management style of
Canada Packers under its former owners, the McLean family, and its new
foreign owners, see Winson (1993: 195).

9 In the United States, Cargill's subsidiary Excel, together with IBP and
ConAgra, produces 82 per cent of the boxed meat. For further details on
Cargill, see Kneen (1990).

10 An interview by one of the authors with management of Ontario's largest
beef slaughter facility in 1994 further confirmed the impact of Cargill's
presence, and that what they felt were predatory pricing policies of this
American conglomerate had caused severe distress for other processors.

11 This discussion of the Westinghouse case borrows heavily from Leach and
Winson (1995).

12 New standards for organochlorine levels in pulp mill effluent were set to
take effect in January 1994 in an effort to prevent the formation of dioxins
and furans and their release into river ecosystems (see Madore 1992: 3).

13 An example related to one of the authors by a company technician
illustrates the change. In the sixties and seventies a 6 per cent concentration of mill effluent was killing trout fry in tests of the effluent for toxicity.
Now with the TMP process six out of ten trout fry are said to survive
forty-eight hours in a 100 per cent concentration of effluent (interview by
author, July 1997).

14 Interview with local union executive, July 1997. The labour-displacing
nature of TMP technology was also confirmed in an interview with a
representative of Abitibi Consolidated, June 1999.

15 At a nearby mill, the reduction of their bush crew had been even more
drastic over this time period (interview with International Woodworkers

of America representative, July 1997). This trend has been exacerbated because the use of TMP technology allows the company to buy more and more of its woodstock in the form of woodchips from the nearby Mallette lumber operation in Cochrane.

16 In 1975 the company had also argued that it should have the right to sign individual contracts with workers in each mill, because each mill had different cost structures. The union at that time was the Canadian Papermakers' Union, newly formed after a breakaway from the American-based International Union. The new union had little money and was in a weak position to strike. Nevertheless, the union believed the company's demand would fundamentally weaken workers bargaining rights in the mills, and dug its heals in for what would be a very long and bitter contest with Abitibi Price Company. Without a strike fund workers received virtually no strike pay for more than seven months. They eventually won the right to have all mills included in contract negotiations (*Enterprise*, 8 Oct. 1975; interviews with families of former mill workers, Iroquois Falls, July 1998).

17 Interview with the executive of local 90 of the Communication, Energy and Papermakers' Union, Iroquois Falls, July 1997, and interview with the regional representative of the CEP, June 1997.

18 Interview with the editor of *Enterprise*, 11 February 2000.

19 Workers at one of the company's older mills in Quebec had caved in to company pressure during the strike, and agreed to local contract negotiations. Workers at this mill were reportedly severed from the union, reducing its overall membership.

20 Interviews with local union executive, July 1997, and Abitibi Consolidated representative, Iroquois Falls, June 1999.

21 Interview with a manager in the high technology sector, Arnprior, 1998.

22 Interview with manager of another high technology firm, Arnprior, 1998.

23 The notion of 'good' wages is, of course, socially constructed, and varies among different societies. We refer to a wage that would be viewed as attractive to an individual with high school education, and perhaps some post-secondary education. It would allow one to aspire to own a vehicle, although perhaps not a late model one, and give access to comfortable rental accommodation and some of the accoutrements of a middle-class lifestyle. Such a wage would have to be at least twice the minimum wage, and perhaps a little more, to allow for the lifestyle suggested above. One's marital status, the job status of one's spouse, and the presence or absence of children are some of the key factors that considerably affect an individuals' material circumstances, of course.

24 As one of them said to us, 'merchants talk and say sales are right down. The community attitude is even different. It's very depressing for the whole community. Everyone's depressed because their friends and family are out of work. It's really bad for the whole community, not just for those people who were laid off' (interview, 1994).

25 For a discussion of the types of employer-employee relationships that small communities are thought to foster, see the classic study by David Lockwood (1975).

5. Skidding into the Contingent Work World

1 Statistics Canada has finally begun discussing the conservative biases inherent in the ways in which the federal government measures unemployment, a bias which we might speculate to be politically motivated in that unemployment rates appear artificially low. In a recent bulletin they note, 'using the one year reference period, the unemployment rate for individuals was 17.3% in 1997, [and] 28.2% for families. This translates into almost one in six people in the labour force who were unemployed at one point during the year, and more than one in four families with at least one member in the labour force that was affected.' See Statistics Canada, Daily, 6 September 2000.

2 For more details on these changes and their impacts, see CLC Policy Briefs, 'A Good Program in Bad Times: The Dismantling of Unemployment Insurance' (http:www.clc-ctc.com/policy/dis-ui.html).

3 Qualifying the category of self-employment to say that people are 'deemed' to be self-employed suggests that this is an extremely problematic category. Self-employment usually incorporates a broad range of occupations which includes such low-income occupations as industrial homeworker, tupperware seller, private child-care provider, seasonal vegetable seller, as well as a number of people working on short-term contracts.

4 For example, it excludes workers who have been out of work for less than or more than a prescribed period, and it excludes workers who have voluntarily resigned from their jobs. While this chapter was in preparation, the Globe and Mail (22 September 1999) reported that Statistics Canada is now tracking 'discouraged workers' on a systematic basis. Using their measure to include workers on the margins of the labour market, the unemployment rate for Canada in 1998 would have been 11.5 per cent instead of 8.3 per cent.

5 It is important to note that our category 'not working' indicates simply that the person considered him/herself to be unemployed at the time of

the interview, and does not indicate that he or she fulfilled the official criteria for being considered unemployed.

6. 'Forget All Your Dreams and Good Luck with Your Life': Lay-Off and the New Reality of Contingent Labour

1 While in the early 1990s approximately 90 per cent of newly unemployed workers qualified for benefits, by the end of the decade 'reforms' by the federal Liberal government had reduced this number to around 45 per cent.
2 It was fortunate that the community is blessed with three supermarkets, a large number for a town this size. The largest of these provided employment for some ten full-time and twenty-four part-time workers.
3 During a comprehensive three-hour tour of the mill operations in 1997, one of the authors was able to assess the gender composition of the production labour force. On the day shift at that time, less than 5 per cent of the workers were women. The few who were observed were working solely on the final packaging of newsprint rolls prior to their loading on rail cars for shipment to southern Canada and the United States.
4 In fact the member of the provincial legislature for the northeastern part of Ontario that includes the town of Iroquois Falls indicated it was his strong impression that northern youth who had left for the supposedly better opportunities of southern Ontario were deciding to migrate back to northern Ontario, for these reasons (interview, June 1997).

7. Economic Diversity, Sustainability, and Manufacturing Communities

1 Details on this firm are derived from an interview with company management in October 1999.
2 Interviews conducted in May 1997 and May–June 1998.
3 Details on the reduction of the workforce in the bush were provided by the regional union representative (July 1997). Holmes (1997: 20) notes that the switch to TMP technology in the mills he examined typically resulted in the shift in wood preparation for the mill from unionized labour to independent contractors. The increase in the use of wood chips from lumber mill operators has also had consequences for the size of the company's harvesting crew.
4 Interview with Abitibi Consolidated, Iroquois Falls, June 1997.
5 Again it is a testimony to the strength of the union, and we might even say farsightedness in this case, that it had bargained hard in contract negotiations in 1990 for a job-security package that obliged the company

to look at all available alternatives before laying off employees, including job reassignment, the exercise of 'bumping' provisions of their agreement, and early retirement (interview with CEP representatives, Iroquois Falls, December 1998).

6 We do not imply that there were no other factors here. The fact that the company had invested many millions of dollars in new pulping technology, and the continued existence of a number of harvestable trees within the confines of Abitibi's cutting licence, meant that the company was less likely to threaten to close the mill if the union refused to back down from its position. Employees at other Abitibi mills were more vulnerable to this threat, as the long strike of 1998 proved.

7 Talks with key informants during our fieldwork in the community led us to believe that the 1975 strike has become an important part of community memory. Indeed, some fear of this strike emerged in the long strike of 1998. This is perhaps not surprising given the length, acrimony, and hardship of the 1975 strike, and the significance of its victory over the long term. Some 20,000 workers in nine pulp-and-paper mill towns representing over 400,000 people were affected by the strike. In Iroquois Falls, total employee wages of $220,000 per week were lost for seven months, and without a strike fund the new union was unable to afford strike pay. Neither were workers getting unemployment insurance, according to newspaper reports, while the union accused the company of withholding employees' strike pay that was legally theirs. In the end many workers had to find work elsewhere to survive, and some never returned to the community (see *Enterprise*, various issues (1975)).

8 The Collective Agreement between Abitibi Price Inc. and the Communications, Energy & Papermakers' Union, Local 90, May 1st, 1993–April 30th, 1998 provided, in 1995, a wage scale that ranged from $18.50 per hour for the bottom job classification to $27.40 per hour for the top classification. This put wages in the mill close to the wages negotiated in what is usually considered the 'gold standard' for industrial workers (i.e. the collective agreements between the major auto companies and the Canadian Auto Workers).

9 Details of the 1975 strike were obtained from the *Enterprise* of Iroquois Falls, 1975, various issues.

10 The union reported good support from business people during the five-month strike in 1998, with many joining the picket line (interview with Local 90 representatives, December 1998).

11 For a good discussion of Polanyi's arguments on the salience of political structures in creating a market for labour in early industrial England, see Block and Somers's 'Beyond the Economistic Fallacy: The Holistic Social

Science of Karl Polanyi' (1984). More recent significant contributions of sociologists include Harrison White's 'Where Do Markets Come From?' (1981) and Mark Granovetter's 'Economic Action and Social Structure (1985).

12 These so-called careful logging practices involve the use of special machinery that attempts to replicate the practices of loggers before the 1940s, who used hand-operated bucksaws in the bush and horses to haul logs out. This is very different from the current practices of clear-cut logging, where everything in sight is cut to the ground. The new practice uses one operator on a logging machine that cuts one track for the machine several metres wide, and then selectively logs mature trees on each side of the machine's path, stacking the harvested trees behind it as it goes and leaving immature trees uncut on each side. It is believed that this method will cut the regeneration of the forest in half, from about 120 years to around 60 years. The latter figure is the time it has taken the black spruce forest to regenerate from the first cut early in the century using the less damaging technologies of horse-drawn sleighs and bucksaws.

The company hopes that outsiders will view this type of logging as more sustainable than clear-cut practices. It should be noted, however, that the company is not interested in a natural regeneration, but wishes a regenerated forest that is primarily evergreen species. To achieve this result it conducts an aerial herbicide spray program over regenerating areas of forest to kill hardwood species (interviews with Abitibi Consolidated forestry employees, July 1997). The company's argument that it is committed to 'careful logging' practices is also tempered by the fact that it has recently pressed the provincial government to open up new areas of fragile forest in the northern reaches of its domain for exploitation, an area that extends up towards the tree line.

13 Interview in July 1997.

14 Information about the most recent merger was gathered from an interview with key informants in the community (11 Feb. 2000; 9 July 2001), and from the *Globe and Mail*, 10, 11 Feb. 2000: B1.

15 Interview in July 1997.

16 This discussion is based on interviews with local business owners in December 1998.

17 Details about forest land harvested and replanted by province can be obtained from the Statistics Canada on-line database CANSIM (http://www.statcan.ca:80/english/Pgdb/Land/Environment/envir03.h tm).

18 The motivational force of the British Columbia example was suggested to the author during an interview with Abitibi management personnel (June 1997).

19 We refer here specifically to the federal government's Model Forests program over the last few years, in which Abitibi Consolidated and the community of Iroquois Falls have participated. Orchestrated largely by experts with training in the biophysical sciences, this program has achieved some interesting advances in understanding and implementing more sustainable harvesting techniques, but has given relatively little attention to the socioeconomic developments that today are undermining the forestry communities themselves (see http//mf.ncr.forestry.ca/).

20 A knowledgeable key informant told us that overnight stays in Cochrane had risen dramatically with the town's efforts to promote winter tourism, from around 200 overnight stays in the early 1990s to 5000 overnight stays by 1995. As one informant involved in the hospitality industry in Iroquois Falls told us, 'in Cochrane there are now some 300 rooms [to accommodate guests] but here we have 60 and can't fill them' (interviews, June 1998).

21 Interview with key informant who had attended a council meeting in early 2000.

8. Some Concluding Thoughts

1 At least this is true for Ontario, but this is, of course, the province with most of the nation's high technology employers.

2 Nelson and Smith (1999: 184) write that their respondents rarely spoke in a collective voice about possibilities for improving their work lives, or their lives more generally. Rather, 'they openly express attitudes of resentment toward the way they believe the government acts – too intrusive, too much self-interest on the part of politicians, too many broken promises, and too much waste and misspending. [They] see virtue in ... hard work and self-sufficiency. [They] strive to distinguish themselves from others who appear to work less hard and be less self-sufficient' (184). This finding strongly resonates with our experience with many, though not all, laid-off plant workers in the Wellington County communities we studied.

3 Not that this threat is entirely absent, however, especially when the physical plant has been allowed to run down considerably and productivity is relatively low. In these cases, the threat of permanent shutdown is considerably more real, as the experience of the 1998 Abitibi strike demonstrated. Workers at one of its older mills in Quebec felt the threat of closure was indeed a grave one, and chose to sign a separate agreement with the company, breaking union solidarity in doing so.

4 As in many areas, Sweden has been at the forefront of such initiatives, and their policies designed to retain women in northern communities are certainly worth looking at.

Glossary

Casualization of labour   Process by which employment becomes less entrenched in longer-term secure forms of tenure and increasingly subject to the variations in market conditions affecting the employer, without the protection from unpaid lay-offs afforded by unions, and increasingly without assistance from the state as well.

Checkered pattern of employment   Increasingly common form of employment characterized by episodes of job holding interspersed with periods of unemployment, sometimes of considerable length.

Contingent work   Contrasted in the book with stable work; sometimes referred to as 'non-standard' work, it is characterized by considerable insecurity of tenure, typically non-union employment without the protections often afforded by unions against arbitrary lay-off, and usually with minimal or non-existent benefit package associated with the job. Increasingly prevalent form of work since the 1980s in the United States and Canada.

Contingent work world   As used in the book, this term refers to the wider situation faced by workers and their families through engagement in contingent forms of employment. Used in contrast to labour in the stable work world (see below), the contingent work world entails a host of usually disadvantageous situations for employees that are the by-product of lack of job security and low wages, including work schedules that are disruptive of relationships with family and friends, excessive working hours to make up for low hourly pay, difficulty in planning for the future because of the short time frame of employment, the undermining of commitment and loyalty to the job, as well as the possibility of forming durable social relationships.

Downsizing   A cost-cutting measure increasingly employed by corporations adopting lean production methods (see below) that essentially entails reductions to the workforce and typically the collapsing of job responsibilities onto the remaining employees.

Globalization   An imprecise term that has come into fashion to capture, among other things, the increasing vulnerability of individuals and communities to economic forces transcending regions and nations.

Greenfield sites   Refers to the relocation of manufacturing firms in recent years away from urban cores to rural areas where wages are typically lower, as are rates of unionization, prices for land, and local taxes. Also favoured by corporations because of the strong work ethic typically associated with agrarian settings.

Just in time production (JIT)   First used in the Japanese automobile assembly industry it is an inventory management system in which components are delivered to customers, and where materials and components are purchased for the next stage of production immediately before they are needed. Used to cut costs associated with keeping large inventories.

Lean production methods   A variety of management practices, found in different combinations in different countries and different corporations, designed to reduce costs and increase profitability. Typically associated with lean production are such practices as transferring part of the production process to lower cost firms (outsourcing), just in time inventory management, employment of work teams on the job, and the use of total quality management (TQM) programs. These methods are typically associated with (often dramatic) reductions in jobs in corporations employing lean production, and for this reason and also for the way in which work is reorganized lean production techniques are often opposed by labour movements. This resistance is sometimes successful.

'Mom' shifts   Work schedules organized by companies to take advantage of the labour of mothers with children.

Predatory capitalism   A term associated with the new practices of capitalist firms that have come into practice by the 1980s, including lean production practices entailing the contracting out of work to non-union firms, creation of two-tiered wage systems within firms whereby more recently hired workers receive considerably lower wages, increased use of part-time contract labour with little or no job security, and in general the reversion to labour practices not seen since earlier in the twentieth century.

Stable work world   This term is used to refer to employment situations and associated family and community life that is made possible with stable, long term employment at a 'living wage' and typically with a number of employment benefits as well. Such employment has historically been the outcome of trade union struggles in the early decades of the twentieth century, and is usually, but not always, protected by labour contracts negotiated by trades and public sector unions.

Sustainability   A term that has come into widespread use in the 1990s and around which there is much discussion as to how it can be utilized as a meaningful concept. Alex Farrell and Maureen Hart (2001) note that there are two general conceptions of sustainability which are sometimes in conflict. One view tends to focus more on biophysical factors regarding environmental degradation and limits to the Earth's carrying capacity. Another popular conception of sustainability focuses more on balancing social, economic, and ecological goals and thereby meeting a broad range of human needs. The focus on resource limits here is largely missing. Both views, however, are concerned with issues of equity, within and between generations. The relationship between the predominantly socioeconomic and the biophysical views of sustainability are increasingly recognized as important and are the subject of much new research.

References

Articles and Books

Adams, Michael. 1999. 'If Times Are So Good, Why Do We Feel So Bad?' *Globe and Mail*, 27 December, A1.

Allen, S., and C. Wolkowitz. 1987. *Homeworking: Myths and Realities*. Basingstoke: Macmillan.

Andrews, Edmund L. 1996. 'Don't Go Away Mad, Just Go Away.' *New York Times*, 13 Feb., D1, D6.

Apostle, Richard, and Gene Barrett. 1992. *Emptying Their Nets: Small Capital and Rural Industrialization in the Nova Scotia Fishing Industry*. Toronto: University of Toronto Press.

Armstrong, P. 1996. 'The Feminization of the Labour Force: Harmonizing Down in a Global Economy.' In I. Bakker (ed.), *Rethinking Restructuring: Gender and Change in Canada*, 29–54. Toronto: University of Toronto Press.

Aronowitz, Stanley, and William DiFazio. 1994. *The Jobless Future: Sci-tech and the Dogma of Work*. Minneapolis: University of Minnesota Press.

Arrighi, G. 1999. 'Globalization and Historical Macrosociology.' In J. Abu-Lughod (ed.), *Sociology for the Twenty-First Century: Continuities and Cutting Edges*. Chicago: University of Chicago Press.

Ashton, Peter G., and James B. Pickens. 1995. 'Employment Diversity and Economic Performance in Small Resource-Dependent Communities near Western National Forests.' *Society and Natural Resources* 8: 231–41.

Attaran, Mohsen, and Martin Zwick. 1987. 'The Effect of Industrial Diversification on Employment and Income: A Case Study.' *Quarterly Review of Economics and Business* 27 (4): 38–54.

Bagguley, P., Jane Mark-Lawson, Dan Shapiro, John Urry, Sylvia Walby, and Alan Warde. 1990. *Restructuring: Place, Class, and Gender*. London: Sage.

Baker, Stephen, Jan Dobrznski, and Michael Schroder. 1992. 'Westinghouse: More Pain Ahead.' *Business Week*, 7 December.

Baldwin, John R., and Guy Gellatly. 1998. *Are There High-Tech Industries or only High-Tech Firms? Evidence from New Technology-Based Firms*. Research Paper Series, Statistics Canada Analytical Studies Branch No. 120. Ottawa: Statistics Canada.

Baran, Paul, and Paul Sweezy. 1966. *Monopoly Capital*. New York: Monthly Review Press.

Barber, P.G. 2002. 'Militant Particularism and Cultural Struggles as Cape Breton Burns Again.' In W. Lem, and B. Leach, eds., *Culture, Economy, Power: Anthropology as Critique, Anthropology as Praxis*. Albany: SUNY Press.

Barlow, Maude. 1990. *Parcel of Rogues: How Free Trade Is Failing Canada*. Toronto: Key Porter.

Barrett, Stanley. 1994. *Paradise*. Toronto: University of Toronto Press.

Bell, Colin, and Howard Newby. 1972. *Community Studies: An Introduction to the Sociology of the Local Community*. New York: Praeger.

Belous, Richard S. 1989. *The Contingent Economy: The Growth of the Temporary, Part-time and Subcontracted Workforce*. Washington: National Planning Association.

Beneria, L., and M. Roldan. 1987. *The Crossroads of Class and Gender: Industrial Homework, Subcontracting and Household Dynamics in Mexico City*. Chicago: University of Chicago Press.

Berck, Peter, Diana Burton, George Goldman, and Jacqueline Geoghegan. 1992. 'Instability in Forestry and Forestry Communities.' *Journal of Business Administration* 20 (1–2): 314–38.

Betcherman, Gordon, and Rene Morissette. 1994. 'Recent Youth Labour Market Experiences in Canada.' Ottawa: Statistics Canada, Analytical Studies Branch, Study no. 63.

Biddle, Frederic M. 1997. 'Boeing Steers Back into Boom-Bust Cycle.' *Globe and Mail*, 24 October (reprinted from *Wall Street Journal*).

Block, Fred, and Margaret Somers. 1984. 'Beyond the Economistic Fallacy: The Holistic Social Science of Karl Polanyi,' in Theda Skocpol, ed., *Vision and Method in Historical Sociology*. Cambridge: Cambridge University Press.

Bloomfield, Gerald T. 1992. *The Railway Life-Cycle in Ontario*. Guelph: Department of Geography, University of Guelph.

Bloomfield, Gerald T., and Elizabeth Bloomfield. 1989a. *The Hum of Industry: Millers, Manufacturers and Artisans of Wellington County, 1871*. Guelph: Department of Geography, University of Guelph.

– 1989b. *Industrial Leaders: The Largest Manufacturing Firms of Ontario in 1871*. Guelph: Department of Geography, University of Guelph.

- 1990. *Patterns of Canadian Industry in 1871: An Overview Based on the Census of Canada*. Guelph: Department of Geography, University of Guelph.
- 1992. *Industry in Ontario Counties, 1871: A Preliminary Atlas*. Report No. 14 Guelph: Department of Geography, University of Guelph.
Bluestone, B., and B. Harrison. 1982. *The Deindustrialization of America: Plant Closings, Community Abandonment, and the Dismantling of Basic Industries*. New York: Basic Books.
- 1988. *The Great U-Turn: Corporate Restructuring and the Polarizing of America*. New York: Basic.
Bolles, L. (1977) 'Kitchens Hit by Priorities.' In J. Nash and M.P. Fernandez Kelly (eds.), *Women, Men and the International Division of Labor*, 138–60. Albany: SUNY Press.
Bollman, Ray D. (ed.). 1992. *Rural and Small Town Canada*. Toronto: Thompson Educational Publishing.
Boris, E. 1994. *Home to Work: Motherhood and the Politics of Industrial Homework in the United States*. Cambridge: Cambridge University Press.
Boris E., and E. Prugl. 1996. *Homeworkers in Global Perspective: Invisible No More*. New York: Routledge.
Bowles, Roy T. 1982. *Little Communities and Big Industries: Studies in the Social Impact of Canadian Resource Extraction*. Toronto: Butterworths.
Bowles, Samuel, and Herbert Gintis. 1976. *Schooling in Capitalist America*. New York: Basic Books.
Brandth, B. 1994. 'Changing Femininity: The Social Construction of Women Farmers in Norway.' *Sociologia Ruralis* 32 (2–3): 127–49.
Bray, Nicholas. 1998. 'Asian Crisis Is Rippling over to Europe.' *Wall Street Journal*, reprinted in *Globe and Mail*, 8 July, B11.
Bryden, J. (ed.) 1994. 'Introduction.' *Towards Sustainable Rural Communities: The Guelph Seminar Series*. Guelph: University School of Rural Planning and Development.
Burawoy, M. 1985. *The Politics of Production*. London: Polity Press.
Burke, M., and John Shields. 1999. *The Job Poor Recovery: Social Cohesion and the Canadian Labour Market*. Toronto: Ryerson University, Research Report of the Ryerson Social Reporting Network. www.ryerson.ca/vacollections/research/ors/research/job.html
Burman, Patrick. 1988. *Killing Time, Losing Ground: Experiences of Unemployment*. Toronto: Thompson Educational Publishing.
Cameron, Duncan. 1991. 'Beyond the Market and the State: How Can We Do Better?' In D. Drache and M. Gertler (eds.), *The New Era of Global Competition: State Policy and Market Power*. Montreal: McGill-Queen's University Press.

Canadian Labour Congress. 1998. 'Impacts of Free Trade on Canadian
    Workers.' In *CLC-NAFTA-The Social Dimensions of North American Economic
    Integration 2*. File:///A1/impactoncaworkers.htm.
Carbert, L. 1995. *Agrarian Feminism*. Toronto: University of Toronto Press.
Chossudovsky, Michel. 1996. *The Globalization of Poverty: Impacts of IMF and
    World Bank Reforms*. Atlantic Highlands, NJ: Zed Books.
Christensen, K. 1987. 'Women and Contingent Work.' *Social Policy* 17 (4):
    15–18.
CLC Policy Briefs. 'A Good Program in Bad Times: The Dismantling of
    Unemployment Insurance.' http: www.clc-ctc.com/policy/dis-vi.html.
Cohen, M. 1985. 'The Decline of Women in Canadian Dairying.' In A.
    Prentice and S. Trofimenkoff (eds.), *The Neglected Majority*. Toronto:
    McClelland and Stewart.
– 1988. *Women's Work, Markets, and Economic Development in Nineteenth-
    Century Ontario*. Toronto: University of Toronto Press.
Connelly, Patricia M., and Martha MacDonald. 1983. 'Women's Work:
    Domestic and Wage Labour in a Nova Scotia Community.' *Studies in
    Political Economy* 10 (Winter): 45–72.
Conroy, Michael E. 1974. 'Alternative Strategies for Regional Industrial
    Diversification.' *Journal of Regional Science* 14 (1): 31–46.
Cook, Peter. 1998. 'An Asian Headache, and More.' *Globe and Mail*, 8 July, B2.
Corak, M. 1993. *The Duration of Unemployment during Boom and Bust*. Statistics
    Canada, Analytical Studies Branch, No. 56. Ottawa: Statistics Canada.
Corman, J., M. Luxton, D. Livingstone, and W. Seccombe. 1993. *Recasting Steel
    Labour: The Stelco Story*. Toronto: Garamond.
Creed, G., and B. Ching 1997. 'Recognizing Rusticity: Identity and the Power
    of Place.' In Ching and Creed, *Knowing Your Place: Rural Identity and
    Cultural Hierarchy*. New York: Routledge.
Crosby, P.A. 1874. *Lovell's Gazetteer of British North America*. Montreal: Lovell.
Daily Bread Food Bank. 1996. *Who Goes Hungry? A Profile of Food Recipients in
    the GTA Served by Member Agencies of the Daily Bread Food Bank*. Toronto:
    Daily Bread Food Bank.
D'Amato, Luisa. 1996. 'Communities Irreversibly Hurt When Big Firms Shut,
    Study Finds.' *Kitchener-Waterloo Record*, 9 April, 1.
Das Gupta, Satadal (ed.). 1996. *The Community in Canada: Rural and Urban*.
    New York: University Press of America.
Davis, Anthony. 1991. *Dire Straits: The Dilemmas of a Fishery. The Case of Digby
    Neck and the Islands*. St John's: Institute of Social and Economic Research.
Douglas, D., and S. Chadwick. 2000. 'Towards more Effective Economic
    Development in Rural Ontario.' University School of Rural Planning and
    Development, University of Guelph.

'Do We Need an Industrial Policy?' 1985. *Harpers* 270: 35–48.

Drache, Daniel. 1991. 'The Systematic Search for Flexibility: National Competitiveness and New Work Relations.' In Daniel Drache and Meric S. Gertler (eds.), *The New Era of Global Competition: State Policy and Market Power*, 249–69. Montreal: McGill-Queen's University Press.

– 1995. 'Celebrating Innis: The Man, the Legacy and Our Future.' In Harold A. Innis, *Staples, Markets, and Cultural Change*. Montreal: McGill-Queen's University Press.

Drache, Daniel, and Wallace Clement. 1985. *New Practical Guide to Canadian Political Economy*. Toronto: Lorimer.

Drohan, Madelaine. 2000. 'Governments Scared of What Didn't Happen in Seattle.' *Globe and Mail*, 23 February, B2.

Dunk, T. 2002. 'Bicentrism, Culture, and the Political-Economy of Socio-Cultural Anthropology in English Canada.' In W. Lem and B. Leach (eds.), *Culture, Economy, Power: Anthropology as Critique, Anthropology as Praxis*. Albany: State University of New York Press.

Economic Council of Canada. 1990. *Good Jobs, Bad Jobs: Employment in the Service Economy*. Ottawa: Supply and Services Canada.

– 1991. *Employment in the Service Economy*. Ottawa: Supply and Services Canada.

Edwards, R. 1979. *Contested Terrain: The Transformation of the Workplace in the Twentieth Century*. London: Heinemann.

Elliot, Larry, and Dan Atkinson. 1998. *The Age of Insecurity*. London: Verso.

Elson, D., and R. Pearson. 1981. 'Nimble Fingers Make Cheap Workers.' *Feminist Review* (7): 87–107.

Fairley, B., C. Leys, and J. Sacouman (eds.). 1990. *Restructuring and Resistance: Perspectives from Atlantic Canada*. Toronto: Garamond.

Farrell, Alex, and Maureen Hart. 2001. 'What Does Sustainability Really Mean?' In R. Scott Frey (ed.), *The Environment and Society: A Reader*. Boston: Allyn and Bacon.

Felt, L., and P. Sinclair. 1995. *Living on the Edge: The Great Northern Peninsula of Newfoundland*. St John's: Institute for Social and Economic Research.

Finance Canada. 1998. *News Release: Government Announces First Budget Surplus in 28 Years*. Ottawa: Government of Canada, 14 October.

Fink, D. 1992. *Agrarian Women: Wives and Mothers in Rural Nebraska, 1880–1940*. Chapel Hill: University of North Carolina Press.

– 1998. *Cutting into the Meatpacking Line: Workers and Change in the Rural Midwest*. Chapel Hill: University of North Carolina Press.

– 2000. 'Keynote Speech Presented at Workshop on Race, Class and Gender.' Vancouver, B.C., 20 January.

Fitchen, Janet. 1991. *Endangered Spaces, Enduring Places: Change, Identity and Survival in Rural America*. Boulder, CO: Westview.

Francis, Diane. 1993. *A Matter of Survival: Canada in the 21st Century.* Toronto: Key Porter.

Friedmann, H. 1993. 'New Wines, New Bottles: Regulation of Capital on a World Scale.' In J. Jensen, R. Mahon, and M. Bienefeld (eds.), *Production, Space, Identity: Political Economy Faces the 21st Century.* Toronto: Canadian Scholars' Press.

Fuller, Anthony. 1998. 'Changing Agricultural, Economic and Social Patterns in the Ontario Countryside.' In M.J. Trouton and Gordon Nelson (eds.), *The Countryside in Ontario.* Waterloo: Heritage Resources Centre (An Environment Reprint).

Gardiner, Paddy. 1996. *Fifty Years in the Prior: An Historic Look Back at Boeing Canada, Arnprior Canada.* Arnprior, ON: Boeing Canada.

Gaventa, John. 1990. 'From the Mountains to the Maquiladoras: A Case Study of Capital Flight and Its Impact on Workers.' In John Gaventa, Barbara Ellen Smith, and Alex Willingham (eds.), *Communities in Economic Crisis: Appalachia and the South,* 85–95. Philadelphia: Temple University Press.

– 1980. *Power and Powerlessness: Quiescence and Rebellion in an Appalachian Valley.* Urbana: University of Illinois Press.

Gaventa, J., B.E. Smith, and A. Willingham (eds.) 1990. *Communities in Economic Crisis: Appalachia and the South.* Philadelphia: Temple University Press.

Gera, S. 1991. *Canadian Unemployment–Lessons from the 80s and Challenges for the 90s: A Compendium.* Ottawa: Economic Council of Canada.

Ghorayshi, P. 1989. 'The Indispensable Nature of Wives' Work for the Farm Family Enterprise.' *Canadian Review of Sociology and Anthropology,* 26 (4): 571–95.

Globe and Mail. 1998. 'Japan's Slide into Recession Casts Large Shadow.' *Globe and Mail,* 13 June, A16.

Gorz, Andre. 1982. *Farewell to the Working Class.* London: Pluto Press.

Granovetter, M. 1985. 'Economic Action and Social Structure: The Problem of Embeddedness.' *American Journal of Sociology,* 91: 481–510.

Grey, Mark A. 1998. 'Meat Packing in StormLake, Iowa: A Community in Transition,' in Kendall Thu and Paul Durrenberger (eds.), *Pigs, Profits and Rural Communities.* Albany: State University of New York Press.

Habermas, Jürgen. 1989. *The New Conservatism.* Cambridge, Mass.: MIT Press.

Halfacree, K.H. 1993. 'Locality and Social Representation: Space, Discourse and Alternative Definitions of the Rural.' *Journal of Rural Studies* 9 (1): 23–37.

Hansen, Philip, and Alicja Muszynski. 1990. 'Crisis in Rural Life and Crisis in Thinking: Directions for Critical Research.' *Canadian Review of Sociology and Anthropology* 27 (1): 1–22.

Hardy, Quentin. 1998. 'Motorola Ekes out Operating Profit: Asia Woes May Last a While, CEO Says.' *Wall Street Journal,* reprinted in *Globe and Mail,* 8 July, B11.

Harvey, D. 1989. *The Condition of Postmodernity.* Oxford: Blackwell.

Haskell, Benjamin, Bryan Norton, and Robert Costanza. 1992. 'What Is Ecosystem Health and Why Should We Worry about It?' In R. Costanza, B. Norton, and B. Haskell (eds.), *Ecosystem Health: New Goals for Environmental Management.* Washington DC: Island Press.

Hathaway, Dale A. 1993. *Can Workers Have a Voice?* University Park: Pennsylvania State University Press.

Healey, T. 1993. 'Selected Plant Closures and Production Relocations: January 1989–June 1992, Ontario.' In D. Cameron and M. Watkins (eds.), *Canada under Free Trade.* Toronto: James Lorimer.

Heery, Edmund, and John Salmon. 2000. 'The Insecurity Thesis.' In Edmund Heery and John Salmon, (eds.), *The Insecure Workforce.* London: Routledge.

Hillery, George. A. 1955. 'Definitions of Community: Areas of Agreement.' *Rural Sociology* 20: 111–23.

Himelfarb, Alex. 1982. 'The Social Characteristics of One Industry Towns in Ontario.' In R.T. Bowles (ed.), *Little Communities and Big Industries: Studies in the Social Impact of Canadian Resource Extraction.* Toronto: Butterworths.

History of Harriston, 1878–1978. 1978. Mildmay, ON: Book Committee.

Hodge, Gerald, and Mohammad A. Qadeer. 1983. *Town and Villages in Canada: The Importance of Being Unimportant.* Toronto: Butterworths.

Hoggart, K. 1990. 'Let's Do Away with Rural.' *Journal of Rural Studies* 6 (3): 245–57.

Holmes, J. 1997. 'In Search of Competitive Efficiency: Labour Process Flexibility in Canadian Newsprint Mills.' *Canadian Geographer* 41 (1): 7–25.

Howard, Ross. 1998. 'Despair Spreads as Town's Jobs Die.' *Globe and Mail,* 12 June, A1.

Howland, M. 1988. *Plant Closings and Worker Displacement: The Regional Issues.* Kalamazoo, MI: W.I. Upjohn Institute for Employment Research.

Hughes, Everett C. 1963. *French Canada in Transition.* Chicago: University of Chicago Press.

Ip, Greg. 1996. 'The Great Wage Divide.' *Globe and Mail,* 26 October, Section B.

Ireland, Gisele. 1983. *Farmer Takes a Wife: A Study.* Chelsey, ON: Concerned Farm Women.

Jackson, Andrew. 1993. 'Manufacturing.' In Duncan Cameron and Mel Watkins (eds.), *Canada Under Free Trade.* Toronto: James Lorimer.

Jackson, C., and R. Pearson (eds.). 1998. *Feminist Visions of Development.* London: Routledge.

Jahoda, M. 1982. *Employment and Unemployment: A Social-Psychological Analysis*. Cambridge: Cambridge University Press.

Johnson, Leo A. 1971. 'Land Policy, Population Growth and Social Structure in the Home District.' *Ontario History* 62 (March): 41–60.

– 1973. *History of the County of Ontario*. Whitby, ON: The Corporation of the County of Ontario.

Jones, R.L. 1946. *History of Agriculture in Ontario, 1613–1880*. Toronto: University of Toronto Press.

Kates, N., B.S. Greiff, and D.Q. Hagen. 1990. *The Psycho-Social Impact of Job Loss*. Washington: American Psychiatric Press.

Kaufman, M. 1985. *Jamaica under Manley: Dilemmas of Socialism and Democracy*. Toronto: Between the Lines.

Keating, N., and B. Monro. 1988. 'Farm Women / Farm Work.' *Sex Roles* 19 (3/4): 155–68.

Kenney, Martin, and Richard Florida. 1993. *Beyond Mass Production: The Japanese System and Its Transfer to the United States*. New York: Oxford University Press.

Kilborn, Peter T. 1995. 'In New Work World, Employers Call all the Shots.' *New York Times*, 3 July, A1.

Kingsolver, A. 1998. 'Introduction.' In A. Kingsolver (ed.), *More Than Class: Studying Power in U.S. Workplaces*. Albany: State University of New York Press.

Kneen, Brewster. 1990. *Trading Up: How Cargill, the World's Largest Grain Trading Company, Is Changing Canadian Agriculture*. Toronto: NC Press.

Koch, Agnes, and John Gartrell. 1992. '"Keep Jobs in the Kootenays": Coping with Closure in British Columbia.' In C. Neil, M. Tykklainen, and John Bradbury (eds.), *Coping with Closure: An International Comparison of Mine Town Experience*, 208–4. London: Routledge.

Kolko, Joyce. 1988. *Restructuring the World Economy*. New York: Pantheon Books.

Kopinak, Kathryn. 1996. *Desert Capitalism: Maquiladoras in North America's Western Industrial Corridor*. Tuscon: University of Arizona Press.

Korten, David C. 1996. *When Corporations Rule the World*. London: Earthscan Publications.

Krahn, H., and G. Lowe. 1998. *Work, Industry and Canadian Society*. Toronto: Nelson.

Lavoie, Leo. 1984. *The Arnprior Story*. Arnprior, ON: Arnprior and District Historical Society.

Laxer, Gordon. 1995. 'Social Solidarity, Democracy and Global Capitalism.' *Canadian Review of Sociology and Anthropology* 32 (3): 287–314.

Leach, Belinda. 1993. 'Flexible Work, Precarious Future: Some Lessons from the Canadian Clothing Industry.' *Canadian Review of Sociology and Anthropology* 20 (1): 64–82.

– 1996. 'Behind Closed Doors: Homework Policy and Lost Possibilities for Change.' In I. Bakker (ed.), *Rethinking Restructuring: Gender and Change in Canada*. Toronto: University of Toronto Press.

– 1998. 'Industrial Homework, Economic Restructuring and the Meaning of Work.' *Labour/Le Travail* 41: 97–115.

– 1999. 'Transforming Rural Livelihoods: Gender, Work and Restructuring in Three Ontario Communities.' In S. Neysmith (ed.), *Restructuring Caring Labour: Discourse, State Practice and Everyday Life*, 209–25. Toronto: University of Toronto Press.

Leach, Belinda, and Anthony Winson. 1995. 'Bringing Globalization "Down to Earth": Restructuring and Labour in Rural Communities.' *Canadian Review of Sociology and Anthropology* 32 (3): 341–64.

– 1999. 'Rural Retreat: The Social Impact of Restructuring in Three Ontario Communities.' In David B. Knight and Alan E. Joseph (eds.), *Restructuring Societies: Insights from the Social Sciences*. Ottawa: Carleton University Press.

Levine, Donald 1995. *Visions of the Sociological Tradition*. Chicago: University of Chicago Press.

Lim, L. 1985. *Women Workers in Multinational Enterprises in Developing Countries*. Geneva: International Labour Organization.

Lipovenko, Dorothy, 1997. 'Young Men Stuck in Low-Paying Jobs.' *Globe and Mail*, 17 September, Section A.

Little, J. 1994. 'Gender Relations and the Rural Labour Process.' In S. Whatmore, T. Marsden, and P. Lowe (eds.), *Gender and Rurality*, 11–30. London: David Fulton.

Little, J., and P. Austin. 1996. 'Women and the Rural Idyll.' *Journal of Rural Studies* 12, 12 (2): 101–11.

Lobao, Linda, Jamie Rulli, and Lawrence A. Brown. 1999. 'Macrolevel Theory and Local-Level Inequality: Industrial Structure, Institutional Arrangements, and the Political Economy of Redistribution, 1970 and 1990.' *Annals of the Association of American Geographers* 89 (4): 571–601.

Lockwood, David. 1975. 'Sources in Variation in Working-Class Images of Society.' In Martin Bulmer (ed.), *Working Class Images of Society*. London: Routledge & Kegan Paul.

Lowe, Graham S. 2000. *The Quality of Work: A People-Centred Agenda*. Toronto: Oxford University Press.

Lucas, Rex. 1971. *Minetown, Milltown, Railtown: Life in Canadian Communities of Single Industry*. Toronto: University of Toronto Press.

Machlis, Gary E., and Jo Ellen Force. 1988. 'Community Stability and Timber-Dependent Communities.' *Rural Sociology* 53 (2): 220–34.

Mackenzie, F. 1995. 'Is Where I Sit, Where I Stand? The Ontario Farm Women's Network, Politics and Difference.' *Journal of Rural Studies* 10 (2): 101–15.

MacKenzie, R.B. 1985. *Competing Visions: The Political Conflict over Americas Economic Future.* Washington: Cato Institute.

Mackenzie, Suzanne, and Glen Norcliffe. 1997. 'Restructuring the Canadian Newsprint Industry.' *Canadian Geographer* 41 (1): 2–6.

Madore, Odette. 1992. *The Pulp and Paper Industry: The Impact of the New Federal Environmental Regulations.* Ottawa: Library of Parliament, Research Branch.

Mahon, R. 1993. 'The "New" Canadian Political Economy Revisited: Production, Space, Identity.' In J. Jensen, R. Mahon and M. Bienefeld (eds.), *Production, Space, Identity: Political Economy Faces the 21ˢᵗ Century.* Toronto: Canadian Scholars' Press.

Malizia, Emil K., and Shanzi Ke. 1993. 'The Influence of Economic Diversity on Unemployment and Stability.' *Journal of Regional Science* 33 (2): 221–35.

Mander, J. 1996. 'Facing the Rising Tide.' In Mander and E. Goldsmith (eds.), *The Case against the Global Economy and for a Turn toward the Local.* San Francisco: Sierra Club Books.

Mander J., and E. Goldsmith (eds.). 1996. *The Case against the Global Economy and for a Turn toward the Local.* San Francisco: Sierra Club Books.

Mantoux, Paul. 1961. *The Industrial Revolution in the 18th Century.* London: Jonathan Cape.

Maple Leaf. 1991. *Maple Leaf Annual Report.*

Marchak, Patricia. 1983. *Green Gold: The Forest Industry in British Columbia.* Vancouver: University of British Columbia Press.

– 1991. *The Integrated Circus: The New Right and the Restructuring of Global Markets.* Montreal: McGill-Queen's University Press.

Marsden, Terry, Philip Lowe, and Sarah Whatmore. 1990. *Rural Restructuring: Global Processes and Their Responses.* London: David Fulton Publishers.

Marshall, Jason. 1998. 'Boeing Hot Topic at Chamber Meeting.' *Arnprior Chronicle-Guide,* 10 January 1998.

Massey, D. 1994. *Space, Place and Gender.* London: Polity Press.

Mawhiney, A., and J. Pitblado. 1999. *Boom Town Blues: Elliot Lake, Collapse and Revival in a Single-Industry Community.* Toronto: Dundurn Press.

McCallum, John. 1980. *Unequal Beginnings: Agriculture and Economic Development in Quebec and Ontario until 1870.* Toronto: University of Toronto Press.

McCarthy, Shawn. 1997. 'Anxious Workers Await Decision on Helicopters.' *Globe and Mail*, 22 December, A6.

McDowell, D., and D. Massey. 1984. 'A Woman's Place?' In D. Massey and J. Allen (eds.), *Geography Matters!* 128–47. Cambridge: Cambridge University Press.

McKenna, Barrie. 1998a. 'More Firms Flock to Mexico.' *Globe and Mail*, 8 July, A1.

– 1998b. 'Japan's Slump Hard on Canadian Firms.' *Globe and Mail*, 29 July, B9.

McKenzie, R.B. 1985. *Competing Visions: The Political Conflict over America's Economic Future.* Washington: Cato Institute.

McKinley Wright, M. 1995. '"I Never Did any Fieldwork, but I Milked an Awful Lot of Cows!" Using Rural Women's Experience to Reconceptualize Models of Work.' *Gender and Society* 9 (2): 216–35.

McQuaig, Linda. 1995. *Shooting the Hippo: Death by Deficit and Other Canadian Myths.* Toronto: Viking.

Menzies, Heather. 1996. *Whose Brave New World? The Information Highway and the New Economy.* Toronto: Between the Lines.

Milner, Brian. 1998. 'GM, UAW Playing Game of Chicken.' *Globe and Mail*, 18 July, B1.

Miner, Horace. 1963. *St. Denis: A French Canadian Community.* Chicago: Phoenix Books.

Moody, Kim. 1997. *Workers in a Lean World.* London: Verso.

Morissette, Rene. 1996. 'The Growth of Earnings Inequality in Canada.' Statistics Canada, Survey of Labour and Income Dynamics, Research Paper Series, Catalogue No. 96–08.

Morisette, R., J. Myles, and G. Picot. 1993. *What Is Happening to Earnings Inequality in Canada?* Statistics Canada, Analytical Studies Branch. Ottawa: Statistics Canada.

Mount Forest District Chamber of Commerce. 1998. *Welcome to Mount Forest.* Mount Forest, ON: Mount Forest District Chamber of Commerce.

Naples, Nancy. 1994. 'Contradictions in Agrarian Ideology: Restructuring Gender, Race-Ethnicity, and Class.' *Rural Sociology* 59: 110–35.

Nash, J. 1989. *From Tank Town to High Tech: The Clash of Community and Corporate Cycles.* New York: Columbia University Press.

– 1994. 'Global Integration and Subsistence Insecurity.' *American Anthropologist* 96 (1): 7–30.

Naylor, R.T. 1972. 'The Rise and Fall of the Third Commercial Empire of the St Lawrence.' In Gary Teeple (ed.), *Capitalism and the National Question in Canada.* Toronto: University of Toronto Press.

Nelson, Margaret K., and Joan Smith. 1999. *Working Hard and Making Do: Surviving in Small Town America.* Berkeley: University of California Press.

Noland, Fred. 1975. 'Strike Is Appalling Say Unions.' *Enterprise*, 8 October.

Nord, Mark. 1994. 'Natural Resources and Persistent Rural Poverty: In Search of the Nexus.' *Society and Natural Resources* 7: 205–20.

Noyelle, T. 1987. *Beyond Industrial Dualism*. Boulder, CO: Westview.

O'Hara, P. 1994. 'Constructing the Future: Cooperation and Resistance among Farm Women in Ireland.' In S. Whatmore, T. Marsden, and P. Lowe (eds.), *Gender and Rurality*. London: David Fulton.

OMAFRA 2001. *Report of the Task Force on Rural Economic Renewal*. Toronto: Queen's Printer for Ontario. Available at: http://www.gov.on.ca/OMAFRA/english/about/galttaskforce/index.html

Orr, D. 1996. 'The Rise of Contingent Employment and the Decline of Pension Coverage.' *Review of Radical Political Economics* 28 (3): 126–34.

Oxford Concise English Dictionary. 1991. Oxford: Oxford University Press.

Palmer, B. 1994. *Capitalism Comes to the Backcountry: The Goodyear Invasion of Napanee*. Toronto: Between the Lines.

– 1996. *Working Class Experience: A History of Canadian Labour*. Toronto: McClelland and Stewart.

Palmer, Craig, and Peter Sinclair. 1997. *When the Fish Are Gone: Ecological Disaster and Fishers of Northwest Newfoundland*. Halifax: Fernwood Publishing.

Parr, Joy. 1990. *The Gender of Breadwinners: Women, Men, and Change in Two Industrial Towns, 1880–1950*. Toronto: University of Toronto Press.

Peck, J. 1996. *Work-Place*. New York: Guilford Press.

Pentland, H.C. 1981. *Labor and Capital in Canada, 1650–1860*. Toronto: Lorimer.

Perring, C. 1979. *Black Mineworkers in Central Africa: Industrial Strategies and the Evolution of an African Proletariat in the Copperbelt, 1911–1914*. New York: Africana Publishing.

Petras, James, and Henry Veltmeyer. 2001. *Globalization Unmasked: Imperialism in the 21st Century*. London: Zed Books.

Picot, G., J. Myles, and T. Wannell. 1990. *Good Jobs/Bad Jobs and the Declining Middle; 1967–1986*. Statistics Canada, Analytical Studies Branch, No. 28. Ottawa: Statistics Canada.

Picot, G., and W. Piper. 1993. *Permanent Layoffs and Displaced Workers: Cyclical Sensitivity, Concentration, and Experience Following the Layoff*. Statistics Canada, Analytical Studies Branch, No. 55. Ottawa: Statistics Canada.

Piore, Michael J., and Charles F. Sabel. 1984. *The Second Industrial Divide*. New York: Basic Books.

Popaleni, K. 1989. 'Shouldering the Burden for Canada Post: Privatization's Impact on Rural Women.' *Resources for Feminist Research* 17 (3): 136–8.

Rayside, David M. 1991. *A Small Town in Modern Times: Alexandria, Ontario*. Montreal: McGill-Queen's University Press.

Redclift, N. and S. Whatmore. 1990. 'Household, Consumption and Liveli-hood: Ideologies and Issues in Rural Research.' In T. Marsden, P. Lowe, and S. Whatmore (eds.), *Rural Restructuring: Global Processes and Their Responses*. London: David Fulton.

Rifkin, Jeremy. 1995. *Technology, Jobs and Your Future – The End of Work: The Decline of the Global Labor Force and the Dawn of the Post-Market Era*. New York: G.P. Putnams Sons.

Rinehart, James W. 1987. *The Tyranny of Work: Alienation and the Labour Process*. Toronto: Harcourt Brace Jovanovich.

Rodwin, L. 1989. *Deindustrialization and Regional Economic Transformation*. Boston: Unwin Hyman.

Rose, D., and M. Villemaire. 1997. 'Reshuffling Paperworkers: Technological Change and Experiences of Reorganization at a Quebec Newsprint Mill.' *Canadian Geographer* 41 (1): 61–87.

Ross, R., and K. Trachte. 1990. *Global Capitalism: The New Leviathan*. Albany: State University of New York Press.

Ryerson, Stanley. 1973. *Unequal Union: Roots of Crisis in the Canadas, 1815– 1873*. Toronto: Progress Books.

Sachs, Wolfgang. 1993. *Global Ecology: A New Arena of Political Conflict*. London: Zed Books.

– 1996. *Gendered Fields: Women, Agriculture and Environment*. Boulder, CO: Westview.

Sayer, Andrew, and Richard Walker. 1992. *The New Social Economy: Reworking the Division of Labour*. Cambridge, MA: Basil Backwell.

Scase, R. 1992. *Class*. Minneapolis: University of Minnesota Press.

Schallau, Con H. 1989. 'Sustained Yield versus Community Stability: An Unfortunate Wedding.' *Journal of Forestry* 86 (9): 16–23.

Schatan, Jacobo. 1990. 'The Deceitful Nature of Socio-Economic Indicators.' *Development* 3/4: 69–75.

Schneider, J. 1995. 'Introduction: The Analytic Strategies of Eric R. Wolf.' *Articulating Hidden History: Exploring the Influence of Eric R. Wolf*. Berkeley: University of California Press.

Schneider, J., and R. Rapp. 1995. *Articulating Hidden History: Exploring the Influence of Eric R. Wolf*. Berkeley: University of California Press.

Seccombe, W., and D. Livingstone 1996. 'Down to Earth people: Revising a Materialist Understanding of Group Consciousness.' In D.W. Livingstone and J. Mangan (eds.), *Recast Dreams: Class and Gender Consciousness in Steeltown*. Toronto: Garamond Press.

Sennett, Richard. 1998. *The Corrosion of Character: The Personal Consequences of Work in the New Capitalism*. New York: W.W. Norton.

Shortall, S. 1993. 'Canadian and Irish Farm Women: Some Similarities, Differences and Comments.' *Canadian Review of Sociology and Anthropology* 20 (2): 172–90.

– 1994. 'Farm Women's Groups: Feminist or Farming or Community Groups, or New Social Movements?' *Sociology* 28 (1): 279–91.

Shucksmith, M. 1994. 'Conceptualising Post-industrial Rurality.' In J. M Bryden (ed.), *Toward Sustainable Rural Communities: The Guelph Seminar Series*. Guelph: University School of Rural Planning and Development.

– 2000. 'Social Exclusion: Bounded Choices and Sustainable Livelihoods in Rural Britain. Paper presented to the 10th World Congress on Rural Sociology, Rio de Janerio, Brazil.

Skeggs, B. 1997. *Formations of Class and Gender*. London: Sage.

Smith, Eldon. 1990. 'Economic Stability and Economic Growth in Rural Communities: Dimensions Relevant to Local Employment Creation Strategy.' *Growth and Change* (Fall): 3–18.

Smith, P. 1992. 'Beyond "Add Women and Stir" in Canadian Rural Society.' In D.A. Hay and G. Basran (eds.), *Rural Sociology in Canada*. Toronto: Oxford University Press.

Statistics Canada. 1881–1996. *Census of Canada*. Various years.

– 1991. *Profile of Urban and Rural Areas*. Ottawa: Statistics Canada.

– 1999. 'Labour Force Update: An Overview of the Labour Market, 1998.' *The Daily*. 27 January.

– 2000. 'Unemployment kaleidoscope.' *The Daily*, 6 Sept. www.statcan.ca.80/Daily/000906/d000906a.htm

Stull, Donald D., and Michael J. Broadway. 1990. 'The Effects of Restructuring on Beef Packing in Kansas.' *Kansas Business Review* 14: 10–16.

Swift, J. 1995. *Wheel of Fortune: Work and Life in the Age of Falling Expectation*. Toronto: Between the Lines.

Teeple, G. 1995. *Globalization and the Decline of Social Reform*. Toronto: Garamond.

Thirsk, Joan. 1984. *The Rural Economy of England: Collected Essays*. London: Hambledon Press.

Thorning, Stephen. 1986. 'T.E. Bissell of Elora, Ontario: A Small Town Manufacturer and His Milieu.' Masters thesis, McMaster University.

Thorning, Stephen. 1991a. 'Bissell Firm Finally Declared Bankruptcy in 1954.' *Elora Sentinel*, 18 June, 6.

– 1991b. 'Business Eventually Boomed after 1937 Fleury-Bissell Merger.' *Elora Sentinel*, 11 June, 6.

– 1991c. 'Elora's Carpet Factory Had a Volatile History.' *Elora Sentinel*, 7 May, 6.

- 1991d. 'Mundel Furniture Company Reached Maturity in the 1920's.' *Elora Sentinel*, 29 Jan., 10.
- 1991e. 'Prosperous Years for the T.E. Bissell Co.' *Elora Sentinel*, 21 May, 6.
- 1991g. 'T.E. Bissel: A Shrewd Implement Maker Lured from Fergus.' *Elora Sentinel*, 14 May, 7.
- 1991h. 'T.E. Bissell Rebuilt after the Disastrous 1918 Fire.' *Elora Sentinel*, 28 May, 6.
- 1991i. 'T.E. Bissell Suddenly Sold His Company in 1928.' *Elora Sentinel*, 4 June, 6.

Tuck, Judy. 1978. *A History of Harriston*. Mildmay, ON: Town Crier.

Urry, J. 1996. 'Sociology of Time and Space.' In Bryan S. Turner (ed.), *The Blackwell Companion to Social Theory*. Oxford: Blackwell.

van der Plas, L. and M. Fonte (eds.). 1994. *Rural Gender Studies in Europe*. Assen: Van Gorcum.

Vernon's Directory for Wellington County. 1867. Hamilton, ON: Henry Vernon and Son.

Waltner-Toews, David. 1994. 'Agro-Ecosystem Health Care.' *Agro-Ecosystem Health Project*, Discussion Paper No. 2.

Warnock, John. 1988. *Free Trade and the New Right Agenda*. Vancouver: New Star Books.

Warr, P.B. 1987. *Work, Unemployment and Mental Health*. Oxford: Claredon Press.

Whatmore, S. 1990. *Farming Women: Gender, Work and Family Enterprise*. London: Macmillan.

Whatmore, S., T. Marsden, and P. Lowe. 1994. *Gender and Rurality*. London: David Fulton.

White, Harrison C. 1981. 'Where Do Markets Come From?' *American Journal of Sociology* 87: 514–47.

Wiebe, N. 1995. 'Farm Women: Cultivating Hope and Sowing Change.' In S. Burt and L. Code (eds.), *Changing Methods: Feminists Transforming Practice*. Toronto: Broadview Press.

Wilkinson, Kenneth. 1986. 'In Search of the Community in a Changing Countryside.' *Rural Sociology* 51: 1–17.

Williams, R. 1983. *Keyword*. London: Flamingo.

- 1973. *The Country and City*. Oxford: Oxford University Press.

Winson, Anthony. 1985. 'The Uneven Development of Canadian Agriculture: Farming in the Maritimes and Ontario.' *Canadian Journal of Sociology* 10 (4): 411–38.

- 1993. *The Intimate Commodity: Food and the Development of the Agro-Industrial Complex in Canada*. Toronto: Garamond Press.

- 1997. 'Does Class Consciousness Exist in Rural Communities? The Impact of Restructuring and Plant Shutdowns in Rural Canada.' *Rural Sociology* 62 (4): 429–53.
Wolf, E. 1982. *Europe and the People without History*. Berkeley: University of California Press.
World Commission on Environment and Development. 1987. *Our Common Future*. Oxford: Oxford University Press.
Yalnizyan, A. 1998. *The Growing Gap: A Report on Growing Inequality Between the Rich and Poor in Canada*. Toronto: Centre for Social Justice.
Yalnizyan, A., T.R. Ide, and A.J. Cordell. 1994. *Shifting Time: Social Policy and the Future of Work*. Toronto: Between the Lines.

Newspapers, Reports, and Directories

Abitibi Consolidated Inc. 1997. *Annual Report*. Montreal.
- 1996. *Annual Report*. Montreal.
Abitibi Price. 1996. *Environmental Compliance Report*. Montreal.
Arnprior Chronicle Guide. Various issues, May, July 1999.
Business Week. 17 February 1992, 7 December 1992.
Collective Agreement between Abitibi Price Inc. and the Communications, Energy & Papermakers' Union, local 90, May 1st, 1993–April 30th, 1998.
The Enterprise. 8 October 1975.
Financial Post. 15 March 1989.
Fortune. 4 November 1991.
Globe and Mail.
Harriston Review.
Kitchener-Waterloo Record.
Mount Forest Confederate. Various issues, Aug. 1906–Oct. 1979.
Mount Forest Olds. April–May, 1996.
PDR Notes. April 1989, 7 February 1991,
Scott's Directories. Ontario Manufacturers. Don Mills: Southam Information Products Group (various editions).

Index

Studies in Comparative Political Economy and Public Policy